Veloce *Classic Reprint* Series

EDWARD TURNER

the man behind the motorcycles

VELOCE

The official biography by Jeff Clew

Also from Veloce Publishing:

Speedpro Series
Harley-Davidson Evolution Engines, How to Build & Power Tune (Hammill)
Motorcycle-engined Racing Car, How to Build (Pashley)
Caring for your scooter – How to maintain & service your 49cc to 125cc twist & go scooter (Fry)
How your motorcycle works – Your guide to the components & systems of modern motorcycles (Henshaw)
Motorcycles – A first-time-buyer's guide (Henshaw)

Enthusiast's Restoration Manual Series
Beginner's Guide to Classic Motorcycle Restoration, The (Burns)
Classic Large Frame Vespa Scooters, How to Restore (Paxton)
Ducati Bevel Twins 1971 to 1986 (Falloon)
How to Restore Classic Off-road Motorcycles (Burns)
How to restore Honda CX500 & CX650 – YOUR step-by-step colour illustrated guide to complete restoration (Burns)
How to restore Honda Fours – YOUR step-by-step colour illustrated guide to complete restoration (Burns)
Triumph Trident T150/T160 & BSA Rocket III, How to Restore (Rooke)
Yamaha FS1-E, How to Restore (Watts)

Essential Buyer's Guide Series
BMW Boxer Twins – All air-cooled R45, R50, R60, R65, R75, R80, R90, R100, RS, RT & LS (Not GS) models 1969 to 1994 (Henshaw)
BSA 350 & 500 Unit Construction Singles (Henshaw)
BSA 500 & 650 Twins (Henshaw)
BSA Bantam (Henshaw)
Ducati Bevel Twins (Falloon)
Ducati Desmodue Twins (Falloon)
Ducati Desmoquattro Twins – 851, 888, 916, 996, 998, ST4 1988 to 2004 (Falloon)
Harley-Davidson Big Twins (Henshaw)
Hinckley Triumph triples & fours 750, 900, 955, 1000, 1050, 1200 – 1991-2009 (Henshaw)
Honda CBR FireBlade (Henshaw)

Honda CBR600 Hurricane (Henshaw)
Honda SOHC Fours 1969-1984 (Henshaw)
Kawasaki Z1 & Z900 (Orritt)
Moto Guzzi 2-valve big twins (Falloon)
Norton Commando (Henshaw)
Piaggio Scooters – all modern four-stroke automatic models 1991 to 2016 (Willis)
Royal Enfield Bullet (Henshaw)
Triumph 350 & 500 Twins (Henshaw)
Triumph Bonneville (Henshaw)
Triumph Thunderbird, Trophy & Tiger (Henshaw)
Velocette 350 & 500 Singles (Henshaw)
Vespa Scooters – Classic 2-stroke models 1960-2008 (Paxton)

Those Were The Days ... Series
Café Racer Phenomenon, The (Walker)
Drag Bike Racing in Britain – From the mid '60s to the mid '80s (Lee)

Auto-Graphics Series
Lambretta Li Series Scooters (Sparrow)

Biographies
Chris Carter at Large – Stories from a lifetime in motorcycle racing (Carter & Skelton)
Edward Turner – The Man Behind the Motorcycles (Clew)
Jim Redman – 6 Times World Motorcycle Champion: The Autobiography (Redman)
'Sox' – Gary Hocking – the forgotten World Motorcycle Champion (Hughes)

General
BMW Boxer Twins 1970-1995 Bible, The (Falloon)
BMW Café Racers (Cloesen)
BMW Custom Motorcycles – Choppers, Cruisers, Bobbers, Trikes & Quads (Cloesen)
Bonjour – Is this Italy? (Turner)
British 250cc Racing Motorcycles (Pereira)
British Café Racers (Cloesen)
British Custom Motorcycles – The Brit Chop – choppers, cruisers, bobbers & trikes (Cloesen)

BSA Bantam Bible, The (Henshaw)
BSA Motorcycles – the final evolution (Jones)
Ducati 750 Bible, The (Falloon)
Ducati 750 SS 'round-case' 1974, The Book of the (Falloon)
Ducati 860, 900 and Mille Bible, The (Falloon)
Ducati Monster Bible (New Updated & Revised Edition), The (Falloon)
Ducati 916 (updated edition) (Falloon)
Fine Art of the Motorcycle Engine, The (Peirce)
From Crystal Palace to Red Square – A Hapless Biker's Road to Russia (Turner)
Funky Mopeds (Skelton)
Italian Cafe Racers (Cloesen)
Italian Custom Motorcycles (Cloesen)
Japanese Custom Motorcycles – The Nippon Chop – Chopper, Cruiser, Bobber, Trikes and Quads (Cloesen)
Kawasaki Triples Bible, The (Walker)
Kawasaki Z1 Story, The (Sheehan)
Lambretta Bible, The (Davies)
Laverda Twins & Triples Bible 1968-1986 (Falloon)
Moto Guzzi Sport & Le Mans Bible, The (Falloon)
Motorcycle Apprentice (Cakebread)
Motorcycle GP Racing in the 1960s (Pereira)
Motorcycle Road & Racing Chassis Designs (Noakes)
MV Agusta Fours, The book of the classic (Falloon)
The Norton Commando Bible – All models 1968 to 1978 (Henshaw)
Roads with a View – England's greatest views and how to find them by road (Corfield)
Scooters & Microcars, The A-Z of Popular (Dan)
Scooter Lifestyle (Grainger)
SCOOTER MANIA! – Recollections of the Isle of Man International Scooter Rally (Jackson)
Triumph Bonneville Bible (59-83) (Henshaw)
Triumph Bonneville!, Save the – The inside story of the Meriden Workers' Co-op (Rosamond)
Triumph Motorcycles & the Meriden Factory (Hancox)

Triumph Speed Twin & Thunderbird Bible (Woolridge)
Triumph Tiger Cub Bible, The (Estall)
Triumph Trophy Bible (Woolridge)
Triumph TR6 (Kimberley)
TT Talking – The TT's most exciting era – As seen by Manx Radio TT's lead commentator 2004-2012 (Lambert)
Velocette Motorcycles – MSS to Thruxton – New Third Edition (Burris)
Vespa – The Story of a Cult Classic in Pictures (Uhlig)
Vincent Motorcycles: The Untold Story since 1946 (Guyony & Parker)

From Veloce Publishing's other imprints:

Battle Cry!
Soviet General & field rank officer uniforms: 1955 to 1991 (Streather)
Red & Soviet military & paramilitary services: female uniforms 1941-1991 (Streather)

Hubble & Hattie
A dog's dinner – Practical, healthy and nutritious recipes for REAL dog food (Paton-Ayre)
A tale of two horses – A passion for free-will teaching (Gregory)
Among the wolves – Memoirs of a wolf handler (Shelbourne)
Animal Grief – How animals mourn (Alderton)
Babies, kids and dogs (Fallon & Davenport)
Bonds – Capturing the special relationship that dogs share with their people (Cukuraite, Pais)
Camper vans, ex-pats and Spanish hounds – The strays of Spain: from road trip to rescue (Coates)
Cat Speak – recognising and understanding behaviour (Rauth-Widmann)
Charlie – The dog who came in from the wild (Tenzin-Dolma & Bekoff)
Clever Dog! – life lessons from the world's most successful animal (O'Meara)
Detector dog – A Talking Dogs Scentwork Manual (Mackinnon)

Dieting with my dog – One busy life, two full figures ... and unconditional love (Frezon)
Dinner with Rover – Delicious, nutritious meals for you and your dog to share (Paton-Ayre)
Dog Cookies – Healthy allergen-free treat recipes for your dog (Schops, Pick)
Dog Games – Stimulating play to entertain your dog and you (Blenski)
Dog Relax – Relaxed dogs, relaxed owners (Pilguj)
Dog Speak – recognising and understanding behaviour (Blenski)
Dog-friendly Gardening – Creating a safe haven for you and your dog (Bush)
Dogs on wheels – Travelling with your canine companion (Mort)
Emergency first aid for dogs – at home and away (Bucksch)
Exercising your puppy: a gentle & natural approach – Gentle Dog care (Robertson, Pope)
For the love of Scout – Promises to a small dog (Ison)
Fun and games for cats! (Seidl)
Gymnastricks – Targeted muscle training for dogs (Mayer)
Helping minds meet – Skills for a better life with your dog (Zulch, Mills, Baumber)
Home alone and happy (Mallatratt & Murphy)
Know Your Dog – The guide to a beautiful relationship (Birmelin)
Life skills for puppies – Laying the foundation for a loving, lasting relationship (Millsm, Zulch, Baumber)
Living with an Older Dog – Gentle Dog Care (Alderton, Hall)
Miaow! Cats really are nicer than people! (Moore CBE FRS)
Mike&Scrabble – A guide to training your new human (Dicks)
My cat has arthritis ... but lives life to the full! (Carrick)
My dog has arthritis ... but lives life to the full! (Carrick)
My dog has cruciate ligament injury – but lives life to the full! A practical guide for owners (Häusler, Friedrich)

My dog has epilepsy ... but lives life to the full! (Carrick)
My dog has hip dysplasia ... but lives life to the full! (Häusle, Friedrich)
My dog is blind – but lives life to the full! The guide to every aspect of a happy life with a blind or sight-impaired dog (Horsky)
My dog is deaf – but lives life to the full! (Willms)
My Dog, my Friend. Heart-warming tales of canine companionship from celebrities and other extraordinary people (Gordon)
No walks? No worries! Maintaining wellbeing in dogs on restricted exercise (Ryan, Zulch, Baumber)
Partners – Everyday working dogs being heroes every day (Walton)
Smellorama! Nose games for dogs (Theby)
Swim to recovery: canine hydrotherapy healing – Gentle Dog Care (Wong)
The Complete Dog Massage Manual – Gentle Dog Care (Robertson)
Tara – The terrier who sailed around the world (Forrester)
The Rex Factor – my dog, my friend (Gordon)
The quite very actual adventures of Worzel Wooface (Pickles)
The truth about wolves and dogs – Dispelling the myths of dog training (Shelbourne)
Unleashing the healing power of animals – True stories about therapy animals – and what they do for us (Preece-Kelly)
Waggy Tails & Wheelchairs – The complete guide to harmonious living for you and your dog (Epp)
Walking the dog – Motorway walks for drivers and dogs (Rees)
When Man Meets Dog (Blazina)
Winston ... the dog who changed my life (Klute)
You and Your Border Terrier – The Essential Guide (Alderton)
You and Your Cockapoo – The Essential Guide (Alderton)
Your dog and you – Understanding the canine psyche (Garratt & Walters)

www.veloce.co.uk

First published in July 2006 by Veloce Publishing Limited, Veloce House, Parkway Farm Business Park, Middle Farm Way, Poundbury, Dorchester DT1 3AR, England. Fax 01305 250479 / e-mail info@veloce.co.uk / web www.veloce.co.uk or www.velocebooks.com. This edition February 2017 ISBN: 978-1-787111-41-7 UPC: 6-36847-01141-3.

The Blue Plaque

In October 2009, Southwark Council recognised Edward Turner for the contribution he had made not only to Southwark but to the motorcycle industry with the unveiling of a coveted Blue Plaque by his son Edward Turner Junior, along with his sisters Jane Meadows and Charmian Hawley. The event took place at the motorcycle designer's former home and was attended by the Mayor of Southwark, Erum Waheed (who campaigned for the plaque), politician and Triumph fan Tony Benn, as well as ex-Meriden factory men and members of the local community. Edward Turner built his first bike in 1927, a 3-speed, 350cc OHC single. A photo of this machine entitled 'The Turner Special' was published in the The Motor Cycle magazine, marking the beginning of a legendary career and an extraordinary influence on the motorcycle industry the world over.

The Blue Plaque at 8 Philip Walk, London SE15, the address at which Edward Turner lived and worked during the 1920s.

Contents

Acknowledgements

No book could have got off to a better start than when Edward's eldest daughter, Jane, sent me a highly detailed, 85-page biography she had compiled about her father. It provided so many hitherto unpublished facts about him and his family's private life that I have used them almost verbatim throughout the book. Jane also provided a copy of his birth certificate, and a number of intriguing items of correspondence from his personal files.

I also visited the home of Edward's other daughter, Charmian, where we were able to sit and discuss much of the detail which I had by now absorbed, and listen to some tapes of broadcasts he had made whilst travelling abroad. It was here that I came across the portraits of Edward and his first wife Marion, which had been painted by his sister.

Others supplied much otherwise unobtainable material, such as John Nelson, a former executive of the Triumph Engineering Company, whom I have had the privilege of knowing for many years. John and I have much in common when it comes to motorcycle service manuals and books, and he very kindly agreed to check the accuracy of my manuscript to ensure it was free from any unintentional errors and, I am pleased to say, write the Foreword.

Much needed input came from Don Brown, a former executive of Johnson Motors Inc. of California. I had met Don on one of my earlier visits to the USA, and he provided detailed information about Triumph's (and Ariel's) first major distributor in that country. It is only with his help, and the aid of a tape he sent, that the chapter on the American market became a reality.

I must also thank Ken Mellor, who gave me permission to use extracts from a tape he had produced when Jim Lee, a former Ariel employee, interviewed Edward at his home in Ockley. Quite by coincidence, the interview took place only six weeks before Edward's death.

The illustrative content of this book came from a wide variety of sources. Jane kindly provided her late father's entire personal photograph collection and those from the Turner family's albums. Many are rare and will be seen here for the first time. I am also grateful to Charmian for all those that she contributed. More photographs came from Vida Wickes, from her late father's collection to which he had promised me access when we first met. These were supplemented by many original factory photographs which John Nelson had not only selected, but also supplied with a very useful aide-mémoire as a guide to originating their captions. Barry Pladdys of the Daimler and Lanchester Owners Club came up at very short notice with the photographs and CD Roms of the Daimler SP250, and also the four and a half litre engine which Edward had designed. Ken Middleditch very kindly let me photograph, also at short notice, five of the Triumphs he has restored to his usual high standard. My thanks are also due to Kawasaki Motors (UK) Ltd for the photograph of their W650 retro ohc twin, reminiscent of an earlier Turner-inspired design.

To all of the foregoing I am truly grateful, as their contributions have ensured that this book has a much better illustrative content.

All photographs used without an acknowledgement are from Edward's personal collection, or are copyright of the old Triumph Engineering Co., Ltd. Those kindly supplied by others have been given the appropriate acknowledgement. Where there has been no indication of the copyright holder I can only apologise for their use without an acknowledgement, especially as some were pasted into their owner's albums.

Last, but certainly not least, I must express my gratitude to Triumph Motorcycles Limited for permission to use the old Triumph logo on the cover of my book, and illustrative material that is copyright of the Triumph Engineering Co. Ltd. This has been granted on the understanding that Triumph Motorcycles Limited bears no responsibility for the content of this book, having had no part in its origination or preparatiion.

Jeff Clew
Queen Camel
England

Foreword

It is now more than fifty years since I had that unforgettable interview with Edward Turner, when, having returned from wartime service in the forces, I was looking for future employment; difficult at the age of twenty seven, when an apprenticeship was demanded to complete the requirements of an engineering career! Edward Turner, already a Member of the Institute of Mechanical Engineers, was the only one out of many to fully understand my quest, and the interview went along these lines until he asked where I had completed my army service. I had spent two years in Basra, Iraq, and Edward Turner confirmed he had also spent time there whilst in the Merchant Navy. My interview became a reminiscence of his early days as a young wireless officer: oh! how I now wish I had really listened and remembered his curriculum vitae! At that point I was sure I had secured my future career!

It is therefore with renewed and absolute pleasure that I have read, and re-read, Jeff Clew's biography of Edward's career and progress through life, having been set on my own way into his care and supervision following that strange initial meeting and interview. (I can now safely refer to him as Edward, though no-one would have dreamed of doing so in my day, or addressing him as anything other than Mr Turner; he was referred to as E.T. within the organisation, but never within his hearing.) Those of us who had the privilege of working with and for him acquired tremendous respect for this man, particularly as we shared the view that he knew each of our jobs inside out, and, if he had had the time, would have been able to do it better. This fact each of us quickly discovered after being summoned to appear before him in order to answer for some circumstance within our domain of control or action. I always likened such a meeting to a visit to the dentist, where you knew he was bound to prod where it hurt most! And it did hurt because we knew instantly - and in no uncertain manner - where we had fallen down and failed him. His demands and standards were high, and he would explode at shortcoming or failure. His command of English was immaculate, his verbal admonishment absolute, and his order for revised or alternative action rang in your ears! But that was the end of it: in twenty five years I can remember only one case where he dismissed someone, and the two occasions upon which I incurred his wrath (both barrels) were never referred to again, and did not impede my progress through the system. Life for us was never tranquil, for it was not known where and when he would next appear, and on what quest. This gave rise to a sort of collective camaraderie within the organisation, which meant that we all knew what was going on elsewhere, producing a co-operative and harmonious team spirit as a combined means of self-preservation and defence from the possible impending wrath of the gods!

Although E.T. rarely spoke of his earlier years, occasionally, during a meeting, he would state that 'he knew his metals' as a result of working in his grandfather's forge in his youth. When it came to a discussion of anything nautical, we were all fully aware of his previous merchantile involvement. Indeed, he had his own boat, and most of the staff at Meriden studiously avoided being involved and ensnared in that activity. On the other hand, I spent more than one Atlantic flight seated next to him, and learned of his enthusiastic and deep interest in such subjects as astral navigation, the movement of the stars and the migration of species across the face of he earth. On many such prolonged overseas visits he would tape his own stories (often grisly but always exciting) for his two young daughters, to be played in his absence at their bedtimes.

We had all come to appreciate that E.T. was not the man he seemed to be and ritually portrayed in the media. None of us, sadly, made the effort to reveal our own understanding of his character as actually experienced collectively by us. Three of us did make a start, but faltered as the Grim Reaper took his toll. So it was with tremendous gratitude that I learned Jeff Clew also felt he should attempt to put the life and achievements of this remarkable man into perspective, and write, not so much a biography, but more a description of E.T. and his achievements as they unfolded over his lifetime career. Naturally, as you will readily deduce, I have deeply enjoyed reading this book and sincerely trust you will also.

John R Nelson MA (Eng)., Cantab., Chartered Engineer. M.I. Mech.E.

Introduction

The notion of a book about Edward Turner was conceived many years ago when I was Editorial Director of the Haynes Publishing Group. The most obvious author would have been Jack Wickes, but, at that time, he was working in the USA following the demise of the Triumph Engineering Company to which, as chief stylist and project engineer, he had devoted most of his working life. As an alternative I tried to interest Ivor Davies in the project, Triumph's former advertising and publicity manager. Before any plans could be discussed in detail, however, fate took a hand and Ivor developed a brain tumour from which he never recovered. It was not until after I had retired in 1991 that I began to think seriously about writing the book myself.

After Jack returned from America I was able to contact him through Hughie Hancox, and visited him during December 1994. As a result of our discussion, I decided to go ahead with the project, albeit with some trepidation. I had intended to visit Jack on several more occasions, as and when I could begin to ask him sensible questions as my research progressed. Sadly, fate once again intervened when Jack died in July 1997, just as things were beginning to progress nicely.

Fortunately, during the intervening period, I had been able to contact Edward's two daughters, Charmian and Jane, from his second marriage. They were extremely supportive right from the start, and it's fair to say that, without their encouragement and help, it is unlikely this book would have been written.

A great deal has been written about the British motorcycle industry and the many enterprising designs it produced during its heyday, yet, surprisingly little has appeared in print about those responsible for them. Apart from the occasional magazine feature, or a brief mention in a marque history, their names were rarely known by those who purchased their end products. It is likely that only a few of those who restore and/or ride a classic motorcycle today could name a half dozen of them.

One name above all others deserves widespread recognition: that of Edward Turner. No single person had such a dynamic effect on the industry over a span of more than four decades. Possessing a unique combination of talents as designer, stylist and engineer from the day he joined Triumph as Chief Designer and General Manager in 1936, until his retirement 28 years later, the names of Turner and Triumph were inseparable. Long after his retirement, Turner's association with the company continued as a consultant.

Only a short while before his death in 1973, Edward Turner originated yet another new design, intended to offer a serious head-on challenge to the Japanese. Even if the other major manufacturers had failed to acknowledge the threat of impending competition from the Far East, he had visited Japan in 1960 to appraise the situation for himself. His report left no doubts about what lay ahead if the British motorcycle industry persisted with its head-in-the-sand attitude. That he was correct in his observations is now only too obvious.

Much has been written about his irascible temperament, his

Edward Turner, Managing Director, the Triumph Engineering Co. Ltd.

intolerance, and his autocratic style of management, some of it based on hearsay by those who had never met him and were unable to form their own opinions. So prevalent has the denigration of some of Britain's former 'captains of industry' now become that it is regarded as accepted practice - with, of course, the benefit of hindsight. Yet, whatever management style Turner adopted, and in the knowledge that he ran a very tight ship, the indisputable factor is that his company was highly successful and one in which his employees took pride and felt privileged to be a part of.

That he also originated a number of design trends which the industry followed for many years was an added bonus, as was his determination always to keep one jump ahead of the competition. It was no coincidence that letters from overseas bearing only the company's slogan as the address - The Best Motorcycle in the World - were invariably delivered to Triumph's Meriden factory. Even today his motorcycles have a considerable cult following.

This book brings to light many hitherto unknown facts and hopefully will help redress some of the misrepresentations of others so that they can be seen in their true perspective. It reveals many details not previously published about Edward Turner's early life, and shows another side of this remarkable and very talented man that few will realise existed.

Jeff Clew
Queen Camel
England

AUTHOR'S NOTE

Although this book contains much information about the individual Triumph models, and previews of new model programmes, it was never intended that this information would be fully comprehensive due to space considerations. Other books are available which provide this information in fine detail, and readers seeking this are advised to refer to the bibliography at the end of this book where such sources of information are listed.

Chapter 1: Early days in Edwardian London

When Edward VII ascended the throne on 24th January 1901, he was in his 60th year. Many viewed his accession with apprehension due to his earlier philanderings; yet, if anything, the Edwardian era, which experienced many exciting new developments despite Edward's relatively short reign of just over nine years, brought with it a sense of gaiety.

Hotels were no longer mere resting places for their guests: now they began making greater use of their banqueting suites and ballrooms, in which they would host social events. Hotel bars became more welcoming, too, no longer catering only for residents. The working class, unable to afford such extravagancies, found consolation in the newly established ABC and Lyons tearooms. By 1910 there were 98 Lyons tearooms in London, and these were described by Lyons as 'luxury catering for the little man'.

They also proved a boon to the West End shopper. The Edwardian era was also the age of the department store: although some already existed, none matched Selfridges, which opened the doors of its new Oxford Street branch in March 1909. With 130 departments, the new store could boast a staff of no less than 1300. Many other stores began to open multiple outlets so that names such as Boots, Liptons, and Home and Colonial became well known in various cities and towns around the country. The corner shop, however, remained the province of the lower paid, as it could provide small quantities of virtually everything, including food, and if needs be, 'put it on the slate'.

The motorcycle and the car, although still in their infancy, were beginning to show their potential as serious means of transportation, albeit for the more affluent. The Locomotives on the Highways Act of 1896 had given them greater freedom of movement, without being restricted to 4mph and having to be preceded by a person on foot to give warning of their approach. The already good railway network was still being expanded, having broadened the concept of travel to include those who previously had not strayed far from home.

Electricity was now playing a part, too. Electrification of the Circle Line on the underground was completed in 1905 and helped ease traffic congestion in the centre of London, which still had its high quota of horsedrawn vehicles. The electric tram was yet another form of cheap transport for the masses. When the construction of the Kingsway tunnel had been completed, a by-product of a serious effort to clear slums in the Aldwych area, the tramway systems north and south of the Thames were linked. Soon, the motor bus would replace the horsedrawn buses, in much the same way as the motor taxi would replace the hansom cab. 7600 hansom cabs had been in use at the turn of the century, but, by 1912, their numbers had dwindled to 400.

Aviation captured public imagination after Louis Bleriot's successful first crossing of the English Channel on 25th July, 1909. It would not be long before flying would become yet another means of transport, offering many the prospect of rapid inter-continental travel.

Perhaps one of the best remembered attractions of the Edwardian era was the music hall, which really came into its own, providing cheap (and often bawdy) entertainment for the masses. Interest in the theatre blossomed, too; several new ones were built in London's West End and the premises of existing theatres expanded.

It was against this background that Edward Turner was born on Thursday, 24th January 1901 in the sub-district of St. Peter

Edward's birth certificate.

Edward's sisters (left to right): Winnifred, Maud and Florence. Maud had an artistic streak and studied at the Slade School of Art.

Two of Edward's brothers, William and Horace, in school uniform. Edward is dressed in a velvet suit, holding a tennis racket.

Walworth, Southwark, in the County of London. Queen Victoria had died two days previously, and on the day of Turner's birth Edward VII was proclaimed King.

Edward Turner was the third son in a family of seven children, comprising three other boys - William, Horace and Alec - and three girls - Florence, Maud and Winnifred. In those days large families were quite common, despite a high rate of infant mortality. Medical science still had a long way to go, and many childhood ailments which are now regarded as trivial were life threatening then. The Turners were by no means immune from this distressing situation: a further son and daughter, Maurice and Fanny, died in infancy, allegedly from drinking unpasteurised milk. Edward came near to an early demise at the time of his birth when his father became somewhat nervous and agitated and dropped him. His cries of protestation left no doubt about his survival!

At the time of Edward's birth the Turner family was living at 32, Bronti Place, and previously had lived at number four in the same road, where Maud had been born. It would seem that William, the father, whose occupation was Master Mechanical Engineer, had a somewhat restless disposition and would seldom stay for long in the same place. Records show the family was inclined to move home about every nine months, and on at least one occasion as far afield as the outskirts of Brighton to get away from the smoke and pea souper fogs for which London was renowned. Yet, the family always returned to London again soon after. By the time it finally settled, the family had changed addresses something like seventeen times, which suggests rented accommodation.

The Turner family had an engineering background. Edward's grandfather had started out in life as a blacksmith, as confirmed by his marriage certificate in 1864. At his son's wedding in 1891, he described his occupation as engineer. Edward's father seems to have undergone more formal training along traditional lines. After completing an apprenticeship, he progressed to journeyman and probably master blacksmith before acceptance as a master

mechanical engineer. By then it seems likely there was only a thin dividing line between the professions of blacksmith and engineer. Edward's mother Frances was the daughter of James Hillman, and from that side of the family came an involvement with coach building and harness making. Winnifred, one of Edward's sisters, claimed their mother's family had been wheelwrights. She also confirmed that one of Frances' brothers became involved with Hillman cars at a later date; an interesting early connection with the motor industry, and particularly the internal combustion engine.

It has been suggested in some quarters that it was from the family's association with coach building that Edward derived his flair for styling, influenced by some of the shapely curves and graceful flowing lines. He would recall being impressed at an early age by a huge drawing of a horsedrawn carriage that occupied an entire wall. If nothing else it instilled in his mind the importance of accurate drawings as the basis for any new project. William Turner Senior had a succession of occupations that involved running a farm and a public house for brief periods. He even contemplated retiring whilst in his early thirties, which accounted for the family's brief removal to the Brighton area.

In 1913 the Turners moved to Peckham Rye in south east London, where William Turner bought a light engineering works which allegedly made the lightning conductor that graced Nelson's Column, and wrought iron gates for some of the larger houses in and around London. The works also manufactured wooden-backed steel wire flue brushes which, during the 1914-18 war, were supplied under War Office contract to the Royal Navy. They were used for cleaning gun barrels and sweeping the funnels of coal-fired warships. It proved a profitable venture for a small factory of about twenty employees.

Edward seemed pleased to have been the first Edwardian born in the family, virtually at the beginning of a new century. He had little feeling for the Victorian age which, with rooms overladen with ornaments, dark, ugly furniture, and walls covered in dark wallpaper, gave him a sense of foreboding. Even everyday clothing was sombre. Collectively, it created in him a claustrophobic feeling synonymous of a bygone age and directly conflicted with his interests, which lay in the present and the future.

From his many recollections of that bygone era Edward would recall his childhood days with obvious pleasure. He was allowed to travel all over London on the top of a double-decker bus at the age of six or seven, with only a playmate of his own age to accompany him. They were each given a penny and told to "go off". He would also recall the purchasing power of a penny or two in the early 1900s,

A studio portrait of Edward's parents, William and Frances, taken circa 1910 when they were aged about 40.

was when he showed how good he was at drawing, a gift which most of the family seemed to possess. His eldest sister, Florence, drew flowers, whilst Maud showed such exceptional artistic ability that she later went on to the Slade School of Art. Edward impressed his art master, who used to joke that he must be related to William Turner, perhaps the most brilliant English painter of all time. It's quite possible his pupil felt an affinity with this painter through the similarity of their surnames, and because his teacher had shown such an interest in him. He once mentioned that, as a boy, his favourite painting had been Turner's Fighting Temeraire. His sister Winnifred recalls her brother showed artistic talent at an early age and was always drawing boats and engines in detail.

Edward had already begun to display ingenuity. When he was still quite young he saw his mother and sisters trying unsuccessfully to fit a very large side of beef horizontally into the oven. After watching them for a few moments he went off to the blacksmith's shop to fashion a large hook, which he attached to the top of the oven so that the beef could be cooked whilst suspended vertically. Later, he installed a low voltage electric butt welder in his father's factory to speed up production. It replaced the traditional blacksmith's hearth used to make the wire brushes. In those days the electricity supply was not too reliable, and the local cinema audience would curse whenever the screen suddenly went dark as the butt welder allowed surges of power that disrupted the supply system!

Edward's relationship with his parents was somewhat uneasy as they never seemed to have much time for their children, being preoccupied with each other. It was to his sister Florrie, some ten years older, that he turned for reassurance, encouragement and approval, and it was she who virtually brought him up. His favourite sibling was his sister Maud, who was the closest to him in age. As mentioned earlier, she showed the most talent in the family and he felt sorry for her when she was brought back from art college to help at home. An accomplished pianist, her extensive classical repertoire never elicited parental appreciation. As far as his brothers were concerned, Edward regarded them as lazy and unwilling to motivate themselves. He found William, his father's favourite, overbearing and inclined to 'lord it' over both himself and the other members of the family when he came home from school. Horace was his mother's favourite and possibly Edward regarded him in much the same light. If anything, he was fond of Alec, whom he considered had a nice character. Being the youngest member of the family, his parents were inclined to spoil Alec a bit, which seemed to have stifled any desire to achieve anything. This, Edward found especially disappointing.

On 4th August 1914 a state of war was declared between Britain and Germany. The news broke whilst Edward was attending a wild west show, and, to his surprise, was greeted by a loud cheer from the audience. Although Britain was ill-equipped for this conflict, there was widespread belief that the war would be over by Christmas. Kitchener's infamous "Your Country Needs You" poster, with its pointing finger, was intended to encourage 100,000 volunteers in the age range 19-38 to join up in the shortest possible time. The response from those wishing to offer their services overwhelmed the recruiting and medical personnel. Many lied about their ages if they were below or above the age limit, but as few questions were asked, no documentary evidence was requested, and the cursory medical examination meant few had difficulty enlisting.

William was the first in the Turner family to take up arms, but somehow managed to secure for himself a 'safe' job in the stores, so was not sent to the front and didn't miss a single Sunday lunch at home. Edward held him in contempt for this because he considered his brother should have put his intelligence to better use. Later,

which, not unexpectedly, related to the purchase of sweets and comics. Even a farthing (a quarter of an old penny) would buy quite a large number of sweets. Another childhood memory was the smell of the streets; a mixture of gas from the street lamps and the aroma of the horses, most of the transport at that time still being horsedrawn. During the summer months this smell was almost overpowering.

His parents moved home so frequently that his schooling became somewhat disjointed. When he was about ten years old one of the highlights of his schooldays was earning a place in a choir school because he had a good voice. To his dismay his parents considered he was sufficiently intelligent not to require expensive tuition, so he was not sent to either a private or a public boarding school like his three brothers, of whom he was envious. For a while he attended Ongar Grammar School in Essex, although not for long. Bullied by a gang of older boys, who threatened to "bash his brains out on the wall", he played truant at about the age of thirteen to work in a chemist's laboratory. He ran errands and carried out odd jobs until eventually his father got to hear of it and he had to return to complete his schooling. An early indication of Edward's talents when younger brother Horace turned up in army uniform, his mother fainted in horror. Within a couple of weeks or so, Horace was blown up by a shell and invalided out of the army, so he was not sent to the front either. Although Horace's hearing was permanently affected, this incident undoubtedly saved his life. Edward was, of course, far too young to offer his own services when war had been declared, but was anxious to enlist as soon as he became 16. The need for new recruits was even greater because so many had perished on the battlefields of Verdun, the Somme and Passchendaele. On 1st July 1916, when the British army made a major but abortive attempt to breach enemy lines, 57,000 officers and men were killed, wounded or went missing. By 1st November that number had risen to 450,000.

The chances of survival whilst on active service were slim, irrespective of which branch of the services a volunteer joined, but this did not deter Edward from wishing to do his bit. Unfortunately, lying about his age was not an option because of his youthful appearance , but after making some enquiries he found a way in which he could volunteer at the age of sixteen. The Marconi International Marine Communication Co. Ltd. had a scheme whereby it would train sixteen year olds to become telegraphy officers and serve with the Merchant Navy, and Edward joined the scheme in June 1917. Wireless messages were at that time transmitted in morse code and he was so keen to pass his course that he would shut himself away for long periods so that he could practice sending and receiving messages with speed and accuracy. He became so proficient that he obtained a posting ahead of several of the older boys. What appealed most to him was that telegraphy officers did not have to follow the usual chain of command, but were answerable to the Captain. Though still only a teenager, he would have responsibility for a ship's safety. Edward was not the kind of person able to fit easily into any kind of hierarchy, preferring instead to take responsibility and show initiative, It was his proud boast that he became a Junior Telegraphy Officer at the age of sixteen and a half and a Senior Officer by the time he was seventeen.

Edward was at first shocked by what he saw and heard when he went to sea in the Hindustan, an armed merchantman manned by a particularly rough crew. He would joke about not getting much to eat other than bully beef and hard biscuits infested with weevils, and show how the biscuits had first to be knocked on the table to dislodge their

Aged 16 or 17, Edward is wearing the Merchant Navy uniform of a Marconi Telegraph Officer in the 1914-18 war.

occupants before they could be eaten. He also complained about the salt diet which brought him out in pimples. Overall, he was proud of the responsible position he now held and would recount how he used to listen to the wireless at night, often under hazardous conditions. He strove always to keep alert, especially at night when events often seemed to be leading to some kind of climax.

When the armistice came about on 11th November 1918, William and Frances Turner could count themselves lucky that all three of their sons had survived the 1914-18 war. Few others were as fortunate: whole streets lost at least one family member in the conflict. William and Horace returned to the family business after they had been demobilised, but Edward's new-found career at sea was so absorbing that he did not advise Marconi of his intention to resign until 8th July 1920. His immediate release was agreed without need for a contractural month's notice.

Edward found himself at a crossroads, uncertain what to do after his years at sea. Although the government had pledged that ex-servicemen would have jobs waiting for them, a sharp recession coincided with the time when so many young men were coming on to the labour market after demobilization. Jobs were few and far between and Edward did not relish the thought of joining the family business which provided for both his parents and his two older brothers. He considered it quite possible the firm might become another victim of the recession as it was still supplying many of its products to the navy.

Initially, he considered a career in the theatre, probably because his parents had a number of friends who were keen theatre-goers, adored the musical hall and knew some of the best music hall artists of the day. In later years, Turner mentioned he had been an impressario on one or two occasions, working in London's West End. He had been put off, however, by some of the seedier aspects of theatrical life, with its 'casting couch' and young girls willing to 'sell themselves' in their eagerness to get a part. He had nothing but contempt for the men who exploited these girls, many of whom were far too young to understand what they were getting themselves into. Turner made a hesitant attempt to tread the boards himself, as he had a fine baritone voice and had been approached on a number of occasions when he had sung at parties. However, after securing only a few small parts and going hungry on several occasions, he decided his true vocation lay in engineering.

Eventually he secured work as a fitter and turner, then as works manager of a small company making boiler accessories and fittings for ship's engine rooms. By attending technical classes in the evening he was able to further improve his knowledge. Conscious of the fact that he was still not heading in quite the right direction, he swallowed his pride and went cap in hand to ask his father for a job. Although he was taken on as works manager, it was at a lower level than that of his two brothers, which only added to his humiliation as it meant he would be earning less than they were.

It soon became obvious to Edward that working for his father had its limitations, so he decided to strike out on his own and

Chepstow Motors, in Peckham Road, south east London, Edward's first business venture.

become independent. Using what was left of his wartime gratuity after his release from the navy, and whatever else he had managed to save during the years that followed, he bought a motorcycle business, Chepstow Motors, in Peckham Road, south east London. How the shop got its name is no longer known, as it was far removed from the Welsh border town of the same name in Monmouthsire. Jim Oliver, a member of the Vintage Motor Cycle Club, recalls calling at Chepstow Motors when he was a schoolboy and lived close by. He was always made welcome by Edward, who acknowledged his youthful enthusiasm and would patiently answer all his questions. His encouragement was not misplaced: in later years Jim ran his own car and motorcycle business in that area.

Chapter 2: On the brink of a new career

Chepstow Motors was a typical small motorcycle business, buying, selling and repairing secondhand light cars and motorcycles, and stocking a range of accessories. An added asset was that it had an agency for Velocette motorcycles.

Although Veloce Limited was only a relatively small, family-owned manufacturer in Birmingham, the company had an enviable reputation for its range of high quality, 250cc two-stroke singles. In 1923, when it decided to add an entirely new 348cc overhead camshaft four-stroke to the range, motorcyclists began to sit up and take notice. The overhead camshaft engine was seen as representing a significant advance in design, and had reached the stage where it was considered reliable. Capable of improved performance when compared with a push rod-operated overhead valve model of similar capacity, the concept was by no means new - Peugeot had a double overhead camshaft racing twin before the 1914-18 war, for example. Unfortunately for Peugeot, metallurgy in those early days had not advanced sufficiently for materials to be available that would withstand the greater stresses and temperatures imposed in this type of engine. As a result the model had been unreliable.

By the mid-twenties there was a better understanding of metallurgy, and Veloce Limited was amongst the first to attempt a breakthrough in 1925, although it would be another year before this actually happened. The inevitable teething troubles inherent in any new design had first to be ironed out, but the company's perseverence paid off in 1926 when a 348cc overhead camshaft Velocette won the Junior TT in the Isle of Man, to finish more than ten minutes ahead of runner-up Jimmy Simpson's AJS. A runaway victory such as this created a hefty demand for the new model, so that any dealership with a Velocette agency benefited from an influx of orders. Veloce Limited received so many orders it had to move to larger premises the following year, and this success also encouraged other manufacturers to compete with the Veloce design and offer their own overhead camshaft models.

Edward's first ride on a motorcycle was in 1915, whilst he was still in short trousers. It was a Light Tourist New Imperial, fitted with a 293cc side valve JAP engine and a two-speed Albion gearbox. At the time he regarded it as "a most formidable machine of uncontrollable power". Later, when his brother William bought a vee twin Harley Davidson, Edward had a 496cc flat twin ABC, which was a constant source of embarrassment to his brother. It was reliable and always in good running order, whereas William had constantly to tinker with his Harley Davidson to keep it going. At weekends, Edward delighted in taking to what he described as "the relatively empty roads to Brighton" and being able to speed along stretches of long, flat road. The national speed limit then was only 20mph, so on several occasions he fell victim to police traps set up to catch speeding motorists and

Chepstow Motors had a valuable asset; a Velocette agency. Edward is sitting on one of the top-of-the-range K series ohc models.

motorcyclists. Once he had to spend the night in police custody until his father arrived to pay his fine and bail him out.

Aware of the significance of the overhead camshaft engine and the interest it was beginning to create, Edward decided to design and build his own motorcycle powered by this type of engine. Rooms on the first floor of Chepstow Motors directly above the showroom had lettering on the windows that proclaimed the existence of the Turner Equipment Company. It was here, after the shop had closed for the day, that the Turner motorcycle began to take shape.

Motorcyclists first became aware of Edward Turner's name when the 16th April 1925 issue of *The Motor Cycle* published the drawings of a single cylinder, overhead camshaft engine he had designed, along with a brief description of some of its more interesting features. It would seem likely he originated these drawings before he acquired Chepstow Motors, in view of the date of publication. His knowledge of the local foundry trade would have made it relatively easy for him to find a local pattern maker to produce the basic castings. All he needed then was to acquire suitable premises and the appropriate workshop equipment so that he could machine them on his own lathe, and use the other machine tools at his disposal for the subsequent milling or drilling operations. His previous work as both a fitter and a turner, and his tuition at evening classes, had given him the necessary skills to undertake all this work entirely unaided. It is alleged he made his own cutting tools from ordinary carbon steel which, when hardened and ground, were good enough to retain their

cutting edge long enough to make the full set of parts he needed for his first prototype.

It was his skill at machining that earnt him great prestige in a quite unexpected way at the Triumph Engineering Company a good many years later. Then the company's Managing Director, he was on the shop floor when he came across a skilled turner having difficulty machining the exact form of a fillet. Asking him to stand aside, Edward carried out to perfection the entire operation, earning him the respect and admiration of the workforce.

His drawings related to a single cylinder ohc engine of 348cc capacity with bore and stroke dimensions of 74 x 81mm, those of the Velocette. Overall, his design approximated that of a conventional, high performance engine, but also incorporated several ingenious features, to which the weekly magazine drew the attention of its readers. Designed to be mounted in a special frame, the engine had a traditional two bearing crankshaft assembly, supported at its right-hand end by a casting that formed an extension of the crankcase to house the valve operating mechanism. The cylinder barrel was sunk deep into the crankcase mouth, the whole assembly kept rigid by sturdy holding-down bolts that screwed into the underside of the cylinder head and had shoulders at their lower end. It was accepted practice to have the lower ends screw into threads cut in the aluminium alloy of the crankcase mouth, but, in Edward's opinion, this was not an ideal arrangement. Cast iron, used for the cylinder head and barrel, has a different rate of expansion to that of aluminium alloy. In consequence, there was always the risk of the threads pulling out of the crankcase in a highly stressed engine. To avoid this Turner arranged for the holding-down bolts to thread into sleeve nuts, which were retained by eye bolts.

The overhead camshaft was driven by a train of spur gear pinions enclosed within the previously mentioned casting, which extended up the right-hand side of the engine and above the top of the cylinder head. A lug cast into the top of the casting acted as a steady when it was clamped to the lower tank tube of the frame. With the traditional front and rear mounting crankcase lugs, this gave the engine an extra fixing point which,

it was claimed, would counteract whip caused by vibration and torque reaction. The camshaft, on which the rocker arms bore directly, lay transversely across the cylinder head. The ends of the rockers in contact with the valve stem end caps were fitted with adjustable tappets, each of their inner ends having a steel roller that bore on the hardened flanks of the cams. The train of spur gear pinions within the casting dispensed with the need for a bevel driven camshaft, as there was no need to turn the drive through ninety degrees, as would have been the case had a vertical drive shaft been used. Furthermore, the cylinder head could be removed without disturbing the valve gear after first detaching the exhaust pipe, carburetter and sparking plug lead. An additional spur gear pinion drove the rear-mounted magneto, taking its drive from a large diameter intermediate idler pinion in the timing gear train.

There is no indication that this design got any further than the drawing board, possibly because it would have been expensive to produce, or perhaps because Edward had still to acquire premises and the workshop equipment with which to begin making a prototype. Enquiries about the engine were invited by contacting Edward at his home address of 87, Rye Hill Park, London, SE15, in the hope that someone might be sufficiently interested to help finance its production.

Nothing more was heard of Edward's design until the 6th January 1927 issue of *The Motor Cycle* published a photograph of a complete machine fitted with a different type of ohc engine which he had patented, accompanied by a detailed description. He had taken

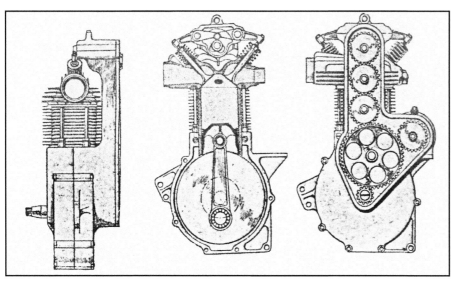

Edward's original design of an overhead camshaft engine, which contained a number of interesting features. These drawings were published in The Motor Cycle *dated 16th April 1925.*

The first Turner Special, the engine of which was an improved version of Edward's earlier design. A complete machine, he entered it in the 1927 London to Exeter Trial, and also raced it at a 'path' race meeting in the grounds of Crystal Palace.

shaft which acted also as the camshaft. It was driven by bevels from the right-hand end of the crankshaft. A second smaller diameter bevel, slightly higher up the camshaft, drove a transversely-mounted magneto at the rear of the casting. The cams were formed on the upper end of the vertical shaft and the valves were operated by short, horizontally-located tappets. A phosphor bronze gasket was interposed between the cylinder head and barrel, the two being clamped together by a yoke, one end of which was attached to lugs on the camshaft casing, and the other joined to the crankcase by two screwed members connected by a sleeve nut. Again, these holding-down bolts were not directly threaded to the crankcase mouth, although a slighty different arrangement was used.

As in the previous design, the cylinder head could be removed to leave the valve mechanism undisturbed. Although the cylinder head had only a single exhaust port, it led to a circular finned 'muff' across its front. An exhaust pipe emerged from each end of this muff, at right angles to the frame, before sweeping back, one each side of the frame, to meet up with its respective silencer. Internally, an aluminium alloy piston with two compression rings, and a fully floating gudgeon pin, gave a compression ratio of 5.75:1. The crankshaft, with a conventional flywheel assembly, was supported by a double roller bearing on the drive side, and by a self-aligning ball race on the timing side. Total loss lubrication was effected by a Best and Lloyd oil pump fitted at the base of the camshaft. It supplied oil directly to the top of the camshaft, which fell into a well from which centrifugal force fed it through small holes in the leading faces of the cams. From here, it drained down into the crankcase.

The cycle parts comprised a rigid loop frame into which the engine was mounted using a three-point fixing, a bolt-up clamp anchoring the top of the camshaft casting to the lower tank tube to form the additional point of attachment. A Webb girder front fork provided the front suspension and both wheels were fitted with 7 inch diameter internal expanding brakes. The gearbox was a proprietary three-speed Sturmey-Archer, with a hand change gate fitted to the right-hand side of the one and three quarter gallon nickel-plated saddle tank. The machine shown in an accompanying photograph appeared to be in semi-racing trim, having a straight through exhaust pipe, dropped handlebars, no kickstarter and a saddle that sloped to the rear. Registered with the London County Council for road use, it bore the registration YP 9286.

It was intended that the Turner Special would be in production by early 1928, and to test it in open competition Edward entered it in the 1927 London to Exeter Trial held on New Year's Eve. A report on the trial appeared in the *The Motor Cycle*, its rider being his best friend, Alf Russell. Russell left London soon after midnight on a bitter cold

his new engine to *The Motor Cycle* offices in Tudor Street, EC4, where it was inspected by Nitor, one of the magazine's staffmen. The new engine had a face cam arrangement, no doubt influenced by the design of the engine used by Dougal Marchant to record a speed of 100.81mph over the flying kilometre during April 1924. Dougal used a much modified 348cc Chater Lea engine to achieve, for the first time, 100mph from a 350.

Listed as the Turner Special, Edward's latest design was described as an experimental prototype, the only similarities it shared with its predecessor were that the engine had the same bore and stroke dimensions (74 x 81mm), the same cubic capacity (348cc), and its cylinder barrel sunk into the crankcase mouth. A long, narrow, oblong casting up the right-hand side of the engine now carried a vertical

Alf Russell, Edward's best friend, whom he employed in his workshop at Chepstow Motors. Alf is seen here on a Norton sidecar outfit, with Edward sitting on the nose of the sidecar. The venue would appear to be Brooklands race track.

The final version of the Turner Special: Edward's flair for styling was becoming evident.

New Year's Day, to arrive in Exeter after negotiating without incident the test hills included in the route. After the obligatory breakfast stop in Exeter, his ascent of Salcombe Hill on the return run was described by the magazine's reporter as fast and unusually steady. Sadly, there

is no further mention of him after this as it was later recorded that he had been forced to retire without completing the course. Even so, for its inaugural competitive event, the previously untried Turner Special seems to have acquitted itself reasonably well and shown promise.

The production model was expected to retail at £75.00 after several minor modifications had been made, and it was listed in the 17th February issue of *The Motor Cycle* Buyers' Guide at this price. Unfortunately, two factors tended to handicap its sales prospects severely. Aesthetically, the prototype showed little sign of the styling which, in later years, would become the hallmark of any Turner-designed machine. Furthermore, for the same price, a model KSS Velocette could be bought, which had a guaranteed maximum speed of 80mph and was virtually identical to the model on which Alec Bennett had won the 1926 Junior TT. Not unexpectedly, It was the latter model that Chepstow Motors sold.

Like many of his contemporaries, Edward had an interest in motorcycle racing and had ridden his brother's Harley Davidson at Brooklands. He also raced at the path racing track in the grounds of the Crystal Palace which opened on 21st May 1927. He entered the Turner Special at the second meeting on 6th August, one of 60 competitors in the 350cc Kempton Cup Race. Against strong opposition, he – not surprisingly – failed to finish amongst the race leaders, many of whom already had a wealth of racing experience. Rising star Gus Kuhn won the race, and made a habit of lowering the track record at every meeting he entered.

In the meetings that followed, Edward rode a 348cc Velocette. At the 12th August 1928 meeting he won the 350cc Middlesex Cup Race, a somewhat hollow victory as there had been a poor entry at this particular meeting due to the counter-attraction of speedway racing. In what is best described as a 'three horse race' (his opponents rode a Velocette and a Sunbeam), the report on this meeting was nonetheless complimentary. His Velocette was described as having infinitely better acceleration, and the report went on to say that Turner led the two mile race for the last one and a half laps. Clearly, he knew a thing or two about machine preparation ...

Now regarded as a rider-agent, Edward's business was likely to be more heavily patronised by members of local motorcycling clubs, in the knowledge that they would be dealing with an expert. By the end of the year, it would seem that Edward no longer regarded his Turner Special as a viable proposition, for it was not listed in the Buyers' Guide published in the 24th November 1927 issue of *The Motor Cycle*. The decision to withdraw it was most likely due to the fact that the cheapest 348cc overhead camshaft Velocette could now be purchased for as little as £58, which considerably undercut the Turner Special price of £75. As a hand-built machine, it would have left precious little scope for any cost-cutting to make it anywhere near competitive in price. Having a Velocette agency was a definite asset!

A second complete Turner Special seems to have been built during 1928, with the same face cam engine basic design but much more attractive overall. The engine had been 'cleaned up' by reversion to a single exhaust port cylinder head, and with the vertical shaft - which also doubled as the camshaft - enclosed within a chromium-plated outer tube that replaced the previous ugly casting. A more modern Sturmey Archer gearbox, complete with kickstarter and foot-operated gearchange, replaced the hand gearchange of its predecessor, with a shapelier oil tank mounted above it. Although the frame design appeared unchanged with a Webb girder fork, the wheels had larger section tyres and larger diameter brakes. The whole appearance was heightened by a chromium-plated saddle tank, with a painted panel on each side and an oblong plate inscribed 'Turner Special'. It was registered for use on the road by the London County Council and bore the number YX 3750.

Exactly when or why this machine was made remains uncertain, as no attempt was made to publicise it in the pages of *The Motor Cycle*, or to give it a price. Yet, for the first time, Edward had shown his styling skill to good effect. This was the machine that led indirectly to the breakthrough into the motorcycle industry he had so urgently been seeking.

Before that could happen, though, something else occurred that would also have an affect on his future. One day, an attractive young lady came into the shop; her brothers were keen motorcyclists and she wanted to enquire about getting one of her own. Edward was much impressed by her enthusiasm for motorcycles and her depth of knowledge about them. A friendship began which resulted in their marriage on 7th July 1929. Edward was then 28 years old and his bride, Edith Marion Webley, four years younger.

This photograph of Marion, Edward's first wife, was taken when she and Edward went on a cruising holiday with some friends on the Norfolk Broads.

Edward with Wilfred Sutcliff, his best man, taken on his wedding day.

Marion with Wilfred Sutcliff.

Chapter 3: The breakthrough – a job with Ariel

As no-one had come forward to offer the financial backing to get his Turner Special into production, not even for the latest re-styled version, Edward went to Birmingham to see whether he could get a major manufacturer interested in his design. It is alleged BSA showed tentative interest at first, but when nothing came of it he called on Ariel.

Here, he was seen by Vic Mole, Ariel's Sales Manager, who showed more interest in a rough sketch of an unusual layout for a four cylinder engine that Edward had brought with him. On paper, this engine had much to commend it, although the details of this second design amounted to no more than a rough sketch drawn on the back of an opened-out Wills Woodbine cigarette packet. However, it seems scarcely believable that someone as well organised as Edward would approach a major motorcycle manufacturer with such an intriguing proposition presented in this manner. Possibly, he took it with him as a second option, should there be little interest shown in his ohc single cylinder design. A designer would often rough out a sketch like this whilst he had an idea in his mind, before committing himself to finer detail. Whatever the reason, it was this second engine design that appealed most to Vic Mole.

A second meeting was arranged at Ariel Works Limited, to which Turner was driven from his London home by one of Ariel's directors. This time he was seen by Val Page, Ariel's Chief Designer, who had read about the Turner Special and been impressed by the thoroughness of its design. Jack Sangster, the company's Joint Managing Director, who had a reputation as an entrepreneur and a financier, was also at the meeting. There could be no suggestion of the Turner Special being made by Ariel because the company was already fully jigged and tooled to make its own motorcycles. Sangster was intrigued by the novel arrangement of Edward's four cylinder engine, an outline of which had already been given him by Vic Mole.

The Sangsters were well-known in the car and motorcycle trade. Jack's father, Charles, had joined Cycle Components Manufacturers in 1895, who acquired the Ariel name only a few years afterwards. By the time his second son, Jack, had joined the business, Ariel Works Limited was part of the renamed parent company, Components Limited, of which Charles Sangster was now Managing Director. No newcomer to motorcycling, Jack had won a silver medal in the 1914 Paris to Nice Road Trial riding an Ariel. Later, after service in the army, he designed a 998cc cyclecar and joined the Rover Co. Ltd. as Assistant Works Manager in order to make it. Such was the Rover Eight's success that, in 1922, Jack Sangster re-joined Components Ltd. as Assistant Managing Director, and became involved with the design of a rival to the Rover, the 999cc Ariel Nine. Sadly, the Ariel car was beset with problems from which it never really recovered,

sustaining heavy losses for the company. Thereafter, the company concentrated on making motorcycles.

Jack Sangster was visibly impressed by Edward's compact 500cc, four cylinder motorcycle engine that had its cylinders arranged in the form of a square. Although the concept of a four cylinder motorcycle engine was by no means new, it was unusual to have the cylinders arranged in this manner. It was like having two vertical twin engines, one behind the other, with their crankshafts coupled together; an arrangement that conveniently overcame the effects of any primary out-of-balance forces. Until then, an in-line four configuration had been the most favoured, with the engine unit in line with the frame. Although this arrangement lent itself to shaft final drive, it tended to give a machine an undesirably long wheelbase after a gearbox had been added. Furthermore, there was always a tendency for the rearmost cylinders to overheat because they were well out of the cooling air stream. The alternative, to arrange the cylinders transversely, created its own problems as it had preferably to be contained within the frame without too much overhang and, if shaft drive was desired, the final drive had to be turned through 90 degrees.

Air-cooled vee-fours also had an overheating problem, because the front two cylinders almost completely masked those that lay behind them. A 'square four' cylinder arrangement was alleged to overcome all of these problems, and it was surprising that no-one had given it serious consideration before.

Jack Sangster decided to give Edward his big chance, and it was as well he did, otherwise Edward might well have accepted a job in the aircraft industry: he had received a firm offer on the day he went for his interview with Ariel. In a letter dated 8th November 1928, Jack Sangster wrote to Edward to confirm his appointment as Designer and Engineer in the company's Development Department, under the control of Val Page. He was to be engaged at an annual salary of £450, and was asked to take up his duties as soon as possible, after he had cleared up his own business arrangements and commitments. It was also made clear that any of Edward's patentable ideas would be the property of the company and not shared. Edward accepted the offer, although from what followed later it was evident that he was not happy about having to relinquish his patent rights.

In January 1929 took up his appointment after disposing of his business in Peckham and moving to Birmingham. Unfortunately, 1929 was not a good year in which to join the industry, even though Val Page's appointment as Chief Designer during late 1925 had injected new life into Ariel's model range. Whilst his revamped Ariel range more or less managed to hold its own, without having to resort to such drastic measures as price-cutting, production statistics were beginning to show an annual decline in the number of machines made in the UK. As the recession deepened, concern throughout

the industry grew, with some justification. Of the 147,000 machines made during 1928 the figure fell to 126,000 in 1929 and by 1930 had slumped even more dramatically to 74,400 - half the 1928 production figure. Recession was indeed biting deeply.

Although fears about the effects of the recession must have caused Edward some concern for his future, his immediate priority was to get his four cylinder model up and running as soon as possible. To assist him with this task a young draughtsman was seconded to him so that the necessary plans could be drawn up to help meet their target. The draughtsman was Bert Hopwood, who had joined the company a few years earlier at the age of 18. Val Page, after discovering that Hopwood had won a college memorial prize for design engineering, had asked to see him and had offered him a job. It seems remarkable that, quite by coincidence, three very talented individuals came together to work under the same roof - Page, Turner and Hopwood - even though the latter two had still to prove themselves. Writing about those early days in his book *Whatever Happened to the British Motorcycle Industry*, Bert Hopwood disclosed: "I made sure that I graduated to the drawing board under the tuition of the best engineering draughtsman I have ever known (Val Page). At a later stage in my career I employed a similar approach with Edward Turner, whom I admired mostly for his down-to-earth business common-sense and for his ingenuity".

On completion the 498cc engine had bore and stroke measurements of 51 x 61mm, with all four cylinders arranged in the previously-mentioned 'square four' configuration within an air-cooled, cast iron cylinder block. Also of cast iron, the monoblock cylinder head casting had two vertical valves per cylinder, operated by rocker arms actuated by a single chain-driven overhead camshaft driven

indirectly from the front offside cylinder. A second chain, running on a sprocket behind the lower camshaft sprocket, drove a Lucas Magdyno at the rear of the cylinder block. All four flywheel assemblies were of the overhung crank type, mounted in pairs parallel to each other. Helically cut gears were located between the front and rear flywheel assemblies to couple them together, running in a separate, oil-filled chamber within the centre of the crankcase.

From the coupling gear in the middle of the rear crankshaft the drive was taken to a three-speed, hand change gearbox built in unit with the engine. The aluminium alloy crankcase casting was massive by conventional standards and separated horizontally, its lower half comprising the sump which contained a twin gear-type oil pump and two filters. A 'dipper' on the end of each of the forged chrome nickel steel connecting rods directed oil from troughs below to the roller bearing big ends. A separate, four pint oil compartment at the rear of the crankcase served as the main oil reservoir.

Separate cases were attached to the offside of the crankcase, one of which enclosed the chain drive to the overhead camshaft, which had a vernier coupling to ensure accurate valve timing. The other enclosed the chain drive to the Lucas Magdyno. A distributor on the nearside of the camshaft carried the ignition leads to the sparking plugs. A single, forward-facing Amal carburetter was fitted with a special air intake to prevent water and other material being ingested. It supplied the mixture to all four cylinders through a cruciform induction manifold. Twin exhaust pipes flanked it on each side, each serving a pair of cylinders. After running the engine on the test bench, it seemed very promising.

Anxious to begin road testing, Edward took a standard production, 250cc single and managed to squeeze the four cylinder

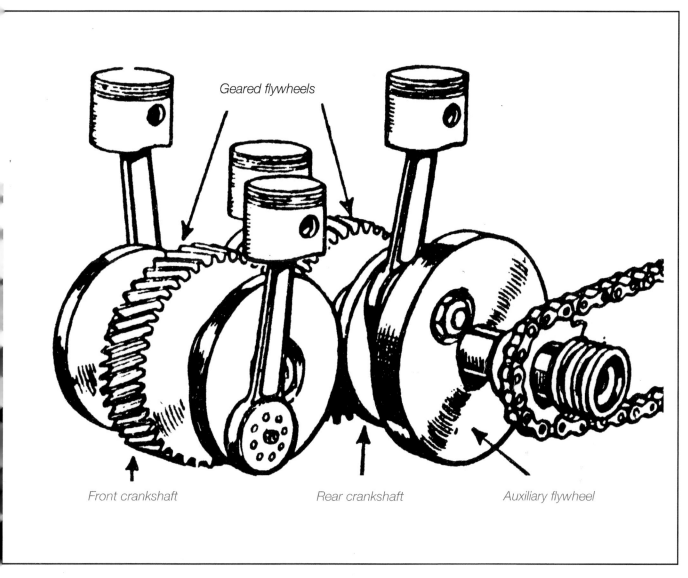

Geared flywheels

Front crankshaft   Rear crankshaft   Auxiliary flywheel

How the crankshaft assembly had to be modified so that a separate proprietary gearbox could be fitted.

engine into its frame by bending the tubes. It was a tight fit, made possible only because the engine was built in unit with the gearbox. A light motorcycle for its capacity, it weighed about 280lbs. Edward carried out much of the initial road testing and, winding it up along the Redditch road, he watched the speedometer soar into the 85-90mph range. He found the four easy to handle and was pleasantly surprised by its exceptionally good acceleration, due to a favourable power-to-weight ratio. It had an exciting 'zooming' exhaust note, too, yet, when idling, would tick over with what Bert Hopwood described as "a sewing machine noise".

Few problems were encountered during the test periods, the most serious of which was the characteristic knock of the coupling gears, which was not bad enough to require further attention. It was one of the testers who caused the greatest concern as he rode the machine with such zest that he frequently came off it. Edward referred to him as his "ball of leather" because he spent much of

his time coming off the machine, rolling along the hard road curled up like a ball!

Soon, a second prototype was on test and overall results were proving so encouraging that both Edward and his assistant were convinced they had a world-beater, which would put the company firmly back on its feet. This might well have been the case, but neither of them had any real concept of its costing, or what effect commercial economies would have when the four went into production and had to sell at a competitive price. Jack Sangster brought them back to reality by insisting they would have to use the frame and cycle parts of the newly-introduced 497cc SG31 'sloper' single. This went against Edward's principles, as throughout his entire career it had always been his intention "to make the metal work". Furthermore, the engine would have to be modified so that it could be used in conjunction with a standard Burman gearbox. This latter requirement would involve no small amount of redesign, as the rear nearside flywheel assembly would have to be changed by the addition of an another flywheel outboard of the big end. This was necessary so that a sprocket could be fitted to the rear mainshaft to transmit the primary drive to the gearbox by chain. Overnight, their world-beater had become overweight and had lost the edge of its performance.

The production model made its debut at the 1930 Motor Cycle Show with a £70 price tag, plus an additional £5.10s if ordered with lighting equipment. Ixion, the legendary journalist on the staff of *The Motor Cycle*, was fortunate enough to be lent for a week one of Turner's two prototypes, and reported on it in very favourable terms in the 18th September issue. He was particularly impressed by its quietness and complete lack of vibration: a brimming glass of water could be rested on it with the engine running, without fear of spilling a drop. He also found the four very flexible, so much so that it would pull evenly down to about 5mph in top gear. A road test of a production model was carried out by Dennis May on 30th September, in advance of its debut at that year's Motor Cycle Show. Writing for *Motor Cycling* under the pseudonym Cyclops, it was he who coined the nickname Squariel, which stood the test of time, always to be associated with this model.

Even with economies to get the machine into production with sufficient profit margin, the revamped model was still expensive and sold in quite small numbers. With the recession in the background and sales at a low level, it is difficult to understand why the model was kept in production, albeit it much modified, until Ariel ceased making four strokes in August 1959. Was such drastic modification of the original design, to achieve commonality of parts throughout the Ariel range, really necessary? Although it made good sense at the time, viewed in retrospect it could be argued that the four might have sold better if the original, higher performance prototype had been put into production using the much lighter 250cc frame. Enthusiasts are often prepared to pay just that little bit extra for something a cut above average.

As an interesting aside, it should be mentioned that, as an experiment, Edward and Val Page ran an engine after removing the front crankshaft, reversing the throws to give a 360 degree crank location, and dividing and retarding the camshaft to reposition the cam correctly. The hastily improvised 250cc vertical twin ran so well that it made Val Page wonder why they had bothered with a four! Experiments were also carried out on the four to determine why the engine had a tendency to overheat when pressed hard. Val Page thought the problem might be due to flexing of the crankshafts, because they were of insufficient thickness due to space limitations that precluded any serious enlargement of them or their bearings. To measure any deflection, the crankcase was tapped in several places and lead-tipped bolts threaded in until they just touched the crankshafts. The amount of lead worn away would indicate just how much the crankshafts had flexed under load. When the high speed test concluded, the results revealed they had flexed by as much as fifteen thousanths of an inch! When this occurred, the heat generated sapped the power of the engine: the faster it ran, the hotter it got and more power was lost. Furthermore, the mesh of the crankshafts coupling teeth was also affected so that the engine became noisier.

This led to thoughts of increasing engine capacity. The now somewhat overweight model 4F/31, which went into production during 1931, had already begun to show some limitations. As mentioned, it would overheat when pressed hard, so to help offset this the amount of finning on the cylinder head was increased. Furthermore, as performance tended to fade when a sidecar was attached, even when the overall gear ratios had been changed to suit, there was only one option: increase the capacity to 601cc by opening up the bore size by 5mm to give bore and stroke measurements of 56 x 61mm.

The larger capacity model, designated the 4F6, went on display at the 1931 Motor Cycle Show, alongside the original 498cc 4F5 model, which continued in production as the 4F5 until the end of the following year.

Edward and his assistant, Bert Hopwood, were not confined to working solely on the four cylinder models. Amongst the many other projects with which they became involved was assisting with the development of the new range of models for the 1931 season, which included designing a four valve cylinder head for an alternative version of a new 500cc ohv 'sloper'. Such was the pressure of work that they often found themselves working late into the night to get it all done.

By this time, Edward and Marion had married and were living at 102, Green Road, Moseley, Birmingham. Marion was able to find local employment which not only provided some extra money to help pay some of the bills, but also meant she was not left on her own in the house all day whilst Edward was working long hours trying to prove himself in his new job. At weekends, however, they made the most of their leisure time together.

An Ariel four was first used in competition when Somerville Sikes, an employee of Forced Induction Limited, entered a supercharged version in the 1931 Senior TT. By fitting one of his company's vane-type Zoller superchargers, and using special valves and pistons, the engine was expected to produce about 40bhp at 5000rpm with a blower pressure of 15psi. Unfortunately, preparation of the bike was not completed until the day of the race, so Sikes was not able to take part in practice. In the race the engine seized and Sikes was forced to retire early, so no-one will ever know if the modified engine would have matched up to expectations.

The Bickell brothers, Brooklands habituees just like Somerville Sikes, were determined to win The Motor Cycle Cup by using a supercharged Ariel four. The cup was to be awarded to the first British rider of a British-made, multi-cylinder machine of under 500cc capacity to cover more than 100 miles in the hour on a British track. Iliffe and Sons, publisher of the weekly magazine, had put up the cup to encourage a resurgence of interest in multi-cylinder machines, which had tended to be overlooked during recent years. Although the two brothers tried very hard, the four always failed to achieve their goal. Running the engine on methanol and having a Powerplus supercharger, they used a sleeved-down, 601cc four with cylinder bores reduced to the original 51mm size. Time and time again, the brothers recorded speeds in excess of 100mph, but were never able to maintain it long enough before the cylinder head gasket blew, or some other failing put them out of contention. The former problem was an inherent weakness that excluded the supercharged 500cc four from any sustained high speed work, no matter how meticulously the engine had been prepared.

Having won the prestigious Maudes Trophy on two previous occasions, the Ariel board decided to go for the hat trick in 1931. The perpetual trophy was the inspiration of George Pettyt, of Maudes Motor Mart. To his mind, speed should not be the sole criteria for assessing the quality of a motorcycle. He believed other factors - such as reliability, ease of maintenance, comfort and economy - were just as important and, to make his point, he donated a valuable silver vase to the Auto-Cycle Union in 1923. It was to be awarded annually to the manufacturer whose machines achieved the most meritorious certified test to uphold the prestige of the two wheeler, closely supervised by the ACU.

Ariel devised a series of unusual tests, all of them built around the figure seven, for its attempt to win the Trophy for the third time in October 1931. Seven of Ariel's latest production models would be taken and each of them subjected to a different but ambitious test, the whole operation taking a month to complete and each test embodying a different 'seven' theme. One of them involved a 600cc Model 4F/6 four, the objective being to cover 700 miles in 700 minutes at Brooklands. The first attempt failed after the machine had covered 301 miles at an average speed of 66mph when the engine seized and the test had to be abandoned. Another engine was built from parts randomly selected by the ACU observer, but on this occasion it was assembled more carefully and partially dismantled after being run on the bench for three hours. Any high spots were then removed prior to reassembly - all these operations carried out under ACU observation. After reassembly, the replacement engine was installed in the original cycle parts and the machine ridden to Brooklands for resumption of the test. By the time darkness had set in, 570 miles had been completed satisfactorily, so the machine was locked away in an ACU sealed garage until the following morning.

The next day, after a safety check, during which some minor adjustments were made, the test recommenced and by the time the 700 miles had been covered, 688 minutes, 14 seconds had elapsed. Some further minor adjustments were made before the machine was timed during a flying start lap of Brooklands Outer Circuit. An average speed of 87.4mph was officially recorded; a very commendable result to mark the conclusion of the test. As the other six tests had also proved successful, Ariel was awarded the Maudes Trophy for the third time in succession.

With the addition of another two draughtsmen to the team, another ambitious range of Ariels was made available for the 1932 season after a lot of hard work. Larger and more graceful chromium-plated petrol tanks, some with a red coloured top panel, improved appearance, and wheel rims were chromium-plated with a red painted centre. These were the famous Red Hunter models. The 499cc, four-valve VH32 model made its debut at the 1931 Olympia Motor Cycle Show, followed a couple of months or so later by a 346cc twin exhaust port model in the same range, its engine forward inclined in the frame.

This new range of models, all of which had a specially tuned engine, were given their name by 'Big' Bill Wheeler, the Sales Manager, who suggested the word Hunter. Jack Sangster agreed but thought Red Hunter would sound even better, so Red Hunter it was. It was a name that fitted in well with the horse's head logo already used by the company in advertisements, which thereafter continued in use for a very long time. The earlier 'Sloper' models, machines in which the engine inclined forward in the frame at a pronounced angle, continued in production. This was a design trend campaigned by BSA in the late twenties, even though it had no particular advantages, and was just another passing fad.

Despite Ariel putting on a brave face, the recession was beginning to bite very deeply into its financial structure. Economy was now the order of the day and only token support was given to the works riders in competition events. The parent company, Components Limited, had been particularly hard hit and, by the middle of the year, was faced with irresolvable financial problems. At its peak, the parent company had employed 3500 workers, and was the largest manufacturer of cycle components in the world. The end came in September 1932 when Ariel went bankrupt and the Official Receiver was called in. The parent company and all its subsidiaries were liquidated and the assets put up for sale.

It was at this point that Jack Sangster, from all accounts now a relatively wealthy man, stepped in to rescue the motorcycle side of the business. By virtue of some astute dealing, Sangster bought most of the production machinery from Ariel Works Limited. Having also bought the Endless Rim Company, he was able to transfer this machinery to the latter company's premises. Any that could not be accommodated was taken to the old Ariel car factory, already his property. When these arrangements had been completed it was possible to resume manufacture of Ariel motorcycles at Selly Oak, Birmingham, after Sangster registered Ariel Motors (JS) Ltd. as a new private company. When the manufacture of motorcycles recommenced a month later, it is alleged he had over-stretched himself and the first week's wages were paid from a bank overdraft!

It had been a traumatic time for everyone, not least Charles Sangster, who died soon after the collapse of Components Limited. The formation of the new company called for some restructuring and Jack Sangster took Edward aside to explain what action he proposed taking. His first move would be to "get rid of Val Page", to use his own words, as he considered Page had been making too many mistakes. Unfortunately, Edward's reaction was not what he had expected. Whilst agreeing that Val had indeed made mistakes, he said this was only to be expected as he had been working under too much pressure. Personally, he held Val in high regard because he was a first-class practical engineer who was willing to offer advice whenever it was needed. A modest, kindly man, a true gentleman in every sense of the word, Val was unquestionably a very talented designer, and had already proved himself whilst working for JAP. When he joined Ariel he had taken the company out of the doldrums by designing an entirely new range of models that continued until the end of the thirties and beyond.

What caused Edward the greatest concern was that Jack Sangster intended promoting him to the position of Chief Designer in Val's place. This put him in a most awkward position: whilst he appreciated the offer of promotion and was ambitious for it, he did not like being asked to accept it at the expense of a colleague he held in high regard. He told Sangster he would take the job only if Val was given an equivalent position in the organisation. Fortunately, the situation resolved itself when Val accepted the post of Chief Designer with Triumph and left of his own accord.

Triumph was also in the doldrums with a range of unimpressive models, and needed someone of Page's calibre to project a new model range for the 1934 season. In a letter dated 17th October 1932, Jack Sangster wrote to Edward to confirm his appointment to the managerial staff, giving him permission to use the courtesy title Technical Director when signing letters. His salary would be £400 per annum, plus 5% of the net trading profits of the company, and expenses at the rate of £100 per annum, paid monthly. However, his commission on the net trading profits of the company would be limited to £500 per annum, and was only payable if the monies owed to the company exceeded book debts.

The agreement also restricted Edward's entitlement to purchase anything from the company, unless he could do so at a lower price than he would expect to pay elsewhere. Any such purchases would be invoiced and had to be settled by the 10th of the month following delivery. He was expected to meet petrol and car expenses out of his own pocket. Undeniably, it was a tight deal for a potential member of the board, as one might expect from a shrewd businessman, and was one that Edward needed to consider very carefully before committing himself. In arriving at a compromise, Edward raised the question of royalty payments in respect of his four cylinder engine design, and other patents with which he had been associated. In a reply dated 21st December, Jack Sangster agreed to pay him one fifth of any royalties due to the company from outside companies in respect of these patents (which then totalled seven), with the proviso that they would only be paid if the company was on a profit-making basis. Interestingly, the letterhead now showed A.S. Lucas and H.J. Hughes as Sangster's fellow directors, and gave the company name as Jack Sangster Limited.

By this time Bill Wheeler was another who had left to join Triumph, and Tom Davis had been appointed Sales Manager in his place. Bert Hopwood continued to work closely with Edward and had been elevated to the position of Chief Draughtsman. The 1933 model range was probably one of Ariel's most memorable, as it marked the beginning of the Red Hunter models that continued until World War 2, then carried on after the war until late 1958. The opportunity had been taken to reduce the number of models in Ariel's range to just twelve; with limited production facilities, it made good economic sense to base the single cylinder model range on one motorcycle, and to use it as the basis of a number of different models with alternative finishes and variations in the specification of the engine fitted. The 601cc Square Four was continued, with bore and stroke dimensions changed to 50.4 x 61mm (which reduced capacity to 599cc), an improved lubrication system, and straight cut coupling gears. It was now 25lbs lighter.

The Bickell brothers valiantly continued to try and win The Motor Cycle Cup with their supercharged four. Something always happened to put an end to their endeavours, despite some encouragement from having completed a flying start lap at Brooklands at a speed of 111.42mph. A blown cylinder head gasket continued to be the main reason why the bike was unable to sustain consistent high speed, although it was also plagued by trivial problems that must have caused the brothers great annoyance. In the end, they had to concede defeat when, on 1st August 1934, 'Ginger' Wood on a New Imperial vee-twin completed an hour at Brooklands at an average speed of 102.27mph to take the Cup.

For the 1934 season the Ariel range continued with detail modifications, and the addition of a new 499cc ohv VG model. Towards the end of 1933, at the time when salaries came up for review, Jack Sangster told Edward he was no longer prepared to honour the arrangement which entitled Turner to draw 5% of the company's profits (the company made a profit of £11,000 that year). To offset this, Sangster proposed to pay him a bonus the following year which, in all probabilty, would amount to more. This did, in fact, prove to be the case, as Edward received £100 more in bonus payments, although it did not escape his notice that the profits had again substantially increased too!

Edward's immediate reaction to this proposal was to involve himself in every aspect of the company's business, including new designs, technical research, publicity, motorcycle competitions, advertising and technical assistance on export matters. In short, any area where company interests could be furthered. Although he did this unofficially, it helped give the company a much broader profile and, by the end of 1935, turnover had more than trebled.

During 1935, Edward redesigned his original Square Four engine to increase capacity to 997cc and eliminate any shortcomings. Starting with the bottom end, he discarded the overhung crankshaft assembly and replaced it with two, one-piece crankshafts, each with a central flange to which was bolted a flywheel. One flywheel was bolted to the left-hand side of one flange and the right-hand side of the other, so that the flywheels overlapped and could be increased in diameter. As they could no longer be coupled by teeth on their peripheries, two straight cut pinions in a compartment on the drive side of the crankcase took care of this function. The connecting rods were of RR56 light alloy, with split white metalled big ends. The crankcase now divided vertically instead of horizontally, and had a renewable oil filter. Operated by duralumin push rods, the valve gear was actuated by a single camshaft between the crankshafts.

The camshaft was driven by a Weller-tensioned chain from the half-time sprocket on rearmost crank, which also drove the rear-mounted Lucas Magdyno and distributor. A twin plunger oil pump took its drive from the camshaft's right-hand end and drew oil from a separate six pint oil tank. The cruciform-shaped induction passage of the cylinder head was retained, but its single induction port now faced to the rear and was fed by a large bore Solex carburetter. Designated the 4G, the new 995cc ohv model made its debut at the 1935 Motor Cycle Show and two years later there was an alternative 599cc 4F version.

Although Edward and Jack Sangster had always enjoyed a good working relationship, their earlier negotiations over salary and bonus payments may well have planted the first seeds of discontent for Edward. Bearing in mind how much he had contributed to the success of the rejuvenated company, he must have felt the remuneration he was receiving did not represent a fair return. Now involved in virtually every aspect of the company's business, he had reached the end of his tether. He told Jack Sangster that unless he could achieve a more secure position with the opportunity to earn a better living, he would have to look elsewhere.

Edward timed his approach particularly well, in the knowledge that Triumph was in financial difficulties and intended to close its motorcycle business. Triumph had overspent heavily on car production and, in order for this side of the business to continue, motorcycle production had to be sacrificed to reduce the deficit. Edward suggested that if Sangster was prepared to buy Triumph's motorcycle business, he would run it for him. The thought of buying Triumph's motorcycle assets had already crossed Sangster's mind, and, saying he would give Edward's proposition further consideration, he began negotiations. His initial approach failed as Triumph had already advised the press that its motorcycle business was to be terminated.

However, it took more than this to deter a skilled negotiator. Using all his charm and powers of persuasion, Sangster eventually succeeded in buying the goodwill of Triumph's motorcycle business on very favourable terms during mid-January 1936. Having learnt that the Lloyds Bank's Official Receiver, a Mr. Graham, would be going to London the following day, he met him at New Street station and, by the time they reached London, the deal had been negotiated. Sangster purchased the motorcycle business, its goodwill, assets and plant and machinery for close on £50,000; this also included the lease of a part of the factory and use of the plant that was to be sold at the end of the lease. He even arranged to sell the existing stock of Triumph spares on commission and reclaimed £8000 from the sale of scrap material! Even so, as had happened when he acquired Ariel, the first week's wages had to be paid from an overdraft.

Edward had achieved his objective and was appointed Director and General Manager of the new company, registered as the Triumph Engineering Co. Ltd. to perpetuate the old Triumph name. His salary was commensurate with his new board appointment, and included a commission of 5% of the net profits of the new company. He was now a shareholder, too, with 4.9% of the equity. At the age of 35 this was a significant step forward in his career. As he said many years later, although he was now working hard and getting only five to six hours' sleep a night, the three years that followed the acquisition of Triumph were the happiest of his life.

Chapter 4: The happiest years of his life

To inaugurate the new company, a luncheon was held at the Kings Head Hotel, Coventry, on 27th January 1936, to which Seigfried Bettmann, founder of Triumph in 1886, was invited to take the Chair. Also invited were many Triumph suppliers and dealers, in order to show that the newly-formed Triumph Engineering Company had every intention of maintaining old links and upholding the old company's high standards.

Stanley Evershed had been appointed Chairman of the new company, but this was just a temporary measure as he was a partner of Evershed and Tomkinson, the company's solicitors. Within a few months he was replaced by Seigfried Bettmann; this was an astute move which gave the new company an air of integrity. His appointment was shortlived, but only because it was his wish to end his 50 years of active commercial life with Triumph. His position was then taken by Jack Sangster.

The part of the old Triumph factory occupied by the Triumph Engineering Company amounted to the first three floors of the five storey building. The remaining two upper floors were used as overflow space, to house the repair stores and a small museum. The new management moved in to take charge of a very experienced workforce, with a full range of supporting facilities: there was everything one could expect to find, even a canteen and a surgery. At the centre of the organisation was the vast sales and dealer network which operated on a worldwide basis with the Dale Street factory its focal point.

Although the workforce could not have realised it at the time, it was witnessing a takeover by two quite exceptional men, who became one of the most successful financiers ever associated with the motorcycle industry, and a designer and managing director who headed one of the most successful and profitable small companies of any kind to operate in this country.

Before the re-formed company could commence operations, Edward's and Jack Sangster's first task was to go through the works to conduct a machine-by-machine inspection of available equipment, in order to decide what to keep and what to discard. Having just acquired a complete motorcycle manufacturing unit, any additional expenditure at this time was quite out of the question. Edward's forward manufacturing plans would be largely influenced by the machine tools at his disposal, and this is why he was obliged to retain the bolt-up crankcase with its vertical split - and to continue with it for his twin cylinder models, as it could be made on capstan lathes. He always regretted this and the limitations of the plant at his disposal. To put it into his own words "we were obliged to cut our coat in accordance with the Dale Street cloth".

The workforce had to accept a cut in salary, albeit a small one, but there was little dissent; most were only too pleased to keep their jobs, especially after so much doubt about the future of Triumph motorcycles. The employees took great pride in their work, and were pleased to be associated with such a well-known name now that their future seemed assured.

Eager to get started, Edward ordered an area in the assembly shop to be partitioned off for his office. The drawing office was to be adjacent, on his left, and entered through one door, and the general office was to be positioned in front of him and approached through the other door. From his position at the 'back of the class', he could view the entire area through the glass partitions. Whilst he was in his office, everyone made sure they kept their heads down!

Having reviewed the machinery, Edward and Jack Sangster had next to take a close look at the staffing situation. A workforce of approximately 850 - management and staff - had been employed by the old company on the motorcycle side of the business. Most were retained in their previous positions. One such employee was Alf Camwell, the Works Manager. He had risen from the shop floor of the old company via the Tool Room, and played a leading role in helping unravel previous motorcycle activities at the time of the takeover. He did so with great competence and minimum unheaval. With an excellent knowledge of the equipment at his disposal, and the capability of the workforce, Camwell helped to establish the manufacturing side of the company in its early years, and became what Edward recognised as a key figure. Although outwardly he appeared softer, gentler and more approachable in nature than did Edward, his quiet confidence and persistence produced results. In the beginning his workforce had, of necessity, to make do on a shoestring, but as time passed employees demonstrated ingenuity and an ability to improvise that was to stay with Triumph. As Edward once remarked "they may be a home-spun lot but they certainly know how to get you out of trouble".

When Edward's new designs began to appear, Alf knew his team would need all the ingenuity it could muster. He once said that provided he could keep his team around him he could cope with all that Edward was likely to throw at him. A staunch Coventrian with a strong sense of humour, he once conceded that, although his old company owed its salvation to Selly Oak, the only good thing to come out of Birmingham was the Coventry road! He was very, very popular with his workforce and was later appointed Works Director. His achievements commanded respect from all and his pleasant personality and enormous contribution to the success of the company earned him great affection, which Edward openly showed in later years.

Val Page, Triumph's former Chief Designer, had departed four months before the takeover. With the collapse of the old company's motorcycle side of the business now inevitable, largely because of neglect, Page had moved on to BSA. Working in a similar capacity there, he was about to design a new series of single cylinder four-strokes that would bring some order to that company's bewildering range of models. Frank Anstey had taken his place at Triumph, only to find his job no longer existed four months later. With understandable annoyance he promptly left to join Ariel as its Chief Designer and started planning the 1937 range.

As mentioned earlier, Bert Hopwood had left Ariel with Edward to continue working with him. He was already familiar with Edward's methods, and, more importantly, his temperament, as he had worked with him during the latter's entire time at Selly Oak. At Triumph, Bert set a standard of engineering draughtsmanship which has been copied over the years by draughtsmen all over the world. As the company grew and Edward provided the flair, courage, and often the cheek to initiate new designs, Bert often had to undertake the more difficult task of perfecting the engineering within a tight financial framework. Edward always regarded his own drawings as sacrosanct and took a great deal of convincing that there was any reason for them to be amended. Sometimes the only way to do this was surreptitiously.

Ted Crabtree, the Chief Buyer, was another expatriate from Ariel. He, too, quickly became an important member of the team, with his wealth of experience in motorcycle purchasing. Bright, fresh and confident, he was what Edward described as 'a self-starter'. He knew his motorcycles, had a wide knowledge of materials and their uses and costs, and made a vital contribution to the new projects and the speed with which they were completed. He did not always see eye-to-eye with the Managing Director and relationships became somewhat strained, but of necessity they soon returned to normal in the daily turmoil of day-to-day life. Ted drove himself very hard and Bert Hopwood jokingly claimed he kept a notebook by his bedside so that if he woke up during the night he could jot down what he was thinking about! Above all else he generated a respect and confidence throughout the trade that would help the company through difficult times, when supply priorities would be vital to maintain dispatches and safeguard the goodwill and prosperity of the company. An ambitious man, he set his sights high but left the company in 1950 to return to Selly Oak as General Manager.

The most radical change took place within the Sales Department, as Edward considered that sales ought to be negotiated whilst on the road, rather than in a centralised office. Harry Perrey, the Sales Manager at the time, found himself without either an office or a title! The country was dividied into three separate areas, each with its own manager. Harry was allocated the area that extended outwards from Coventry to Cornwall and Wales; Jack Welton, previously Harry's assistant, remained at the Coventry works and dealt with all of the paperwork generated by the three area managers.

In January 1936, Edward appointed newcomer, Charles Parker, as Company Secretary. A trained accountant, Charles had put his profession aside because he was a motorcyclist at heart and wanted to work for one of the weekly magazines. He joined

the staff of *The Motor Cycle* as both journalist and road tester. At Triumph it soon became obvious that he was a strict disciplinarian in matters of management and office etiquette, but, above all, was a fair administrator and first-class accountant and businessman. His tight and sometimes ruthless control of the financial reins, under the watchful eye of Jack Sangster, helped the company progress to prosperity and success, making him another of Edward's key figures. During the new company's first trading year, profit was in excess of its purchase price the year before. In recognition of his services, Charles Parker was appointed a director of the company in 1938.

Freddie Clarke, employed as Chief Development Engineer in charge of the Experimental Department, joined the management team in 1936, in time to play a part in the development of the Speed Twin. A brilliant engineer and sharp witted, too, Freddie was indisputably a cockney at heart and by accent. Habitually taciturn, he had a boyish, jockey-like figure, and a shock of copper-red curls. Having earlier achieved fame at Brooklands with a 249cc 2/1 Triumph he had prepared himself, Freddie had to toe the line when he joined Triumph in view of its non-racing policy. However, he was still able to have the occasional ride at Brooklands. On an immaculate 249cc Tiger 70 he had prepared himself, he won a three lap handicap race on 12th March 1938 at 92.06mph, with a fastest lap of 97mph. As related later, he was killed in a road accident soon after he left Triumph to work for Associated Motor Cycles Limited in London.

One of the younger staff who had interviewed for employment with the new company was Jack Wickes, aged 21. He had joined the old Triumph Company, where his father worked as Despatch Manager, when he left school. His job was that of print boy, which involved delivering blueprints to all the different departments for a weekly wage of 8s. 4d. He had started attending engineering classes at the local technical college and, as his creative ability developed, went on to study art. His father encouraged him to better himself by getting a job as a draughtsman and, at the time of his interview, he was poised to join New Imperial in this capacity. During his interview he sensed that the Triumph Engineering Company held a bright future for him, and changed his mind, agreeing to become Edward's personal

Woodside, Gibbet Hill Road, the Turner's new home, which lay just off the A429 Coventry to Kenilworth road.

assistant, with an increase in salary. It made sense to Edward to take him on as Jack knew everyone in the factory and could help with forward planning. It was a wise choice as Wickes continued to work for Edward even after the latter's retirement. It was Jack who transformed Edward's sketches into general schemes and sometimes into full colour illustrations. He also submitted his own ideas for approval which, if completed in the office and accepted, could be seen on future production models. His design of the now familiar Triumph headlamp nacelle is just one example. A very good working relationship developed between the pair; Jack had a high regard for his boss who, although not a qualified engineer, was a very shrewd person. Edward would often refer affectionately to Jack as "my pencil", an understatement if ever there was one!

Now working in Coventry, and in a more senior position with an improved salary, Edward bought a detached house, Woodside, in Gibbet Hill Road, just off the A429 Coventry to Kenilworth road. He was working even longer hours and Marion would see little of him except at weekends, when they made the most of their time together. In their new environment they made lots of friends, and travelled around in their cars with three other couples. He even found time to take Marion away on a cruise.

The most urgent priority at work was to project an entirely new range of motorcycles for the 1937 season, and to have them ready in the autumn so that their details could be released to the press. Edward and Bert Hopwood weren't strangers to working well into the night on a wide variety of projects that had ranged from car and motorcycle engines to diesel engines with a modular concept, and, on one occasion, a four cylinder light aircraft engine. Once again, late night sessions became necessary which prompted Edward to set up a drawing office in his new home. On many occasions he would return home, snatch a quick meal and retire to the office for the rest of the evening. When he failed to come to bed, Marion would often find him still working at his drawing board.

Val Page left behind at Triumph a legacy of nine new models, one of them a 650cc vertical twin, and some interesting prototypes. The latter included a side valve engine with hydraulically-operated valves, an overhead camshaft engine having similarities with the Velocette design, and a pressed steel frame like that used by Coventry Eagle for its Silent Superb model. Initially, Edward decided the existing Triumph model range should be continued virtually unaltered, because the takeover had happened whilst the factory was stocking up for the spring sales boom. The Despatch Department was full of new models waiting to be sent out, and there were even more on the assembly track. To move them out to the dealers as quickly as possible was an urgent priority.

After clearing the old Triumph models, Edward's next objective was to commonalise as many parts as possible across the whole model range as an effective way of cutting costs. With this in mind, he projected eleven single models for 1937, all of which would receive just enough attention to give them a new image. They were the first Triumphs to show evidence of his flair for styling. Top of the range were the three aptly-named "Tiger" models, a 250, a 350 and a 500, based respectively on Page's L2/1, 3/2 and 5/5 models. Finished in silver sheen with blue lining, offset by a great deal of chromium-plating, the engines were specially tuned for optimum performance. They were supported by three de luxe roadsters, the 2H, the 3H and the 5H, which had standard engines of corresponding capacity and were distinctive in appearance by virtue of a black and plum red finish with gold lining. The 350, 500 and 600cc side valve models were also retained, reclassified as the 3S, 5S and 6S respectively. All the new models had a four-speed foot change gearbox, with the

positive stop mechanism fully enclosed within the gearbox. The 6/1 twin was discontinued as it had had been a sluggish seller and was camel-like in appearance.

A tremendous air of enthusiasm had been instilled in the workforce, so much so that they got quite used to working on Saturday mornings, often on Saturday afternoons and, if needs be, on Sunday mornings, too. It mattered not to the managerial staff that they worked unpaid overtime; what counted was getting the work done and seeing the new models take shape with, perhaps, the opportunity to ride one of them.

At the 1936 Motor Cycle Show, the last pre-war show to be held in Olympia, the new range of "Tiger" models made quite an impact. Their shapely, bulbous, chromium-plated petrol tanks, with the silver panels outlined in blue, drew the crowds, who were dazzled by the chromium-plated headlamps and wheel rims, polished aluminium alloy chaincases and engine covers, chrome instrument panel and saddle springs, gearboxes with fully enclosed foot gearchange mechanism, and other styling changes. As the show number of *Motor Cycling* so succinctly put it, they were most attractive and colourful, yet did not display any suggestion of flashiness. They were attractively priced, too, at £46 (Tiger 70), £56 (Tiger 80) and £66 (Tiger 90).

Already, the Triumph 'works' team of Ted Thacker, Allan Jefferies and Fred Povey had won gold medals in September's International Six Days Trial on specially prepared versions of models made by the old company , riding 249cc, 343cc and 493cc models respectively.

When Jack Sangster had asked Edward to take up his new position with Triumph, he had said he would be satisfied if the company broke even at the end of eleven months. That target was met with ease and, by the end of the year, the Triumph Engineering Company was £21,000 in profit.

Early in 1937 it was decided that Triumph would make another bid for the Maudes Trophy, in an effort to publicise the Tiger range of single cylinder models. An ACU observer purchased, at random, three stock machines from dealers and used them for the basis of the test, which would take place on the racing circuit at Donington Park. Accordingly, E.B. Ware, who represented the ACU on this occasion, obtained a 350cc Tiger 80 from Glandfield Lawrence of Tottenham Court, London; a 250cc Tiger 70 from W. Brandish and Sons of Coventry, and a 500cc Tiger 90 from Birmingham's Colmore depot.

All three machines were transported to Donington by lorry so that the test could start early the next morning. Preparation of the machines included exchanging the upswept exhaust system for one of the optional downswept sort, fitting a rear mudguard pad, re-jetting the carburetter and fitting a racing plug. There had been a hard frost overnight and in places the track was icy, but, by the time these preparations had been completed, the ice had melted. A last minute change of plan meant that Freddie Clarke rode in place of Wal Handley, who went down with the 'flu. Allan Jefferies rode the Tiger 80 and Ted Thacker the Tiger 70. All three were despatched by Harry Perrey, the test organizer.

Because the machines were new and had not been run in, the riders were asked to first cover ten laps of the inner circuit in second gear, keeping below 20mph. This tedious routine was not helped when persistent, bitterly cold rain set in within the first half-an-hour. Ted Thacker was the first casualty when he was forced to pull in after only eight laps with a rear wheel puncture caused by tyre creep pulling out the inner tube valve. The wheel was changed and he was soon on his way again. After the ten laps had been completed, a further five had to be done at 30mph, after which the riders were free to travel at whatever speed they wished.

Freddie Clarke was soon lapping at around 81-82mph, and

Whichever side you look at, the 1937 343cc ohv Tiger 80 is an extremely attractive machine, with performance to match. Restoration by Ken Middleditch. (Author photos)

Allan Jefferies was only a fraction slower, despite his smaller capacity machine. Even Ted Thacker, on the smallest of the three machines, was going surprisingly quickly. All went well until Freddie came in to say that his machine had lost 10mph, the cause of which was a suspect oil pump. This was changed and he was soon able to lap at over 80mph once more. By now the rain was falling in torrents and, with the riders now bitterly cold, the attempt was abandoned until the following morning for safety reasons. Routine adjustments were permitted under ACU observation, before the machines were locked away for the night.

Next morning weather conditions had improved, so it was decided to start the three hour speed test as soon as possible. Within half-an-hour, the rain had started again, however, and became increasingly heavy. Freddie Clarke was still experiencing oil pump trouble, so the part was dismantled, cleaned, put back together and replaced, all within eight minutes; he had no more problems with it. Whilst all this was going on, Allan Jefferies and Ted Thacker were lapping consistently, and were well ahead of schedule. Refuelling meant lost time, but even this was accomplished with astonishing speed. After one and a half hours (half-time), Allan Jefferies had 44 laps to his credit, Freddie Clarke 41 and Ted Thacker 39. Freddie was rapidly catching Allan until a displaced sparking plug cost him another eight minutes in lost time. Freddie redoubled his efforts to make up the time but overshot one of the corners and slid off in the damp grass, fortunately, without damage to himself or his machine. Undeterred, he pressed on again, thankful that the sun had at last come out. At the finish Freddie was just five laps adrift of Allan's total: 84 to 89. Ted Thacker missed his 80th lap by just 6 seconds.

At the end of the test, it was found that two of the machines had remained remarkably oil-tight. The exception was Freddie Clarke's, from which oil dripped as a result of the work on the pump. On all three machines, the lighting systems still functioned satisfactorily.

Edward was there to offer his congratulations to the riders who, at time, had endured the most apalling weather conditions. For the record the average speeds were: F.W.S. Clarke 54.41mph, A. Jefferies 57.43mph and F.T. Thacker 50.72mph.

The machines were taken to Brooklands in a lorry by E.B. Ware so that the maximum speeds could be recorded the following day with the same riders. The Tiger 90 recorded 82.31mph, the Tiger 80 74.68mph and the Tiger 70 66.39mph. The speeds were calculated after starting with a first flying lap, which also resulted in an advantageous second lap time. On the third lap the riders pulled in.

It had been a worthwhile effort, as was confirmed when the ACU announced towards the end of October that the Trophy would be awarded to Triumph. Too late, unfortunately, for publicity at the 1937 Motor Cycle Show, but very welcome, nonetheless.

Freddie Clarke's earlier successes at Brooklands with a 249cc 2/1 model prompted someone to ask Edward why Triumph had not participated in the Isle of Man TT races in recent years. His reply outlined the policy he had followed throughout his entire career with Triumph. It was his belief that racing was no longer the attractive proposition for manufacturers it had been in the mid-to-late twenties. In those days, a racing machine was based closely on the standard production model, and something like 60% of it was common to both. Now, a racing machine bore little, if any, resemblance to its standard production counterpart. He did not for a moment advocate the abolition of these races, but if they were to be of any value, he believed they should be for stock machines. If that came about, he would be prepared to support such events, as no doubt would other manufacturers. Whether he was right to take this line is open to question because he, like many others, had seen how the Amateur

TT (later to become the Manx Grand Prix) soon came to be known as the 'shamateur TT'. By subtle bending of the rules, works-prepared machines, and even prototypes, were entered under all manner of different guises.

Edward was still not entirely satisfied that he was receiving just reward for his contribution to the success of Ariel and Triumph, even though his personal circumstances had seen a significant, if belated, improvement. Presumably as the result of further approaches by him, Jack Sangster revealed he was considering making Ariel and Triumph public limited companies, with their shares quoted on the Stock Exchange. This would be done through a merchant banker and he asked Edward if he would consider becoming Managing Director of both companies, and a director of the holding company that would own all the shares of both companies. In return, Edward would be expected to sign an agreement binding him to this undertaking for between five and seven years from flotation.

Although Sangster's latest proposition needed very careful consideration, it elicited a somewhat unexpected response. In a two-page letter dated 5th November 1937, Edward did not hesitate to express his disappointment about certain aspects of the proposition, even though he considered he was well able to successfully undertake management of both companies. He, nonetheless, needed to be satisfied that the basis for such an agreement would be satisfactory from his own viewpoint, as he would be unable to give of his best if anything rankled in his mind. In his estimation, the two companies represented an asset worth £350,000 to £400,000 at a conservative estimate, and by the end of the current year would have earned roughly £250,000 since 1933. He felt that he, more than any other, had been responsible for bringing about these results, which was supported by the fact that production had risen from 2700 to over 6000 machines annually. Although Jack Sangster claimed he had not taken anything from the Ariel business other than his salary, except possibly the money used to purchase Triumph, he (Edward) had received nothing more than a salary, and was still awaiting Sangster's response to an earlier promise which he had expected to materialise into something substantial. Had Ariel been floated as a separate organisation, as he had also expected, he'd hoped to receive a cash consideration in recognition of his efforts. Had Triumph been floated in a similar manner, he would have expected a sum considerably in excess of the value of his shareholding, which itself was not commensurate with the effort he had put into the business. If Triumph had been floated for, say £200,000, he thought Sangster's suggestion of a payment of £25,000 fell far short of what he could have expected in view of his efforts over the past five years, let alone the even greater effort that would be needed for the five years to follow.

To tone down his response, Edward conceded that he believed in his own mind that Sangster was anxious to be fair, although he thought the difficulty lay in him being unable to view the whole matter objectively. He was, of course, fully aware of the tremendous efforts Sangster had made to purchase both Ariel and Triumph on favourable terms, and having found the capital to do so had created the basis on which he himself had been able to operate. Yet everything remained in Sangster's hands whilst he was still struggling and holding an insignificant proportion of the equity. Though he had tried to be reasonable, as yet he had little to show for his work. He expected to receive some tangible benefit in recognition of his efforts, before they entered a new era and he assumed responsibility for the futures of both businesses.

To arrive at an equitable compromise, Edward suggested the matter be submitted to an independent arbitrator, if Sangster was willing, in which case he would accept the ruling. Alternatively, his

This page & following two pages: Four photographs of the prototype model T, later catalogued as the 5T Speed Twin, the design with which Edward's name will always be associated. It was so advanced that it sent a cold shiver throughout the British motorcycle industry. The prototype was restored by Dave Jenkin of Yeovil in the blue and silver "Tiger" colours used originally. (Author photos)

shareholding in Triumph could be increased before the flotation took place, and on taking over the management of Ariel, he should receive a percentage of that holding. Jack Sangster's reply to Edward's two-page letter is not available, but subsequent correspondence suggests that the problem was not submitted to independent arbitration. Although Edward eventually agreed to sign the agreement as it stood, the price offered at the time of flotation was inadequate, so the launch was held in abeyance in the hope that the market would become more responsive. The prospect of a re-launch was discussed several times, but never took place. When World War 2 intervened, the idea was abandoned completely.

One can only speculate on what the relationship between Edward and Jack Sangster was that allowed this 'cat and mouse' game to go on for so long. On the surface, at least, they seemed to enjoy a friendship and Edward was never heard to say a bitter word about his employer, yet it is known that their relationship was very fiery at times. Edward was essentially a loyal person and always mindful that Sangster had given him his break in life. Even so, he was very ambitious and had proved he could deliver the goods on numerous occasions, often when working under extreme pressure. His weaknesses lay in his impatience to get things done, completely unaware that he could work at a much greater pace than most and had the ability to do so almost indefinitely. Not too well skilled at motivation, he usually got things done by inspiring others, but if that did not work he would resort to bullying. Jack Sangster had the advantage of being a shrewd entrepreneur who, as Edward noted, would "grab anyone from anywhere if he thought they could do him some good".

Impressed by Edward's skill in getting things done, and his ability to know in advance what the public wanted, Sangster probably also considered him a bit overpowering, and perhaps even likely to challenge his own position in the fullness of time. He must have known the deal he offered Edward at Ariel was hardly what a director designate would expect and, whilst trying to ease the situation a little by appointing Edward Director and General Manager of Triumph, he still did not offer him over-generous terms. Is it possible he became so jealous of Edward's progress and the reputation he had achieved

within the motorcycle industry, that he felt it necessary to put him in his place? Whatever the reason, their friendship persisted even after both had retired, and they would regularly meet for lunch and discuss personal and family matters.

Whatever Edward may have felt, he had of necessity to put these thoughts behind him and devote all his energies to Triumph's new model range for 1938. His conception of a vertical twin now took precedence, and he was able to show his latest design to the motorcycling press at the end of July 1937. Rumour abounded that his new multi would have four cylinders like his earlier Ariel Square Four, in the absence of any knowledge of the experiment he had carried out by uncoupling two of the Ariel's cylinders and running them as though they were a twin. The press had not expected an engine of this type, a design that differed in almost every respect to Val Page's model 6/1 twin.

MINIMUM OIL LEVEL

What surprised the assembled reporters most was that the twin was so compact that it resembled a single in profile, yet weighed 5lbs less than its single cylinder counterpart, despite the obvious need to duplicate many of its components. The cylinders were in a single block casting, with a separate one-piece cylinder head, the crankcase being just a trifle broader than that of a single cylinder model. Internally, the crankshaft was a built-up, three-part assembly, comprising a central flywheel to which a short shaft with a balance weight, a crankpin, and a circular flange, were bolted on each side. The two crankpins were in-line, so that the pistons rose and fell in unison and the firing intervals were evenly spaced. This, and a bore size of 63mm, gave the engine a capacity of 498cc, these being the dimensions of the 250cc single which ensured a commonality of

parts. In consequence, parts were available "off the shelf" as Edward put it. Other features were connecting rods made from alloy forgings, with white metal big end bearings. The whole crankshaft assembly ran on a single ball bearing on the drive side, and a single roller bearing on the timing side. The timing gear was a series of five plain cut pinions, two of which drove the camshafts mounted at the front and rear of the crankcase. The rearmost pinion also drove a Lucas Magdyno mounted at the rear of the cylinder block.

At first, the overhead valve gear was lubricated by a feed taken off the main supply from the oil pump, via a restrictor. As this proved unsatisfactory in service, due mostly to changes in oil viscosity, the feed was transferred to a narrow pipe branching off the return feed to the oil tank, as suggested by Freddie Clarke. The inlet and exhaust valves

29

exact speed recorded during an early road test. An insight into the forethought that went into the design of Edward's Speed Twin engine was given when he was interviewed about it by George Wilson of *The Motor Cycle*. His comments, supplemented by those made later by Jack Wickes, make interesting reading.

Few will deny Edward's original twin cylinder engine was unquestionably the most successful of its kind ever and that it set a trend, worldwide, that would hold good for several decades. The obvious first question was why a twin and not a 500cc single? Quite apart from the fact that Edward's earlier experiments with 'half an Ariel Square Four engine' had shown such promise, there were many other supporting reasons. A twin cylinder of this configuration would provide a better, more even, torque (on the assumption the firing intervals were even) and, because of this it would pull better at lower speeds. Other attributes were that it would be easy to start and have better acceleration, and that it would be easier to silence and run much cooler. Although a single was recognised as the most economic of engines, it had to be acknowledgeded that a twin could run quite satisfactorily with a smaller choke size carburetter, yet show a

were enclosed within separate detachable aluminium alloy rocker boxes, each having two hexagon-headed caps that unscrewed to permit tappet adjustment. Oil drained back through two external branched pipes which connected with the front or rear short tubes that enclosed the push rods. Each cylinder had a curvacious chromium-plated exhaust pipe that led back to a circular silencer clamped to the chainstays of the frame. They gave the machine a nicely balanced look and created the impression of a two port single. A single Amal carburetter served both cylinders through a branched manifold. The dry sump lubrication system was particularly thorough, employing a twin plunger pump within the timing chest actuated by an eccentric pin and a sliding block. It maintained a pressure of 60psi, recorded on the oil pressure gauge mounted in a tank top instrument panel moulded in Bakelite.

The gearbox was the standard four-speed Triumph type with foot gearchange. A nice styling touch was fairing the dome that enclosed the engine shaft shock absorber on the polished aluminium alloy primary drive chaincase. The frame and gearbox were those of the Tiger 90, the former being of the single downtube type with a girder front fork and a rigid rear end. The front wheel was of 20 inch diameter, and the rear 19 inch, with chromium-plated rims, a ribbed tyre on the front and a studded tyre at the rear. The finish of the new twin, designated the model T, was particularly eye-catching, its chromium-plated petrol tank relieved by plum red panels and a metallic Triumph logo. The cycle parts were also finished in the same colour - amaranth red - a name that would soon become familiar to Triumph owners all over the world.

It was claimed that the new twin had been entirely free of problems right from the drawing board, which was confirmed by an experimental model with a sidecar attached that had covered over 10,000 miles on the road in all weathers. Edward had projected a top speed of 90mph when the twin was ridden solo, and this was the

better rate of fuel consumption for a similar power output. This was because the depression in the branched induction manifold was more constant, and any blow-back would be diverted by the carburetter to the other cylinder. The choice of a smaller choke alone would ensure improved vaporisation.

The strength of the engine lay in the rigidity of its built-up crankshaft assembly, which had been patented. Edward decried the need for a centre bearing as he was of the opinion that it was preferable to make a beam inherently rigid rather than restrain it from whipping by a central bearing. To achieve compactness he needed the flywheel to be between the connecting rods, with a mass that would have a moment of inertia capable of resisting shock loadings by its own resistance to movement, and be effective in dampening torque variations and resisting shock loadings from combustion. Since the flywheel was to be in the middle and could not be forged with the crank, the assembly either had to be split or the flywheel threaded over the crank cheeks. By adopting the former line of approach, the result was a crankshaft of immensely rigid construction, which lasted for more than a decade in principle and was used in many thousands of engines. Initially, this crankshaft was serving an engine capable of delivering about 28bhp, but, ten years later, it was still being used satisfactorily in a 650cc engine giving 65bhp on dope. The use of the centre flywheel did, of course, also eliminate the problem of conflicting torsional effects between the flywheel and the internal balance weights, had an external flywheel been necessary. Furthermore, it enabled the large mass of metal to be produced more economically from a high quality cast iron, rather than a steel forging.

An additional bonus was the space between the crank cheeks and the inner periphery of the flywheel flange. It formed a most useful continual centrifuge for the oil supply to the big ends whilst

A blue and silver colour scheme was adopted for the "Tiger" singles, and continued when eventually they were superceded by the Tiger twins. This is a 1938 493cc ohv Tiger 90 in its final year of manufacture; another restoration by Ken Middleditch. (Author photos)

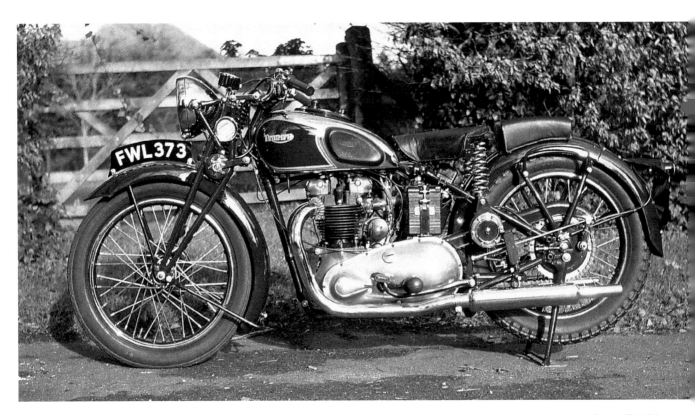

When the 5T "Speed Twin" went into production it was finished in Amaranth Red. This 1937 model is the second earliest "Speed Twin" known, and has an interesting history. It, too, has been restored by Ken Middleditch. (Author photos)

they were being fed at 60psi pressure. The patented big end construction was unique in several respects. Edward used light alloy for his connecting rods, claiming that although it would have been acceptable to use steel rods of no greater weight, the extra mass of metal possible with light alloy helped to stiffen the beam. Moreover, it was his intention to run the light alloy on the upper half of the rod direct on the big end journal, employing a white metalled cap as a safety valve' since, in the unlikely event of oil failure, the white metal would flow and prevent seizure of the cap half only. The material he chose for the connecting rods was Hiduminium RR 56, a Rolls-Royce alloy which provided an excellent bearing material. With no heat break between the bearing and the rod, the heat-carrying capacity of the bearing was very high, sustaining speeds in excess of 8000rpm and extremely high bearing loads without distress. It is interesting to note that Edward is on record as the first person to use RR56 for connecting rods.

There can have been little wrong with his choice as, 35 years on, the same material was being expertly forged by High Duty Alloys for use in Doug Hele's world-beating 750cc three cylinder Triumphs that swept the board in 1972. In the first design, the big end bearing cap was of unique design, being produced from a 100 ton tensile strength nickel chrome steel, with the big end bolts forged integrally with the bearing cap, projecting upwards. The cap's nuts were positioned above the centre line of the big end, not below as was normal practice. Although this construction was quite complicated to manufacture, requiring the bolts to be hollow milled, it saved weight and. moreover. enabled the diameter of the gravity cast crankcase to be reduced, thus increasing rigidity.

Manganese molybdenum alloy steel was used for the crankshaft, heat-treated to 55 tons tensile. To this specification it could still be machined by using specially tipped machine tools without the need for further heat treatment. This eliminated the need for trueing and setting as was first thought would be necessary if the RR56 connecting rods needed to run on a fully case hardened nickel steel journal. This material continued in use even when one-piece crankshafts with a shrunk-on flywheel came into use many years later.

Edward also claimed that greater reliability and durability are inherent in a twin cylinder engine, and went on to explain that this is because the weight of the pistons, the connecting rods and other associated components, is no more than that of their single cylinder engine counterparts. Furthermore, the inertia and centrifugal loadings on each big end, whilst at top dead centre on the exhaust stroke, were less than half those of the single at the same revolutions.

Weight and economics were very much the name of the game and Edward kept a very close watch on the thickness of the crankcase castings, to ensure the sections he prescribed were maintained. It was all part of his policy of cost reduction by letting the metal do the work.

When the range of models for the 1938 season was announced in advance of the 1937 show, it again comprised a total of eleven, one of them the new twin. The singles were similar in specification to those of the previous year, apart from a number of minor modifications. All now featured rubber-mounted handlebars and a single exhaust port cylinder head. Although a speedometer was an obligatory fitting, Triumph, like most other manufacturers, regarded it as an extra and levied an additional charge. A new headlamp (chromium-plated on the "Tigers") had a domed glass, and there was the option of an upswept or a downswept silencer. On two models, coil ignition replaced the customary magneto, a pointer to the future.

As may be expected, the twin was a star attraction at the show, held for the first time at Earls Court. It drew so much attention that most of the other major manufacturers knew they would have to follow suit with something to match it as soon as possible if they were to stay in the hunt. That it retailed at £75, just £5 more than its 500cc single cylinder counterpart, only added to their worries!

During the winter of 1937/8, M. Winslow and I.B. Wicksteed built a supercharged Triumph twin to attempt the 500cc flying start record at Brooklands. Their attempt was made during the Hutchinson 100 race meeting; a bad choice, as it turned out. Held during October 1938, the weather was anything but good, yet, undeterred by a bitterly cold, gale-force wind and a rain-lashed track, the record-breaking attempt went ahead as plannned. A speed of 118.02mph was achieved by the machine's rider, Ivan Wicksteed. Little did he realise at the time that it would stand in perpetuity as Brooklands closed when World War 2 broke out, never to re-open. Triumph now held the 350cc, 500cc and 750cc records at the track. Yet again, Edward's faith in a design that broke new ground had been more than justified, and he was now convinced the only way to go was to drop the single cylinder models and concentrate on twins.

However, before he could do so, he would need to increase the range of the twins, using as many common parts as possible to reduce manufacturing costs. He may not have been too pleased when Allan Jefferies won the British Experts Trial on his much modified 350cc side valve model - Triumph's least profitable model!

For the 1939 range he designed a specially-tuned version of the 500cc Model T, now catalogued as the 5T Speed Twin. Finished in the Tiger range colours, the new model was marketed as the Tiger 100. Essential differences, apart from the colour scheme, were the use of forged alloy pistons to permit the use of a higher compression ratio, and silencers with tapered ends which, when removed, converted them into open megaphones. The extra power of the Tiger 100 made it necessary to hold down the cylinder block by an extra two studs in the crankcase casting. This modification was also made to the Speed Twin so that both models could use a common casting. Supplied with a racing-style pillion pad and a bronze cylinder head available to special order (at extra cost), the Tiger 100 sold fully equipped with lighting for £82.15s. as compared to the Speed Twin's slightly increased price of £76.10s.

Introduction of the Tiger 100 twin meant that the 500cc Tiger 90 single could now be dropped from the range. Only the 249cc Tiger 70 model continued to be a problem. For the first year of manufacture it had been based on the Val Page L2/1 model, which had a unique and integrally forged flywheel and mainshaft. It was widely regarded by competition riders as one of the best 250cc models ever made in this country. Unfortunately, it made virtually no profit and, as Edward put it, "all the 1935 L2/1 Tiger 70s have been sold with a £5 cheque in the toolbox!". His response was to base the Tiger 70 on Page's 2/1 model for the following season as more parts would then be interchangeable with those of the Tiger 80.

No newcomer to winning the Maudes Trophy, Triumph made a further bid to win this prestigious award during March 1939. A Speed Twin and a Tiger 100 were selected at random from two Triumph dealers and checked over at the works before the attempt began. Two Triumph testers, Bill Nicholl (Tiger 100) and Bob Ballard (Speed Twin), rode the two machines from Coventry to John O'Groat's, then to Land's End and from there to Brooklands. There they were met by E.B. Ware, the ACU's observer, who closely monitored the test. At the conclusion of this part of the test, the distance travelled totalled 1806 miles, the route having been shortened because of snowbound roads in the north of Scotland. Both machines had averaged 42mph during this stage. When they arrived at the track, Ivan Wicksteed and David Whitworth shared the Tiger 100 to speed around the track for six hours, whilst Allan Jefferies and Freddie Clarke did the same with the Speed Twin, each rider having a one and a half hour session in the saddle. At the end of the six hour stint, the Tiger 100 had averaged 78.5mph, with a final lap at 88.46mph. The Speed Twin averaged 75.02mph during the same period and completed a final lap at 84.41mph. No mechanical problems of any kind were encountered throughout the test, although the Speed Twin needed to pull in for attention when the oil pipe connected to the pressure gauge in the instrument panel fractured. To effect a hasty repair, its broken end was flattened to stem the flow of oil so that the test could continue with the least possible delay. The Tiger 100 also hit trouble when a nail picked up on the track punctured the rear tyre. A complete spare rear wheel was fitted, which caused a delay of just under four minutes.

When the test had been satisfactorily completed, the riders were met and congratulated by Edward, Charles Parker, the Company Secretary, Eric Headlam, who had organised the test for Triumph, and Jack Welton, the company's Sales Manager. The two machines were ridden back to Coventry in a headwind the following morning at an average speed of 46mph, adding another 106 miles to the total mileage. After lunch, both engines were stripped and examined, and no measurable wear found; even the plain bearing big ends were still as-new. The only signs of damage were on the off-side piston of the Tiger 100 and the near side piston of the Speed Twin, suggesting a recent seizure. It could have had little effect as both machines had been ridden at 65-70mph along the Banbury to Coventry road when returning to the factory.

There was still an air of uneasiness between Edward and Jack Sangster concerning the much discussed agreement mentioned earlier. Since it would bind Edward to a seven year service agreement with Triumph and Ariel, it was essential from his point of view that its terms came closer to resolving the grievances he had expressed. A revised draft, which allegedly took this into account, was submitted to him during May, but after studying it carefully, Edward found it still fell short of his expectations. Working long hours and getting little sleep, he asked for it to be held in abeyance until such time as he had a quiet moment and could go through it carefully.

During the year he gained a further important concession that underlined his staus within the company: he was given his own chauffeur, Frank Griffiths. Although their relationship was sometimes stormy, enough to provoke Griffiths sufficiently to give his notice, or alternatively for him to be sacked many times, the bond between them survived for many years.

During May, the weekly magazine *Motor Cycling* proposed sponsoring a race meeting at Donington, to include some races in which standard sports machines could take part. With this in mind the Manufacturers' Union, which represented British motorcycle manufacturers, thought it would be a good idea if a convoy of machines ridden by their manufacturers' representatives, assembled at The Royal Hotel, Ashby-de-la-Zouch, and rode to the track. There they would be entertained to lunch by Roland Dangerfield, Managing Director of Temple Press Limited, who published *Motor Cycling*. The idea behind this demonstration was to give spectators the opportunity of seeing some of the leading personalities of the British motorcycle industry riding their own products. A good response resulted, over 50 taking part, led by Gilbert Smith, President of the Manufacturers' Union, driving a Norton sidecar outfit. Sir Malcolm Campbell and his son Donald joined the party by riding their own machines from London, and Triumph was well represented by a trio of Speed Twins ridden by Edward, Charles Parker and Jack Welton.

Whilst the more senior members of a manufacturer's staff rarely rode their own products, this could not be said of Edward. Disinclined to believe the reports of the works testers, especially when they were testing a new model, he would often take a machine and tear off down the road in a crescendo of noise, still clad in his pin-stripe suit and with the brim of his trilby hat jammed tightly on his brow. Like as not he would do so on an unregistered machine, too impatient to wait and have trade plates fitted. Anyone who saw him leave the factory in this fashion was left in no doubt about his riding ability and desire to travel at speed. When he returned he would have a confirmed opinion and a positive verdict, with instructions to either proceed forthwith or "put it under the bench and we will look at it later".

Occasionally, Edward would ride out with the testers and exchange bikes. Jack Wickes recalls one occasion when Edward put his head around the Drawing Office door and said "Wickes, I'm taking your machine to Whitley Common with Ballard and Nicholl to compare steering geometry. I trust it's a sound runner?" Jack's reply "It is at present" brought forth a knowing look! An hour later, Edward put his head around the door again and said "I regret to say Wickes that during the investigation your girder front fork got bent. Get it repaired and borrow another machine in the meanwhile". He had been away from Meriden for about an hour and as Whitley Common was only a short distance away Jack had wondered why he had been away for so long. The reason was now all too apparent - Edward had been home to change his suit. As he walked away, his normal seafaring stride failed to conceal a limp! Both Ballard and Nicholls were too discreet to enlarge on the incident.

The Speed Twins were already acquiring a good reputation. They had been used by a motorcycle guard of honour in British

The 1939 499cc Tiger 100, the high performance version of the Speed Twin which replaced the Tiger 90. Note the 'cocktail shaker' silencers which, when the ends are removed, provide open megaphone exhausts.

TRIUMPH TIGER '100'
500 c.c. O.H.V. TWIN

34

Columbia during the 1939 Tour of Canada by King George V and Queen Mary. Furthermore, Sir Malcolm Campbell, three times winner of the World Land Speed Record, had written a splendid unsolicited testimonial, which read as follows:

In my opinion the Triumph Speed Twin has no equal. It is a machine eminently suitable for all purposes, is an extremely sound engineering job, and the workmanship is superb.

I acquired my first Triumph motorcycle in 1908, and never went without one until the outbreak of the Great War in 1914. I now own a Triumph Speed Twin, and a Tiger 100, and so long as I indulge in this pastime I shall continue to use the machines made by this eminent firm.

New Scotland Yard Police had ordered a whole fleet of Speed Twins for its mobile units, soon to be followed by an order from the Metropolitan Police and other police units all over the world. The Speed Twin was making its mark less than two years from inception.

New Imperial was acquired by Jack Sangster during 1939. The company had been declared bankrupt at the end of the previous year, despite the many excellent models it made and its not inconsiderable number of racing successes. It was planned at first to continue manufacture under the original name; there was a need to add a lightweight machine to the range of motorcycles made by Sangster's companies. However, it was eventually decided instead that Edward would design a completely new 200cc ohv single cylinder model to carry this famous name.

Within six months, a prototype was up and running; an unusual machine, some features of which appeared in Edward's later 3TU twin cylinder model, a prototype that was being being developed after World War 2 as a cheap utility model. According to Bert Hopwood, its engine required a very unusual method for the manufacture of its cylinder, starting with thick section tubes, the insides of which formed the cylinder bores. Finning was added in the form of a series of sheet copper pressings interspersed with spacers, the assembly being brazed together as a whole. The machine also used the tiny three-speed gearbox Edward had designed for use on a 3TW military prototype, and disc wheels. Initial tests were handicapped by recurring engine seizure problems and unpredictable handling, but before these problems could be eradicated, priorities in other areas brought all further development work to a halt. As a result the New Imperial name was never resurrected.

In November the ACU announced that Triumph had again been awarded the Maudes Trophy. Yet Edward was completely unable to take in this welcome news. A recent personal tragedy had completely knocked the bottom out of his world.

Saturday 9th July 1939 was the start of another weekend, a day to which Edward and Marion had been looking forward. It had been their tenth wedding anniversary the day before and that morning they were to meet up with three other couples who had become their constant companions. The women wanted to go shopping, so Edward and the three men went to visit the factory. The womenfolk were late returning home so Edward set off to find them, passing a road accident on his way. Unable to find them he returned home, where he was summoned to the hospital. On arrival there he was told that the four women had been involved in the road accident he had passed, and all had died. He was so deeply shocked that, to use his own words from an interview given only a few weeks before his death: "I fainted away like a baby and coming to from that faint is one of the most painful recollections of my life, that will follow me to the grave". According to reports in the 10th and 11th July issues of the *Birmingham Post*, the car Marion was driving had been hit by a lorry from behind on a notoriously tricky part of the road. In those days, cars didn't have head restraints or seat belts, and all four women had suffered broken necks as a result of whiplash.

The other three couples had children, but not Edward and Marion. She had been unable to bear a child and only a couple of months earlier had gone in to hospital for what proved to be a very painful operation, presumably to attend to this problem. Their children might have helped the other three men in their grief, but for Edward it was the beginning of many lonely years. To make matters worse, he had to pass the scene of the accident every day on his way to and from work. He kept in touch with two of the families; the third husband broke off all contact.

It was a very long time before Edward could come to terms with the situation, and he tried to avoid talking about it. It was fortunate that Marion had taken on Jennie, a young girl from a Welsh mining village, to help her with the housework, and that she stayed on after the fatal accident. At least Edward was rarely on his own in the house, even though she lived in a separate part of it. His home must have seemed very cold and cheerless after a long day at work, with only his labrador for company. He spent much of his time listening to the radio or reading, having joined a book club.

The accident failed to deter Edward from driving, probably because he prided himself on being a safe driver. Yet he was always impatient and inclined to take risks. One evening when he was alone, driving Jack Sangster's Rover back home from Birmingham, he drove into the back of a lorry carrying telegraph poles, one of which went through his windscreen. Perhaps that is why he was given a chauffeur!

The Dale Street drawing office in 1939, with a young Jack Wickes in the foreground. (Vida Wickes)

Chapter 5: War, and all manner of problems

When the British Government's ultimatum expired on 3rd September 1939, and Britain once again found itself at war with Germany, there was no longer any possibility of holding a 1939 Motor Cycle Show. Petrol rationing came into effect almost immediately and branded fuels disappeared 'for the duration', to be replaced by 'pool', a low octane petrol that made even restricted travel less pleasant. It not only took the edge off the performance of the more sporting models, but also caused an engine to 'pink' unless a plate was inserted under the cylinder barrel to lower the compression ratio.

Despite this, manufacturers were optimistically giving details of their 1940 model ranges, Triumph included. As had been the case during the 1914-18 war, the manufacture of motorcycles for the civilian market was allowed to continue for a while, with the proviso that their production would be limited as priority would go to making machines for the armed forces. Triumph had booked advertising space on the front cover of one of the motorcycling weeklies to coincide with the release of details of its 1940 model range. It would have featured the new 350cc twin, but the outbreak of war put an end to that. Although the covers had already been printed, all had to be scrapped at the last minute and reprinted with another advertisement. Nine years would elapse before the motorcycling world got a glimpse of the new model 3T.

Announced at the end of October 1939, Triumph's 1940 range comprised nine models. All had higher overall gear ratios to help achieve better fuel economy by the addition of one tooth to the engine sprocket, and revised carburetter settings to weaken the mixture. The Tiger 100 and Speed Twin models continued to dominate the range, the latter having check springs added to its girder front fork so that a lighter main spring could be substituted, and a four gallon petrol tank with recessed knee grips. A contemporary photograph of a Tiger 100 showed it fitted with more deeply valanced mudguards and a rear carrier, features that did little to enhance its sporting image. These parts were, however, catalogued as optional extras, although few ordered them. In due course, the Tiger 100 also featured the check springs fitted to the girder front fork and a lighter main fork spring, to fall into line with the Speed Twin specification.

The other models were four ohv singles, the 2H and 3H de luxe models, and the Tiger 70 and Tiger 80. They were augmented by three side valve models, continuation of the existing 600cc 6S model and two new models, the 3SE and the 5SE, of 350cc and 500cc capacity respectively. The 3SE and 5SE models previously had been destined for export and differed from the others in having a pressed steel chaincase, a rubber pan saddle and a petrol tank without a top mounted instrument panel. A further difference - coil ignition - applied to the 3SE model only. All models, with the exception of the Tigers and the Speed Twin, were finished in black with white lining, the two SE models being distinctive in having gold lining instead. The Tigers retained their characteristic silver finish with blue lining and the Speed Twin its now familiar amaranth red colour.

As may be expected, prices had increased due to the added cost and forseeable shortage of raw materials. To help offset this, the two new SE models were marketed at a more affordable level resulting from the economies made in their specification, as detailed in the foregoing. Notable absentees from the range were the 250cc 2H model and the 500cc 5H. This had been expected as the company had already advised that these two models were nearing the end of production.

During February 1940, Jack Sangster wrote to Edward following a recent conversation in which he had again

The 349cc 3T and Tiger 85 models would have been introduced to the 1940 model range had not World War 2 intervened. This is the Tiger 85 which, although listed after the war, never went into production due to the high demand for the already well-established models. Only its standard 3T counterpart was made.

pressed him to put his signature to the long-proposed agreement. Sangster appeared to be getting a little exasperated that it was still not signed, and made some further concessions to help bring their protracted negotiations to a swift conclusion.

Firstly, Sangster agreed that Edward's 4.7% holding in Triumph could be exchanged for a 10% holding in Colmore Investment Trust Ltd, the holding company for the shares of Triumph and Ariel. He stated quite catgorically that he had no wish to change the name of this company, nor did he wish to increase its share capital, presumably because the proposed flotation of the new holding company necessary to have fulfilled this function had failed to materialise. Secondly, Edward would have to agree to enter into a seven year service agreement (six years from January 1940) with Triumph and Ariel, the terms of which were substantially similar to those of the agreement he had approved the previous May. The agreement would provide Edward with a commission on the combined profits of both companies amounting to two and a half percent up to £100,000, and five percent thereafter. His duties in relation to Ariel would remain flexible and subject to modification, according to developments. Thirdly, sale of his shareholding to a third party would be restricted unless it was also offered to Sangster on similar terms. There was also the option to repurchase Edward's holding for £10,000 in the event of his non-fulfilment of the service agreement. Finally, came the sting in the tail: a £1000 loan made to Edward by Colmore in 1936, which would have been cancelled in the event of a flotation, would have to be repaid by him under the proposed agreement.

Sangster stressed that these points represented the general outline of the changed arrangements, and asked Edward to confirm if he now agreed to accept them in principle. This was necessary because it would involve his solicitors in a considerable amount of work to draw up the amended agreement for signature. Edward's reaction to again being put under pressure to sign is not known, but it seems improbable that, even in its amended form, he would have found the Service Agreement acceptable from what followed at a later date. It offered no solutions to his main bone of contention; the question of the exploitation of his patent rights, and his royalty payment entitlement if Sangster negotiated licensing of these rights outside of his own group of companies.

Other matters now took precedence, the most urgent of which was to secure a contract for the production of a motorcycle suitable for military use. Although motorcycles played a leading role in the 1914-18 war, there still was not a specially designed military motorcycle. The government supply departments had been very diffident in attitude, even though, from time to time in the early thirties, they had placed limited orders for machines such as the Triumph NL3 and the Douglas L29. Even when war was virtually imminent they were still carrying out evaluation tests, the basic requirement being that any such machine should have a capacity exceeding 250cc, not weigh more than 250lbs, have a maximum speed of 60-70mph, and a fuel consumption of 80mpg at 30mph. Furthermore, it should have six inches ground clearance, be capable of stopping in 35 feet from 30mph, and inaudible from a half mile distance whilst being ridden. If a prototype machine fulfilling this specification succeeded in passing the evaluation tests, it would be made under contract to an identical specification by a number of different manufacturers.

Triumph, along with several other leading manufacturers, already had prototype designs under test, including a lightweight 3TW model. None, however, was sufficiently well advanced, and civilian models were pressed into military service, finished in matt khaki. 1400 machines left the Dale Street work in six weeks, and although Triumph's 3S and 5S side valve models were best suited for military service, some twin cylinder models were also included.

Whilst all this went on, work on the 3TW military prototype was now well advanced. Designed by Edward, the 3TW was a lightweight 350cc vertical twin that owed some allegiance to the now 'mothballed' 3T twin. It was unusual in many respects, having only a diminutive three-speed foot change gearbox (as projected for the aborted pre-war New Imperial project), and a welded tubular frame with only a lower top tube, using an internally reinforced petrol tank as a structural member to replace the missing top one. The engine was an ohv twin, its lower end having a characteristically-shaped Triumph timing cover, with an unusual separate circular cover at the base. The timing chest contained the usual assembly of pinions, including a drive to the rear mounted magneto. What broke new ground was the use of an alternator to power the direct lighting system, hence the additional detachable circular cover that formed part of the timing cover. It was the first recorded use of an alternator on a motorcycle.

Triumph's 3TW was one of several prototypes demonstrated to senior army personnel on Bagshot Heath during the early years of the war. It weighed only 230lb, well below the army's 250lb limit, and ascended the one-in-two-and-a-half gradient of the test hill with ease. However, contemporary reports suggest the engine was peaky, producing most of its power from 3000rpm on, and needed a heavier flywheel assembly and smaller choke size carburetter to lower the usable power range. Unfortunately, these modifications increased the weight to just over 260lbs, though not entirely as a result of actually having to fit them. Light alloy had been used wherever possible to help reduce overall weight. Now in short supply due to the heavy demands of the aircraft industry, cast iron had to be substituted, something which had to be taken into account by amending the stipulated weight limit. Army personnel were impressed by the modified 3TW, and when Triumph received a contract to make this machine during July 1940, fate intervened. Full details of the 3TW were published in the 6th March 1941 issue of *Motor Cycling*.

The early part of the war had been much quieter than expected, with only a limited amount of bombing by enemy aircraft, mostly targetted at military installations and in the form of nuisance raids. Most of the action took place in the air, where the Luftwaffe and the RAF battled for supremacy whilst the former's fighter-escorted bombers tried to destroy Britain's airfields. When the Luftwaffe failed to annihilate the RAF to set the scene for an invasion by sea, it switched to bombing under the cover of darkness. When the first bombs fell on London, Winston Churchill ordered the bombing of Berlin in reprisal, which provoked Germany into embarking on a campaign to eliminate most of this country's major cities. On 14th November 1940, Coventry was the chosen target, and the city centre and its ancient cathedral were destroyed in a particularly vicious attack, one result of which was that a new word, blitz, short for blitzkrieg (a swift, intensive military attack), was added to the English language.

The Triumph works in Dale Street lay within the shadow of the cathedral and it, too, was razed to the ground. It was particularly ironic that the first batch of fifty 3TW models was already packed in wooden crates awaiting despatch, only to be destroyed with the factory. With virtually everything gone, it was a question of salvaging whatever was possible in the way of usable and repairable machinery, and finding somewhere else to resume production. Frank Baker was amazed to find that the petrol tank in the yard had survived and still contained 2000 gallons, albeit contaminated by water. When Edward and Jack Wickes visited the site to see for themselves the extent of the damage, Frank was given a crate of beer to keep quiet about his discovery. The water was pumped off and, although the petrol was dyed red to ensure it was used for its designated purpose (a government requirement),

Jack was allowed to draw off a couple of gallons to give to an uncle. The remainder was used to cover many more private miles than official petrol allowances would have permitted.

Early signs of a rift between Edward and Jack Sangster now began to appear. Edward was in favour of having the factory rebuilt well away from Coventry's city centre, as he felt sure that Coventry would be bombed again, as indeed it was only a few months later. Jack Sangster wanted to have it rebuilt on its old site, but the War Damage Commission was not in favour as it and Coventry Council had other plans. Edward went ahead and acquired a site in Meriden six miles from the city centre, just off the A45 main Coventry to Birmingham road, despite initial rejection of the plan by Meriden Rural District Council. To say that Jack Sangster was not best pleased with the outcome is an understatement, as became evident later.

To get things going before the new factory was up and running Triumph personnel took up temporary accommodation in somewhat austere premises, in what was known as The Cape, by the Grand Union Canal, at Warwick. The former home of the Benford Mortar Mix Company, it had an adjoining derelict chapel with a bell tower, its exterior clad in corrugated iron. The chapel housed Triumph's commercial staff, who aptly christened it 'The Tin Tabernacle'.

The 3TW project had to be abandoned completely, as there was no chance of building a replacement batch of machines with everything gone, including the tooling. All that could be produced were military versions of the pre-war 350cc ohv side valve singles, the 3HW and 3SW, and mostly the former. Both gave reliable service in the hands of army personnel. Management as well as shop floor personnel rolled up their sleeves and set about recovering as much plant and equipment as they could, including that which was considered repairable, to get it set up and working in the temporary accommodation.

Lack of drawings, most of which had been destroyed, was the biggest problem. Even if they could be redrawn, all of the measurements and tolerances had to be identical to those of the originals, otherwise none of the new replacement parts would fit.

Hidden danger. An unexploded bomb lies amongst the ruins of Triumph's Dale Street factory in the centre of Coventry.

Fortunately, Jack Wickes had been at a cinema in Leamington Spa when the air raid sirens had sounded to signify the start of the raid on Coventry. With great presence of mind, he went straight to the factory and grabbed as many drawings as he could to take to a safe place. Still others were retrieved from suppliers who held facsimile copies, and from Edward's own files at home, even though they needed updating. Any that were still missing had painstakingly to be re-created. Unfortunately, steel filing cabinets were hard to obtain and the cardboard boxes in which the drawings were filed were savaged by the mice that infested the canalside factory. Sometimes it seemed as though they could never hope to win against such adversity.

The 350cc ohv 3HW model in particular provided sterling service, being similar in most respects to the Tiger 80 model from which it had been derived, apart from the cast-in-one cylinder head and rocker box of cast iron. These models were easily recognised by the circular cover above the push rod tubes. Many

The "tin tabernacle", Triumph's temporary home alongside the Grand Union Canal at Warwick. As much of the production machinery as could be salvaged was moved to Warwick, and all the engineering drawings that had been lost had to be re-created. All that could now be produced was the 3HW, a military version of the pre-war 343cc single.

3HWs continued to give good service after the war, and could be seen at early post-war grass track racing events because the engine responded well to amateur tuning.

Edward's continuing correspondence with his solicitors confirmed that his main grievance with Sangster's proposed agreement - the need to safeguard his patent rights should his skills be sought outside the motorcycle industry - had still not been addressed. Edward was willing to enter into a 50/50 partnership with Sangster, assuming the latter felt such a proposition was worth pursuing and would give it his financial backing. Any such negotiations would, of course, fall outside the scope of the business activities with which he was normally involved, such as the design of a tractor, motor car or aircraft engine. His objective was to limit the extent to which the patent rights and any royalties arising from any of his inventions might be exploited, should Jack Sangster become a partner in any such transactions.

At this time Edward was, after Marion's unfortunate death, still "a miserable little man", to use his own description many years later. Although he had made no attempt to accept Sangster's earlier revised agreement and ease the troubled relationship that existed between them, what he least expected happened. Soon after production had commenced during 1942 at Britain's most modern motorcycle factory, the new Triumph works in Meriden, came the news on 23rd July that Jack Sangster had summarily dismissed him.

Edward had no need to go looking for another job: no sooner had word got around the industry about his departure from Triumph than he was contacted by James Leek, Chief Executive of BSA. Anxious to take him on, Leek asked Edward to come and see him, so that they could discuss how best to make use of his considerable talents. The outcome was an offer from BSA to employ Edward as Technical Director, with what amounted to a roving commission to help solve problems as they occurred within the BSA Group. Some of this work involved investigation of spring problems in Oerlikon guns, and Edward also redesigned the cylinder head of what became the post-war B31 and B33 models.

The design had been evolved from the pre-war B29 model (later re-classified as the B30), which had hairpin valve springs as the result of Joe Craig's involvement with BSA for a short while before the war. Now coil springs were wanted instead as they took up less space. This was followed by a request to design a military model for BSA; like Triumph, BSA was anxious to secure an army contract for its production if it met with army approval. Edward's previous involvement - along with Bert Hopwood - with Triumph's 3TW put him in an ideal position to take this on, although a somewhat bizarre situation arose when this news reached Jack Sangster.

Already far from pleased that Edward had joined BSA, Triumph's greatest rival, the news of BSA's latest project seemed to infuriate Sangster. Triumph still lacked a prototype design after having to abandon its 3TW venture when the factory had been destroyed during the Coventry blitz. Bert Hopwood had been put in charge of Triumph's design after Edward's departure, and Sangster was well aware that there was nothing to replace the 3TW. Once he got to know about BSA's intentions, he was determined Triumph should have a prototype up and running before BSA. That it would be necessary to achieve this within three months in order to meet his target date deadline was of little consequence. To be first was the all-important factor as Sangster had no intention of submitting the machine for evaluation tests: it would be broken up after the press had been made aware of its existence.

A tall order under any circumstances, but one to which Hopwood applied himself readily, knowing he had a head start. Using a modified Triumph twin crankcase with a Tiger 100 crankshaft assembly, he incorporated some of his own ideas, and, by adapting a top end based on the 3TW design, came up with a modified version, a 500cc side valve vertical twin. Evidence of his influence on its design can be found within the timing chest, in which he used a tensioned endless chain to drive the camshaft and a rear-mounted Lucas Dynomatic coil ignition system. Hopwood was not in favour of using a train of straight cut pinions, as he considered they added to the mechanical noise of an engine and would give his prototype the characteristic Triumph twin rattle. The Dynomatic ignition system dispensed with the need for a magneto, and took the form of a dynamo mounted at the rear of the cylinder block, driven at engine speed. The left-hand end of the unit contained a contact breaker-cum-distributor with a two-to-one reduction gear and automatic advance-retard mechanism of the centrifugal type. The ignition coil was mounted separately, immediately below the petrol tank. Hopwood also used a single camshaft for both sets of valves, mounted in front of the cylinder block. This simplified tappet adjustment by having forward-facing detachable covers at its base.

For the gearbox, Hopwood favoured a separate, standard Triumph four-speeder, as he had always considered Edward's tiny three-speed 3TW gearbox inadequate. Interestingly, the prototype was fitted with

The new factory at Meriden in March 1942 after completion, but before occupation. (John Nelson)

a telescopic front fork which gave five and a half inches of movement; the first time this type of fork was used on a Triumph.

When complete, the machine weighed 330lbs, only 6lbs more than the 350cc 3HW single, despite the enforced use of cast iron for the cylinder head and block. It was an easy machine to maintain and repair, and preliminary tests confirmed it would cruise all day at 55-60mph with complete reliability. It was made clear, however, that this model, and the earlier 350cc twin, would not necessarily be offered for sale to the general public after the war.

Sangster's target was met - in seven weeks - and the Triumph 5TW prototype was unveiled to the press during late February 1943, well in advance of BSA's offering. As anticipated, the 5TW was broken up soon after. Hopwood's efforts were not wasted completely, though: later, after further modification, the 5TW eventually emerged after the war as the 500cc TRW side valve twin, as will be apparent later.

Edward's 490cc BSA design resembled that of his earlier 3TW twin in some respects, as it also employed side valves and had a single, forward-mounted camshaft. It had a three-speed gearbox, too, which, in this design, was bolted to the rear of the engine crankcase to give the appearance of unit-construction. This necessitated the use of an adjustable tensioner to retain correct primary chain tension. The final drive chain also had fixed centres and used a movable jockey sprocket to maintain tension; this allowed complete enclosure. Other features included a duplex cradle frame and a telescopic front fork, the latter making its first appearance on a BSA.

Initially, direct lighting was used by mounting a crankshaft-driven alternator on the outside of the primary chaincase, but later the system was modified to include a rectifier and a battery. A Solex carburetter supplied the mixture to the engine. A most unusual feature was location of the toolbox in the top of the petrol tank. The speedometer was also recessed into the tank top, a trend continued on the early post-war BSA models. Ironically, the BSA prototype was not accepted by the army and never got beyond the prototype stage.

Many attempts were made during the war years to keep alive the interest in motorcycling, one of which was a series of papers written by prominent engineers and designers which were presented at local meetings of the Institution of Mechanical Engineers. Edward was asked to prepare a paper on Post-war Motorcycle Development for the Coventry section of the Institition at Coventry Technical College on 11th May 1943. Unlike the first meeting, it attracted a quite different audience, comprised mostly of representatives from the motor car industry and motorcycle accessory manufacturers. His paper was well received and, in the lively discussion that followed, the car manufacturers had some interesting comments to offer. Edward strongly refuted the inference that the evolution of the lightweight car had been largely responsible for the decline in motorcycle sales since 1930. In his opinion, the cause was directly attributable to the apathy of those who professed to have motorcycling's interests at heart. In reply to other questions, he confirmed he was very much an advocate of plain bearings in motorcycle engines and, with remarkable prophecy, claimed transmission by belt would eventually be acceptable, though only in primary drives. Edward also expressed concern about the need to reduce noise and vibration, which acted as deterrents to potential purchasers. In addition, he believed thought had to be given to some provision for carrying luggage.

Now that he was in BSA's employ, Edward once again raised the vexed question of the exploitation of his own patent rights, which led to BSA submitting a draft agreement for his approval. His solicitors advised that he should reject this agreement and 'bind himself' to give BSA the first option on any of his ideas about motorcycles. He was also advised not offer his patents to any other company, in consideration of which BSA should pay him a royalty on the receipts from any of his inventions. Furthermore, he should also ensure the patents were applied for in his own name.

How Edward reacted to this advice is not known, but the matter appears not to have been referred to again, no doubt due to a sudden and unexpected change in Jack Sangster's plans. What followed was to have a dramatic affect on Edward's future with the British motorcycle industry. After Sangster had seen BSA's prototype, he had misgivings about getting rid of Edward, and contacted him soon after to say he would very much like to see him as soon as possible. When the two of them met, Sangster openly admitted he had made a mistake and asked Edward if he would return to Triumph on more acceptable terms.

Chapter 6: Back at Triumph's helm

On 10th August 1943, Edward wrote to James Leek, BSA's Chief Executive, to confirm his resignation from BSA after accepting Jack Sangster's offer to return to Triumph as its Managing Director. Edward had seen Leek the evening before to discuss this, and, in the second paragraph of his letter, he wrote: "It is with very mixed feelings that I request your acceptance of my resignation as I have been very fairly and very courteously treated both by yourself and all members of the staff of BSA".

Although Edward had been very glad to accept Leek's offer to join BSA after his unexpected dismissal from Triumph, it seems likely that, deep down, he had found it very difficult to accept the discipline inherent in such a huge complex. It would have been a very different atmosphere to that he had been accustomed to in a much smaller private company where he alone held the reins and had responsibility for making decisions.

Having been invited to return to Triumph considerably strengthened Edward's hand in negotiating a much better deal with Jack Sangster in terms of salary, commission, allowable expenses and improved personal stake in the company. He took up his new post as Triumph's Managing Director on 1st September 1943, with an eight year contract and a salary of £1500, inclusive of all director's fees. In addition, he was given an allowance of £250 per annum, paid monthly, for running and maintaining his car. Further entitlements included a 5% commission on net trading profits of the company for each year, after charging director's fees and the payment of all salaries, bonuses and commissions, and making the necessary reserves for depreciation and liabilities. The question of patent rights was again raised and it was made clear that, whether or not they related to any of the company's products or methods of production, they were to be retained solely for the company's benefit, which would meet any costs.

The service agreement on which Edward's return to Triumph was based seemed to offer a reasonable compromise, in view of the earlier protracted negotiations, although it failed to resolve in his favour the question of royalties from his patents. That these had been singled out for special mention in the new agreement showed that Sangster was unwilling to yield ground on this contentious issue, which Edward would reluctantly have had to accept when he signed.

His first priority on re-joining Triumph after an absence of almost eighteen months was to take a look at Triumph's 5TW prototype military model design which Bert Hopwood had modified in accordance with his own ideas. The Fighting Vehicle Research and Development Establishment at Chobham had re-drafted the specification, having come to the conclusion that performance was not as important as the ability to provide long, reliable service and a greater degree of flexibility at lower speeds. Overhead valve engines were no longer so much in favour, so lightness and the ability to negotiate rough terrain were virtually the only original requirements still to be met. This meant that a side valve vertical twin now stood a much better chance of being accepted.

Edward reverted to the use of straight cut timing pinions in the timing chest which he had originally specified, and made a few other modifications, after which several prototypes were submitted for extended trials. After the war it was possible to substitute an aluminium alloy cylinder head for the cast iron original, and adopt the running gear used by most of the Triumph range from 1946. Eventually, the TRW prototype, as it was now known, was accepted for military use and received NATO approval. Machines and spare parts went to a number of foreign governments, as well as to the RAF and Marines, and departments such as the Ministry of Defence, for use by dispatch riders. Although BSA's equivalent never got beyond the prototype stage, the method of bolting the gearbox to the rear of the engine to give the appearance of unit construction was used later on the BSA A7 and A10 twins destined for civilian use.

It would be reasonable to expect that Edward and Jack Sangster now enjoyed a more cordial working relationship. However, towards the end of 1943, Edward was astounded to learn that Sangster had agreed in principle to sell Ariel to BSA, the deal to be completed by the end of the following year. Furthermore, it had been agreed that if, at any time, Sangster wished to dispose of Triumph, BSA would have first refusal. Edward was furious that Sangster had not even told him about this, let alone involved him in discussions. Not only was he a shareholder of the holding company, he also had a fond affection for Ariel. So great was his resentment it is alleged that he gave serious thought to handing in his resignation and returning to BSA.

The deal with BSA was completed by December 1944 and, of the various figures bandied about concerning the purchase price, one source has suggested that Jack Sangster's formidable negotiating powers resulted in BSA paying just over £375,000 for Ariel. If this is right, it was almost a fivefold increase on the figure BSA had originally proposed when negotiations started. In later years, Jack Sangster admitted that selling Ariel to BSA had been a serious error of judgement. When Ariel's workforce received the news about the company's sale, immediate reaction was to down tools and go on strike, and it was not until they were convinced that Ariel would retain its autonomy that the strike was called off.

During the early part of 1945, it became increasingly obvious that the war in Europe was drawing to a close, with hostilities likely to end within a matter of months. With an eye to the future, the Triumph Engineering Company sprang a surprise towards the end of February, when it revealed provisional details of a post-war programme. Triumph

After Edward had converted Hopwood's prototype 499cc 5TW side valve military twin back to his original specification, it was eventually accepted for military use and given NATO approval. By then, World War 2 was over, but it was ordered by many foreign governments, the RAF, the Marines, and several ministeries. It was also used for a time by the Royal Signals Display Team, seen here collecting its new machines from Meriden. (John Nelson)

was the first British manufacturer to do this, secure in the knowledge that its already tried-and-tested twin cylinder engine would give it a head start.

The proposed range comprised five models: two 500cc twins, two 350cc twins and a 350cc single. The 500cc twins which formed the backbone of the range were the Speed Twin and the Tiger 100, similar in most respects to their pre-war counterparts apart from a redesigned crankcase casting. This made possible the use of a separate magneto and dynamo, dispensing with the Lucas Magdyno previously mounted at the rear of the cylinder block. A BTH magneto took its place, whilst a Lucas dynamo was slotted through the front engine plates to be driven by an additional pinion within the timing chest. Apart from providing better access to the rearmost nuts holding down the cylinder block, mechanical quietness was improved. Unseen was a timed engine breather attached to one end of the inlet camshaft, which took the form of a spring-loaded ported disc that

located with a similar ported valve in the end of the camshaft bush. A vapour exit in the left-hand crankcase terminated in a short pipe that discharged to the atmosphere. A further modification dispensed with the external oil pipes used previously to transfer oil draining from the rocker boxes to the push rod tubes.

The two new 350cc twins gave the impression of being smaller capacity versions of their 500cc counterparts, yet they actually differed in quite a number of respects. Internally, the crankshaft assembly still took the form of a central flywheel, into which both crankpins - with their integral bobweights - were pressed, but arrangement on these models differed in having the cranks located and clamped by 55 ton heat treated alloy bolts. The cylinder head also differed in having integral rocker boxes. Access to the rocker arms for tappet adjustment was provided by an alloy cover at front and rear, retained by a large diameter screwed knob. The new type of crankcase was used with a separate magneto and dynamo. Not so obvious was

Although the 3H model was not listed after the war in view of Triumph's 'all twins' policy, some 3HWs were converted for civilian use to overcome the initial shortage of new models. Despite a minimum of chromium plating and a utilitarian finish, it nonetheless managed to appeal in its new guise. (John Nelson)

The prototype 349cc 3TU twin might have ended up with New Imperial on its petrol tank after Jack Sangster bought the company when it went into liquidation during 1939. Even Edward later referred to his 3TU as "somewhat agricultural in concept"! It still exists, taken by a dealer in lieu of a bad debt when the Meriden factory finally closed.

the use of a frame of different dimensions, which, at first, appeared similar to that used for the 500s.

The most noticeable feature of all the twins was a telescopic front fork with a 19 inch diameter front wheel, and adoption of a chromium-plated trim around the front number plate. There was also a hint of some future form of unspecified rear suspension. The standard 350cc twin was the 3T model that would have gone into production for the 1940 season, had it not been for the war. It was finished in black with ivory coloured lining. The other 350cc twin was the Tiger 85; in effect, a 3T model with a tuned engine. It was to have been finished in the characteristic silver with blue lining that identified these models, but it never went into production for a number of reasons, not least of which was that when production for the civilian market eventually commenced, Triumph could sell every model it made, so there was little point in adding an extra 350cc twin whilst this situation continued. Furthermore, and perhaps more to the point, its performance never came up to expectation. Even Freddie Clarke, Triumph's very talented Development Engineer, failed to get it to respond as it should. The gap was filled by the 350cc

single, a civilian version of the 3HW military model, finished in black with the tank panels and wheel centres lined in ivory.

There was no attempt to resurrect the 3TU twin cylinder utility model either. Very austere-looking, even Edward described it as " agricultural in concept!". Fulfilment of export orders was the main objective, and everything else had to go by the board.

Despite destruction of the Coventry factory, and the subsequent move to temporary and quite unsuitable premises in Warwick, Triumph made just under 50,000 machines during the war; a quite remarkable achievement. This did not take into account the many and varied other items that Triumph produced to help the war effort, such as aircraft components, track links for tanks, stretcher carriages, steering housings, a power-driven winch for towing aircraft and a generator set for the RAF. The last two applications required an all-alloy engine to provide the motive power. The use of light alloy in their construction was imperative to reduce overall weight, especially as the generator set had been designed for airborne use. That parts of this engine could also be used to advantage in another later engine would soon prove of significance.

Chapter 7: Post-war production commences

It was not until the end of July 1945 that several of the leading manufacturers − Triumph included − received permission to resume production of motorcycles for sale to the general public. Even then, an unnecessarily bureaucratic ruling threatened to delay deliveries.

Before a new machine could be purchased, the buyer had first to obtain a 'Licence to Acquire' from the Ministry of War Transport by completing the appropriate form and waiting several weeks before the licence was granted. It was an absurd requirement because it not only prevented a dealer from carrying stock in the showroom, but also meant that the prospective buyer had to select a machine from catalogues, assuming any happened to be available. There was virtually no chance of being able to see the machine first, let alone sit on it. As if this was not bad enough, the same procedure had to be followed when an ex-WD machine was being purchased - and soon the market would be flooded with them! Fortunately, common sense prevailed and the ruling was soon abandoned, although Purchase Tax had still to be paid, even when an ex-WD machine was sold.

Motor Cycling was able to road test one of the early post-war 5T Speed Twins, a report on which was published in the 17th January issue. Given the opportunity to select one of three models for this test, a Speed Twin, a Tiger 100 or the new 3T twin, the magazine chose the Speed Twin, not only because it was the most popular model in the Triumph range, but also because it could be compared with the 1937 and 1939 models the magazine had tested before the war. The road test report was favourable on almost every count, and ride was enhanced by the added comfort factor provided by the telescopic front fork with its increased range of movement. The only criticisms were the need to move the footrests about an inch further back to allow a more comfortable riding position, a tendency for the rear wheel to lock during heavy braking, and the pronounced 'dip' of the front fork when only the front brake was applied. To anyone used to a girder front fork this last criticism would have been particularly evident simply because a telescopic fork has a much wider range of travel. It was something to which a rider very soon became accustomed, especially as really effective damping systems had still to be devised. The only 'black mark' in the report was given for removal of the handlebar-operated air control, which was replaced by a spring-loaded, push down plunger on top of the single carburetter. It was awkward to get at when wearing gloves, especially in cold weather.

Performance-wise, the Speed Twin had a maximum speed of 86.6mph over a flying start quarter mile, two or three miles per hour below that of the pre-war models. This was to be expected as the engine had now to run on 'pool' petrol of a much lower octane rating, and with a reduced compression ratio. Petrol consumption averaged 77mpg in the country and fell to 66mpg when the machine was ridden in built-up areas. On the credit side the Speed Twin still retained its good looks and clean lines, which were further enhanced by a new 4 gallon petrol tank intended for introduction for the 1940 season, had not war intervened. Although the finish in amaranth red was by far the more popular, it was also possible to order a Speed Twin with an optional black finish.

The price had now risen to £110, to which Purchase Tax added a further £30. 5s. Furthermore, although a speedometer was required by law, it meant having to pay an extra £3. 10s, plus 19s 3d Purchase Tax.

A new employee, Ivor Davies, joined the management team at Meriden during January 1946 as Advertising, Publicity and Competitions Manager. One of his first tasks was to announce to the press that the factory would again be competing in trials and scrambles, with riders that would include Allan Jefferies, as soon as he had been released from the armed forces. Allan had successfully ridden for the factory before the war, and was unquestionably one of the best all-rounders in virtually every aspect of motorcycle sport. He would be joined by Bert Gaymer, and a new recruit, Jim Alves. Jack Welton, Triumph's Sales Office Manager, had seen Jim perform well in trials on a much modified 350cc MAC Velocette, and in scrambles with an ex-WD 350cc 3HW Triumph, both of which Jim had prepared himself. Acting on Jack's advice, Edward attended several meetings to see Jim in action and, impressed, agreed he should be signed to ride for Triumph.

As Triumph was producing only twin cylinder models, the question arose about which would be the most suitable model to adapt for competition use. The 350cc 3T seemed to offer the best prospects, with the added advantage that it could be converted for off-road use with comparative ease. Surprisingly, there wasn't a Competition Shop at Meriden, so the prototype trials model, virtually a 3T twin stripped of all non-essential parts, had to be built in the Repair Shop. If someone now has ENX 674 in their possession they have a remarkable machine that started Triumph's post-war off-road success story.

At the 1946 Cotswold Cups Trial, the first big event in which it was entered, Jim Alves won with ease, even pitted against the might of this country's leading trials riders. Celebrations were much in order at the Amberley Inn on Rodborough Common, near Stroud, Gloucester, where the trial had started and finished.

Motor Cycling got its chance to road test a standard 3T model towards the end of March. It was put through a 1500 mile test, and the magazine gave the impression that the higher performance Tiger 85 model was still expected to be available as an alternative. The 3T, officially catalogued as the de luxe model, received a very favourable report. It could be ridden down to about 15mph in top gear without any evidence of transmission snatch, and would cruise happily within the 30-60mph range. Above 60mph the steering got a bit skittish, to the extent that a touch of steering damper had to be applied. Braking was good and the rider found he could successfully cope with some of the notorious trials hills in the Midlands and Derbyshire if rear tyre pressure was first reduced to 7psi. A security bolt fitted as standard to the rear wheel prevented the possibility of tyre creep on the rim. On the road, maximum speed was 74mph, whilst petrol consumption averaged 76mpg in town and 81mpg in the country. Oil consumption was negligible. In all, it proved a very satisfactory test from Triumph's point of view, with only two minor criticisms - a tendency for the saddle to hit the rear mudguard when riding over rough ground, and a rear chainguard that needed a flared end to prevent excess oil from the chain oiler from getting on to the rider's coat if it had been set too generously. The price of the 3T? £139.14s., inclusive of Purchase Tax, with an extra £4.8s.11d. for the obligatory speedometer. It seems inconceivable that the cost of the speedometer was not included in the overall purchase price, yet many other manufacturers continued to list it as an extra, even though it was a legal requirement. The 3T was a shade heavier than might have been expected, weighing 335lbs with empty tanks.

When Charles Markham, one of *Motor Cycling's* road testers, was at the Bemrose Trial, he asked Ivor Davies if he could borrow Jim Alves' 'works' trials model for a test. His request was granted and ENX 674 was loaned to him for a day so that he could take it over the Cotswold Trial course on which Alves had earlier put up an outstanding performance. It provided the opportunity to find out how much the competition model differed from the standard production 3T model, and what it was like to ride a twin cylinder model off road, where the border line between wheelspin and grip is very fine indeed.

The main differences between the competition model and the standard 3T model comprised the substitution of a 21 inch front wheel shod with a 3 inch section trials tyre retained by a security bolt. The rear was shod with a 4.00 x 19 inch trials tyre, retained by two security bolts. The telescopic front fork was similar to that of the road model, apart from the lack of headlamp brackets and steering damper. The petrol tank, from a Tiger 70, had a smaller capacity and, being narrower in width, could be set further back in the frame to permit a better steering lock for the front fork. An unusual feature not usually seen on twins was an exhaust valve lifter in place of a magneto cut-out button. To improve ground clearance, a two-into-one siamese exhaust system on the left-hand side linked up with an upward sloping silencer.

Set up for a richer than usual mixture, the carburetter provided exceptionally good low speed acceleration yet, surprisingly, it did not have an air filter. Another surprise related to the magneto, which had standard automatic ignition advance rather than manual operation. As may be expected, the gears in the standard gearbox had been changed to give much wider ratios, and a folding kickstarter fitted to keep it out of harm's way whilst the machine was being ridden. Lighter section mudguards provided better clearance and there was a crankcase shield to prevent underside damage by rocks or stones. Saddle height was 4 inches higher than that of the standard model, and ground clearance had increased by one and a half inches to a full seven inches.

Alves preferred to use his own handlebar bend and, because of this, dispensed with the Triumph 'click action' twist grip then in general use. Just as well, perhaps, as some years later it caused a serious road accident in the USA when the spring-loaded plunger jammed in the ratchet teeth whilst the throttle was fully open.

After reducing rear tyre pressure to 8psi, Markham soon found it was not as difficult to ride a twin over a trials course as he had first thought it might be on account of the Triumph's progressive surge of power. Once he had mastered the technique, he found its slow pulling power so remarkable that he could count the individual beats of the engine! Needless to say, any ham-fistedness with the throttle soon ended in disaster, as the border line between grip and wheelspin was very fine. Inevitably, the question arose: should these early successes in 'open' trials be attributed to Alves or to the Triumph? Markham came to the conclusion that it had to be a combination of both, with the accent on Alves' command of throttle control.

The first road race of any significance was the 1946 Ulster Grand Prix, which had to have a title change in order to attract other than British riders. It was decided to call it the Ulster Road Race until such time as riders from the Continent were again able to take part. Eyebrows were raised when the list of entries was published as, amongst them, was the official Triumph 'works' entry of Ernie Lyons on a 500cc twin. When the machine arrived in Belfast it featured a hitherto unseen all-alloy engine, the top end of which was based on that used for the airborne generator set. It also featured rear suspension provided by a wheel with a large diameter spring hub. The entry had been made to give the prototype a trial run under racing conditions, as it was intended to also enter it in September's Manx Grand Prix.

Interestingly, another Triumph twin had been entered privately by Rex McCandless. It had its engine inclined forward at an angle of about forty five degrees, housed in what proved to be the forerunner of his 'featherbed' frame. This frame, of his own design, was destined to change the whole concept of handling at high speed, and was subsequently taken up by Norton. Exactly why Triumph should have decided to enter a machine in a road racing event is unclear, especially in view of Edward's earlier comments about the foolishness of providing works support when the majority of other machines entered bore little or no resemblance to their road-going counterparts. One can only speculate on the underlying reason behind his sudden and unexpected change of policy. Unlike a later clandestine attempt to enter a factory-prepared racer, Edward was aware of the machine's existence. Working late one night, noise from the Development Department caused him to look in and find the engine being run on the test bed.

Admittedly, the new racing Triumph bore a close similarity to the standard, over-the-counter Tiger 100, discounting the all-alloy top end of the engine, and use of the mysterious 'spring wheel' that had been vaguely hinted at in a pre-war press release. In all probability, Edward wanted to see how a Triumph twin built to racing specification would perform in open competition. If it did well it might provide a convenient way of introducing aspiring amateur racers to the sport at relatively low cost, with the prospect of having a reasonably competitive mount. Whatever the reason, the development work carried out at Meriden could only have been sanctioned with his personal approval, albeit perhaps grudging.

The person responsible for building and preparing the machine Lyons was to ride was Freddie Clarke. As mentioned earlier, Freddie was a former Brooklands habituee who had prepared and ridden Triumphs, both singles and twins, with considerable success at that venue. It was he who brought about a useful reduction in the prototype racer's overall weight by grafting a silicon alloy cylinder head and barrel from one of the wartime airborne generator units on to the crankcase assembly of a Tiger 100. The spring wheel, which Edward had designed and patented before the war, had been road tested

Triumph pursued a flexible policy with regard to official support in competition events, continuing its pre-war interest in trials and scrambles. Yet it came as a surprise when the factory entered Ernie Lyons in the 1946 Ulster Road Race on a 499cc twin. The engine had a Tiger 100 bottom end, with an all-alloy cylinder head and barrel from a wartime generator engine. It was intended to give the machine a run prior to entering it in the1946 Manx Grand Prix. This is a similar engine. (John Nelson)

than that of the standard wheel and, as the wheel moved in an arc the tension of the final drive chain remained constant throughout its range of travel.

It would be pleasing to report that the new racing twin acquitted itself well in the Ulster Road Race, but, as so often happens when a prototype makes its debut, an unexpected problem blighted its chances. No sooner did it start to show potential than misfiring set in, slowing it down again. When Lyons had used up all his racing plugs he wisely refrained from retiring so that he could use the rest of the race to try and identify the cause of the problem. It was not until the post mortem held after the race that it was traced to a low petrol level in the remotely-mounted float chamber used to feed the twin carburetters. The resultant weak mixture had caused overheating.

When practice for the Manx Grand Prix began, it was soon evident that Lyon's Triumph had been well sorted, as he was third on the leader board at a speed of 71.50mph on the day of his first appearance. The leader board was headed by Ken Bills' Norton, which was just under 3mph faster. In a later practise session, Eric Briggs on another Norton put in a lap at 78.66mph, which relegated Lyons to fourth on the leader board, even though by then he had improved his own lap time by just under 3mph. When Senior Race day dawned, the weather was so atrocious it is surprising the race was not postponed. It was raining hard and there was the additional problem of mist, to say nothing of the prospect of a large black dog reported to be running loose in the vicinity of Brandish Corner! The race stewards got together to decide whether or not to go ahead with the race, but, as the weather forecasters expected it to improve (unfortunately, a false assumption), the race started on time at 11.00am. Irish road racers are tough men and Lyons had a feeling he could win the race, especially if the roads were wet. Still not too familiar with the thirty seven and three quarter mile TT course, it took all his powers of concentration to maintain his grip on the race, at times standing on the footrests to keep the Triumph under control in such treacherous conditions. Unfamiliar corners meant he had to start braking before they came into view, which he could do only by counting slowly as the warning boards appeared.

During his second lap he ran through a flooded patch of road at Ballacraine, which caused him an anxious moment or two when the engine cut out completely, then ran some way on one cylinder before the second one cut in. As he entered his last lap, he had begun to lose concentration and it was not until he bounced off a kerb in Ramsey that he managed to regain his composure. His problems were compounded when the rev counter stopped working. As he crossed the finishing line, soaked to the skin and completely exhausted, he raised his goggles for the last time to drain the water that had accumulated inside throughout the race. It had been an utterly exhausting ride.

His efforts were rewarded, however, and well applauded, too, as he led the race from start to finish and was 43 seconds ahead of Ken Bills' Norton. It was the first Triumph win in the Isle of Man since 1908, when Jack Marshall had won the single cylinder class at 40.49mph. Ernie's race average in such vile conditions was a very creditable 77.24mph. It was surprising that he even finished because, during the customary post-race examination of the first three placed machines, it was found that the Triumph's front down tube had fractured just above the engine front mounting lug, which, presumably, was when the rev counter had packed up! It said much for the robust construction of the frame that it had held together so well, and had not caused Lyons to suspect that anything so dramatic had occurred. It could not have held out much longer. Externally, the engine was remarkably free from oil leaks, and it is alleged that

in 1941. Although it provided only a limited amount of movement, it was an ingenious way, by simply changing the rear wheel, of converting a rigid frame into a spring frame, without needing to use a welding torch. It was alleged to add only 12lbs in weight, compared to the weight of the original wheel, but in reality this was more like 20lbs. When it later came into general use throughout the Triumph range as an optional extra, it was effective in taking out the initial shock when the machine hit one of the many potholes in Britain's roads as the result of neglect throughout the war. On the debit side, it was cumbersome to remove and replace in the frame when the need arose to mend a rear wheel puncture. Furthermore, when the relatively small diameter cup and cone wheel bearings began to wear and play developed, stability whilst cornering suffered, resulting in a tendency for the rear end to weave. Fortunately, the later Mark II version paid attention to this problem, but not before the wheel had received adverse comment. There were two hidden advantages though: the spring wheel had a rear brake an inch larger in diameter

This is the machine that Ernie Lyons was to ride in the 1946 Manx Grand Prix. It was providential that a longer front mudguard was fitted the night before the race in view of the appalling weather that prevailed throughout the event.

An incorrect weather forecast led to the race being run in steadily deteriorating weather conditions. Soaked to the skin and blinded by the rain, Ernie Lyons picks his way along the gutter to a well deserved win. The longer front mudguard from his own Tiger 100, fitted the night before the race, is evident in this photograph, as is the additional mudguard stay.

petrol consumption averaged around 40mpg. As for the spring wheel, it was still in perfect working order.

It was later disclosed that a big decision had to be made about the Triumph after some last minute carburetter jetting tests had been carried out the evening before the Senior Race. Lyons happened to notice a speck of aluminium on one of the plugs when they were being removed, but Freddie Clarke, Rex McCandless and Freddie Dixon, all of whom were present at the time, hastened to assure him it was nothing to worry about, knowing only too well that as soon as Lyons left they would have to strip and rebuild the engine after requesting an extension for the machine to be 'weighed in' early the following morning. Lyons himself suspected this might happen, but had such faith in his support team that it it did not worry him unduly. He also thought it likely they would lower the compression ratio a shade at the same time, as a safeguard. What he did not anticipate was that they would find time to fit the longer front mudguard from his own Tiger 100, as though they had had a premonition of what conditions were likely to be on race day. There could not have been a more helpful last minute modification.

To win the first post-war Manx Grand Prix at the first attempt must surely have exceeded Edward's most optimistic expectations, especially as it had been accomplished under such dreadful weather conditions. Delighted though he may have been, he took care to avoid giving the impression that he was likely to backtrack on his earlier comments about official support for road racing. In a carefully worded statement, he made it clear that Triumph's success did not mean that they would be going "hell for leather" on a racing programme, although they may be able to offer competitors some reasonable support as a result. By adopting this line he made what was, in effect, a compromise, leaving the door open just a little should future developments necessitate a change in plan.

To mark the success of the Manx Grand Prix win, Edward asked Ivor Davies to arrange a commemorative dinner during October at the Bath Hotel, Leamington Spa, to which the motorcycling press would be invited. As it so happened, the date of the dinner coincided with that of the Shelsley Walsh speed hill climb, at which Ernie Lyons had been entered on the Triumph. This was a happy coincidence as Ernie made the fastest time of the day at Shelsley Walsh, beating the best times of all the cars, including that of Raymond Mays' ERA, the course record holder. Ernie was so late in getting away from Shelsley Walsh that he had no time to change and sat down to dinner still clad in his racing leathers! In his after-dinner speech of congratulation, Edward said that although Triumph would never allow racing to take precedence over the production of standard road-going models, the company would henceforth take a more active interest in racing. This news provided a fitting finale to what had been a very congenial evening.

The news about Triumph's success in the Manx Grand Prix created a great deal of interest in North America, where Edward had already seen the potential of a huge export market. As explained in a separate chapter about Triumph in the USA, he had reached an agreement with Jack Sangster that would allow him to make an annual visit to help set up a sales organisation that would represent Triumph interests in that country. Though he intended marketing the new racing model in limited numbers, it was imperative that a few be exported to the USA, hopefully to add to the prestige Triumph was rapidly gaining there. According to Bert Hopwood, no clear instructions about getting the racer into production had been given before Edward departed on his next visit to the US, so Bert and

A lunch was held the following month at the Bath Hotel, Leamington Spa, to celebrate Ernie's win, to which the Press was invited.

A speed hill climb at Shelsley Walsh was held on the day of the luncheon, at which Ernie put up the fastest time of the day on the same machine to make it a double celebration. The meeting ran late and Ernie had to sit down to lunch still clad in his racing leathers!

Freddie Clarke took it upon themselves to start things moving in this direction. Expecting that Edward would be pleased they had taken the initiative, they were taken aback on his return when, to quote Bert's own words: "He raved at Clarke and was particularly rude to me, pointing out that my duties were to keep things on an even keel whilst he was absent".

Freddie took it particularly badly and handed in his notice. Having married Barbara Laird and set up home in the Midlands only a short while earlier, the uncertainty that surrounded his career and the added responsibilites he now had caused him to seek employment elsewhere. He accepted an appointment as Research and Development Engineer with Associated Motor Cycles, and started work at Plumstead early in the new year. His brief was to concentrate on development of the AJS 'Porcupine' racing twin, but, sadly, his new career was cut short all too soon. With his wife riding pillion he crashed on some spilt oil on the Kenilworth to Stonebridge road in Warwickshire. Although no other vehicle was involved, Freddie lost his life and Barbara was severely injured. The loss to the motorcycle industry was immeasurable.

Bert Hopwood decided he too would leave Triumph at more or less the same time. When Edward had taken him to task about getting the prototype racer into production whilst away in America, he had good reason to query his terms of reference and to wonder exactly where his responsibilities lay, if indeed he had any. It certainly had not helped to be told he had been imagining his own capabilities! Although Bert loved his job, considered himself to be part of a wonderful management team, and was thoroughly steeped in Triumph matters, he reluctantly came to the conclusion that his prospects were virtually nil. When Gilbert Smith of Norton Motors got to hear that Bert was unhappy at Triumph, and was seeking employment elsewhere, he offered him the job of Chief Designer at Bracebridge Street, which Bert readily accepted. When he handed in his notice, it came like a bolt out of the blue to Edward, who had been completely unaware of Bert's discontent. Their working relationship went a long way back to their days at Ariel, and they were widely regarded as a tailor-made pair. Edward did all he could to persuade Bert to change his mind, but when he finally realised his efforts were in vain, he claimed Bert's now imminent departure would be like "losing a limb". Bert was quite taken aback to realise he was held in such high esteem.

Not unexpectedly, British road racers wanted to get their hands on one of the new racing twins as soon as possible. David Whitworth, a rider in the 'Continental Circus', was fortunate enough to be the first to succeed in this respect. Having a good record on the Continental circuits in 1939, and gaining three first places in five races at Scarborough's spring meeting, he was the ideal person to help with development of the new racer. It became available too late for him to ride in the 1947 TT (in which he finished second in the Junior race on a Velocette), but he managed to cover some 2000 racing miles with it before the season ended. He had taken it to first place in Belgium at the Circuit de la Chambre, with a record lap of 80.935mph, and later, third place in the Dutch TT at 82.15mph, despite a persistent misfire. When the cause of this was found and eliminated, he was in great demand by European race promoters, with the promise of good 'start' money.

At the end of the season Whitworth's machine was stripped by Tyrell Smith and Ernie Nott, both of whom now manned Triumph's Experimental Department. The former had worked and raced for Excelsior, and the latter for Rudge, bringing some welcome fresh expertise to the factory. Internally, David's engine was in first class condition, making it difficult to believe that it had covered such an extensive racing mileage. The pistons were unmarked and both cylinder bores had a perfect mirror finish. There was no detectable wear in the big end bearings, or, for that matter, in any of the other bearings, despite the use of ordinary mineral oil and not a castor-based racing oil. The cylinder head had a deep, soft coating of carbon, which showed how well the carburation had been set up. Apart from fitting new valves and springs as a precaution, the engine was cleaned up and reassembled for continued use. What of the spring wheel? That, too, appeared nicely run-in, with no apparent traces of wear, like the remainder of the cycle parts.

Henry Vale, who had first come to the company in 1937 as a repair shop fitter, rejoined Triumph during the year after demobilisation from the army. He was offered a quite unique job - to look after Meriden's Competition Shop. It was, however, a one-man job, as, until then, the Competition Shop had not existed. Furthermore, it did not have even a separate building as the shop was no more than a corner of the Repair Department. Henry was ideally suited for the job; not only was he an active trials rider, but also a self-taught mechanic who had served as a Senior Technical Instructor in the army. It was he who fitted the Speed Twins then being used by the 'works' trials riders with alloy cylinder heads and barrels from the wartime generator engine, to become the forerunners of the TR5 Trophy twin model that made its debut at the 1948 Motor Cycle Show. Black paint disguised the use of light alloy components and gave the impression they were little more than specially adapted Speed Twins.

Thereafter, Henry had responsibility for the factory's ISDT models from 1948 to1966, as well as the 'works' scrambles and trials models used mostly in one-day events. He travelled with the riders to all the major events to offer whatever support was necessary, and played a leading role in masterminding Triumph's three-year run of ISDT successes from 1949 to 1951.

In the meantime, Triumph's programme for 1948 had been introduced: it amounted to just three twins, the 350cc 3T, the 500cc 5T "Speed Twin" and the 500cc T100 "Tiger 100". Only minor specification changes had been made, such as the use of a domed headlamp glass and a re-styled rear number plate. On the larger capacity models, a detachable rear mudguard aided wheel removal in the event of a puncture. The spring wheel now became available as an optional extra (£20. 6s. 5d. inclusive of Purchase Tax), as did a propstand (£1.11s. 8d.). Most of the new models were earmarked for export as Britain still needed every penny to help pay off the massive war-time debts from World War 2.

After Ivor Davies, Triumph's Publicity Manager, had confirmed during early January that Syd Barnett and Bill McVeigh would be riding Triumph racing twins during the now imminent 1948 racing season, Edward issued the following statement to the motorcycling press, to clarify the situation. It read as follows:"In view of the large number of inquiries we have had from well-known motorcycle racing men who wish to acquire a machine similar to that which was successfully raced by Ernie Lyons and David Whitworth, it has been decided that this company will make available to the public forthwith a limited number of these machines, which will be exact replicas of the prototypes already demonstrated.

"This is not to be construed as any change in our previous non-racing policy - this company is not going to race with officially entered teams. Many riders are currently using standard Tiger 100s for racing, for which they were not primarily designed, and we shall now be making a more suitable machine for purely racing purposes.

"Contributory reasons for this decision are that the abolition of the basic petrol [sic] and the restriction of supplies for the home market may endanger the overall interest in motorcycling as a whole,

The production version of the race-winning machine, which was made in limited numbers and marketed as the Grand Prix model.

The Grand Prix model was undoubtedly attractive in appearance, and surprisingly fast. It could also prove quite a handful, as demonstrated by Bob 'fearless' Foster at this Ansty meeting in 1949!

and we feel that we will be making a contribution to the general situation if more racing machines are obtainable. It was the stated intention of at least two well-known riders to use Italian machines in the TT unless they could obtain Triumph racing machines, no other suitable machines being available, and this brought the matter to a head, as obviously these are not good times for British skill to be used for promoting foreign competition.

"Notwithstanding the pressure on our works for standard machines, this company has decided to divert a portion of its productive effort to the manufacture of a limited number of these racing machines for sale to suitable riders. The price of the machine retail will be £270, plus Purchase Tax, and it will, of course, include the spring wheel, rev. counter and all accessories.

"We shall try as far as possible, through our dealers, to ensure that these machines get into the right hands, and that they will also be made available overseas, but as currently we cannot forecast the demand accurately, we are going to confine our activities to making a really good job of a limited number rather than endeavour to sell in quantity".

A few weeks later a full description of the over-the-counter racing twin was published by the motorcycling weeklies, acknowledging that, henceforth, it would be known as the Grand Prix Triumph to

commemorate Ernie Lyon's winning ride. In subsequent conversation Edward disclosed that, during his most recent visit to California, he had ridden one of the prototypes at a speed of over 110mph. How many other Managing Directors could claim that?

Interestingly, the overall weight of the Grand Prix model had been kept to 314lb, and special attention paid to the fine detail. This included the provision of a tension spring retainer for the steering damper knob, and wiring the finned exhaust pipe nuts to the cylinder block to prevent slackening. Obviously, many of the lessons learnt whilst racing the prototypes had paid off, to the extent that the Grand Prix was supplied ready for immediate racing.

As mentioned earlier, the prototype Triumph side valve twin built to the Ministry of Supply's specification, came into prominence again during 1948. It was featured in an article about the service machine of the future, published in the 29th April issue of *Motor Cycling*. One of three prototypes undergoing extended testing at the Fighting Vehicle Research and Development Establishment, it was being evaluated alongside two other twins; a BSA and a Douglas. By now, a Lucas alternator driven by the crankshaft and located within the primary chaincase had replaced the Triumph's earlier Dynmatic ignition system. Furthermore, a four-speed gearbox was about to be bolted to the rear of the engine unit in place of the original separate three-speed unit, before all three prototypes took part in the 1948 Scottish Six Days Trial. In common with the other prototypes, the Triumph's chain was also fully enclosed, using an alloy twin tunnel chaincase with flexible joints.

In the trial, the Triumph was ridden by Staff Sergeant Hird, and both the Triumph and the BSA completed the course, T.A. Tracey qualifying for a Second Class Award on the BSA and S/Sgt. Hird a Third Class Award.

All eyes now focussed on the Senior TT in which eleven Grand Prix Triumphs had been entered. Several well-known riders, such as Syd Barnett, Ken Bills, Jack Brett, Bob Foster, Freddie Frith and David Whitworth, had entered on Triumphs and performed well during practice. Although expectations ran high, hopes were soon dashed as, one by one, the Triumphs dropped out of the race. Not one finished; the last runner was Albert Moule, who was holding 5th position until the final lap.

The thirty seven and three quarter mile TT course is renowned for its punishing nature, and Triumph's racing engine was inclined to be fragile if pushed really hard: mostly unspecified engine problems of one kind or another had been responsible for Triumph's lack of success in the race. It was not all doom and gloom, though, as the Grand Prix racer shone in many events of lesser status, and figured high in the results of Continental races. The ultimate reward came later, when Don Crossley won the 1948 Manx Grand Prix at a record speed of 80.62mph, with Reg Armstrong and Arthur Wheeler in 4th and 5th places respectively. A Manx Grand Prix celebration dinner on Friday 24th September at the Abbey Hotel, Kenilworth, followed, to which all Triumph riders who had finished were invited.

Following closely was the 1948 International Six Days Trial, centred on San Remo, Italy. Triumph had made an official entry comprising Allan Jefferies, Jim Alves and Bert Gaymer, the last two riding specially modified 500c Speed Twins whilst Allan, as Trophy Team Captain, rode a prototype fitted with an all-alloy generator engine of the type used in the Grand Prix racers. From Triumph's (and Britain's!) point of view, the event was an outstanding success. Great Britain won the International Trophy, the major award, the team comprising Allan Jefferies on the 498cc Triumph prototype, Vic Brittain (346 Royal Enfield), Charlie Rogers (346 Royal Enfield), Hugh Viney (498 AJS) and Jack Williams (490 Norton). The team lost not a single mark. Britain also claimed the Silver Vase, the 'A' Team of Jim Alves (498 Triumph), Bob Ray (497 Ariel) and Jack Stocker (499 Royal Enfield) not losing a mark either. This meant that Triumph carried off the prestigious Manufacturers' Team Award, with Jawa's number two team the runner-up.

Edward's reaction to the unfortunate demise of the Triumphs in the TT is not recorded, although it was unwritten company policy that, if a Triumph failed for whatever reason, the factory disowned it! Perhaps it is fortunate that the International Six Days Trial followed so soon afterwards. There was no greater patriot at heart than Edward, who would have been greatly pleased by the success of the British team. The icing on the cake was carrying off the Manufacturers' Team Award and, not very long afterwards, Don Crossley's win in that year's Manx Grand Prix.

In early October Triumph announced its range of models for the 1949 season, inclusion of the Grand Prix racer increasing it to four twin cylinder models. For the road-going models, detail modifications

were the order of the day, with two important exceptions. Especially welcome was removal of the old fashioned-looking, tank-mounted instrument panel that restricted access to the top of the engine. The petrol tank no longer needed to be recessed to accommodate it, so threaded inserts in its top allowed a chrome-plated parcel carrier to be attached as an optional extra, if required. Most noticeable was adoption of a stylish nacelle to enclose the headlamp, switchgear, speedometer, ammeter and ignition cut-out button, and to surround the steering damper knob. From all accounts, this tidying-up of the cluttered area around the steering head can be attributed to Jack Wickes, not that credit was ever given to its originator.

Other lesser - but nonetheless welcome - modifications included the use of a knurled knob for adjusting the friction of the twist grip, and a horn button built into the handlebars, with internal electrical connections. The new Lucas 60 watt dynamo improved the lighting with the less obvious advantage of its armature supported on ball bearings at both ends. Only the Grand Prix racer continued unchanged.

That was not the end of it, however. When the 1948 Motor Cycle Show opened at Earls Court, a fifth twin had been added to the range. Built as an on-off road competition model, it was a virtual replica of Allan Jefferies' ISDT prototype, and given the name "Trophy Twin" to commemorate his success in this event. Fitted with a much 'softer' low compression, all-alloy engine using a Tiger 100 crankcase, different cams and a single carburetter, its high-mounted, two-into-one exhaust system gave it a very functional appearance, an impression heightened by its skimpy alloy mudguards and rear wheel shod with a 4.00 x 19 inch Dunlop trials tyre. In accordance with Triumph practice at the time, it had a 20 inch front wheel, shod with a matching 3.00 x 20 Dunlop trials tyre. With a ground clearance of 6.5 inches, the Trophy Twin was supplied with a wide ratio gearbox, which provided a 5.24:1 top gear for normal road use.

If the Lucas lighting equipment was detached, a blanking-off plate was included with the tool kit for sealing off the now exposed part of the timing chest when the dynamo was removed. The Trophy Twin's finish was offset by its 2.5 gallon, chromium-plated petrol tank, which had silver panels, lined in blue. With matching mudguards it conformed with the now familiar 'Tiger' colour scheme. Catalogued as the TR5 model, it retailed at £195. 11s. 8d. and, although available ready for action ' over the counter', it was also to be used by the 'works' trials riders. Many considered it the best Triumph yet made, and an ideal clubman's mount, especially on account of its quoted low weight of 295lb and its manoeuvrability. With a favourable top gear ratio, it was surprisingly fast on the road, with a maximum speed of almost 90mph, although handling capability at increased speed gave rise to some concern! When 'wound up', it had a very distinctive exhaust note, reminiscent of a swarm of angry wasps.

A spring wheel was not included in the Trophy's specification, although it could be supplied as an optional extra. It is unlikely that many were ordered with this option, since, at that time, rear suspension of any kind was frowned upon by the majority of trials riders, who regarded it as a deterrent to success in off-road events. It was certainly not robust enough for use in scrambles, as some soon discovered to their cost.

During March 1949, *Motor Cycling* road tested the latest 5T Speed Twin. It had been the magazine's practice to single out this

particular model in the past, as it was the first of Edward's twin cylinder models to go into production. By selecting a 5T for road test, it could be compared with its predecessors, demonstrating just how the design had progressed over the years. In this instance, it was the magazine's first opportunity to sample the spring wheel, which formed part of the specification of the machine made available. It received a fair test as some of the test mileage was over roads that had been neglected during the war years, to say nothing of cobbled streets and tram lines. It was observed that the spring wheel absorbed all but the most severe jolts and coped adequately, when the rider of a rigid frame machine would have been bounced about on the saddle. No mention was made of what affect, if any, the wheel had on cornering at higher speeds, although it should be remembered that journalists in that era were inclined to 'pull their punches', ever-mindful that a particularly adverse report could result in a loss to their particular publication of advertising revenue from the manufacturer concerned.

When the list of entrants for the 1949 Senior TT was published, the number entering a GrandPrix model had increased to fifteen. Some, such as Albert Moule and Arthur Wheeler, had entered one of these models, despite their enforced retirement the previous year due to engine problems. A newcomer from New Zealand, Sid Jensen, had been entered by the New Zealand ACU Ltd., having finished second on a Triumph Grand Prix in his homeland's Senior TT in Auckland at the beginning of the year. Although Norton 'works' riders finished first, second and fourth, Sid rode sufficiently well to finish fifth at a speed of 83.17mph. C.A. Stevens was sixth on another Triumph, Bill Petch finished twelfth, and J. Bailey seventeenth, all of them qualifying for a silver replica. Two more Triumphs further down the field qualified for a bronze replica.

This result did much to compensate for the misfortunes suffered by Triumph riders in the 1948 Senior TT, and it was fortunate that Edward made one of his rare appearances in the Isle of Man on this occasion, as he was usually in the USA at this time. He expressed his pleasure by giving Sid Jensen the machine he had ridden in the race in appreciation of his efforts. It was handed over to Sid during a simple ceremony at Meriden, at which all of Triumph's senior staff were present. Later, Edward may have had reason to regret his spontaneous gesture because, as Sid loaded his van to take the Triumph away, he noticed that there was already an AJS twin on board which Sid was taking home with him!

Although the Clubman's TT had been run for the previous two years, the Senior class had been very much regarded as the preserve of the International Norton. Not exclusively, though, by any means; there had been a sprinkling of Triumphs, too, as well as machines from most of the other manufacturers. The Triumph Grand Prix was, of course, excluded on account of its racing specification. Even so, the company's standard production models, like the Tiger 100 or a Speed Twin, could give a good account of themselves. A Triumph ridden by Bill McVeigh had finished fourth in the 1948 Senior Clubman's race, and four other riders had also done sufficiently well to be given free entry in that year's Manx Grand Prix.

In the 1949 Senior Clubman's TT, Triumph entries increased to twenty six, twice the number of those for International Nortons. This year, the Senior race was a separate entity, not run in conjunction with the 1000cc race as before. It is pleasing to record that Triumphs put up the best performance, to finish in second, third, fifth, eighth and ninth places. Allan Jefferies had taken second place, confirming he was probably the best all-rounder this country has ever known. To have been beaten by the rider of an International Norton was no disgrace, as its rider was none other than Geoff Duke, who was at the start of what would amount to an outstanding road racing career.

Early September brought forth the news that Britain had won the International Six Days Trial again, although, sadly, without Allan Jefferies as a member of the Triumph team. Despite his epic ride in the Senior Clubman's TT, Allan had announced his retirement from riding in competition at the end of the previous year. Jim Alves, Bert Gaymer and Bob Manns rode in Britain's Vase 'A' team, losing only one mark and each winning a gold medal. Interestingly, their Trophy Twins were the only rigid frame, multi-cylinder machines to be ridden by team men. Times were changing and rear suspension was becoming acceptable in trials-type events.

Despite the number of free entries in the Manx Grand Prix won by Triumph riders, most of them chose to ride a different make in the Senior Race. One of the exceptions was Don Crossley, who was unlucky enough to have to retire at Ballacraine on the last lap, whilst lying fifth, the by now familiar 'unspecified engine problems' given as the reason. Only two Triumphs crossed the finishing line, J. Smith in thirteenth place and R.E.D. Harrison in twenty first. The winner? Geoff Duke on a Manx Norton!

By the end of the year, Triumph had started a night shift at Meriden so that it could increase production by 20%. Although Triumph production figures have always been a jealously guarded secret, it was alleged that, by the end of 1948, in the order of 250 machines a week were being produced. As a result of the extra shift, the number of models allocated to the home market could be stepped up considerably. Until then, 70% of all Triumphs had been shipped overseas, where they were big dollar earners. Although the company's export policy was to remain unchanged, Edward explained to the Press that exports to North America were going very well. Yet he knew from his own regular visits that Triumph had hardly begun to scratch the surface. It was his intention to maintain the export/home market ratio of 70/30% as he expected 1950 to be a record year for dollar earnings. The underlying reason for his optimism had been the introduction in late September of an entirely new model, with which he expected to enhance Triumph's sales prospects even more, both at home and abroad.

Triumph's successful 1949 ISDT Team, left to right: Jim Alves, Bob Manns and Bert Gaymer.

Edward makes a presentation to Allan Jefferies to mark his retirement as one of Triumph's most outstanding riders. Allan was probably the best all-rounder in British motorcycle sport at that time. He was always successful at whatever he did, and had one of the company's best-known dealerships in Shipley, Yorkshire. (Vida Wickes)

Chapter 8: The Thunderbird makes its debut

Like Ivor Davies, Neale Shilton had joined Triumph after demobilisation from the army, initially as a sales representative. The territory he had to cover was euphemistically described as the South West, although it actually extended as far north as Peterborough and Stamford. Towards the end of 1948, Ivor and Neale were asked to hand in their Speed Twins to the Experimental Department for some unspecified modifications to be made. The request was all the more mysterious because these were their own machines and not the company's.

Ivor and Neale realised that they stood to gain more than they could lose, so handed in their machines as requested. When they got them back it was very difficult to see what had been done to them; that is, until they set off home at the end of the day. The engines now had a good deal more power and responded much more readily to the throttle. Discreet enquiries made the following day revealed a prototype 649cc engine had been fitted to each. By opening up the bore size of the Speed Twin cylinder block from 63 to 71mm, and by increasing the stroke by just 2mm, Edward had increased the capacity by 150cc with comparative ease.

On the road their bikes were capable of a genuine 100mph, and other riders seemed quite perplexed when they were overtaken with ease by what appeared to be a standard Speed Twin. This was demonstrated quite forceably when Ivor and Neale rode to one of the road race meetings at Blandford, Dorset, over a bank holiday weekend. It must have been all the more upsetting for some at being overtaken by Ivor whilst his wife, Doreen, was riding pillion! When the two machines were parked, they were closely scrutinised by a few who had been passed on the way; not that it was possible to detect any external differences. To keep the experimental nature of the engine secret, the Experimental Department had ensured that the engine number had been stamped with the 5T prefix of a standard production Speed Twin.

As related in the chapter about Triumph in North America, the need for a new, larger capacity engine had been generated by impassioned pleas from America, a land where biggest is always best. Used to riding large capacity vee twins with vast amounts of torque, American enthusiasts regarded a Triumph twin as lacking in certain respects. The appeal of its design and appearance was not in doubt, nor its performance in relation to engine size. It had, however, only a 40 cu.in. engine by US measurements, whilst Americans were more accustomed to a machine with a 61, 74 or even 80 cu. in. capacity. The latter would withstand a good deal of abuse, especially with regard to gearboxes. Furthermore, they were built to endure high temperatures when ridden hard over long distances whilst crossing deserts, or during runs along the network of highways that criss-crossed the country. Under these conditions, a British-made vertical twin was inclined to wilt a bit if ridden in the same heavy-handed manner.

The answer was for Triumph to increase the capacity of its engines so that they would be less stressed, and give a better account of themselves, performance-wise, when needed. That it was possible to increase the capacity so easily was a real bonus. A 649cc twin was clearly a step in the right direction, and Edward felt confident it would be welcomed by British and American enthusiasts alike. Officially, the new model was designated the 6T but, with a stroke of inspiration, Edward gave it the swashbuckling name of Thunderbird. The idea had come to him during a regular visit to America, when he was driving to one of the Daytona Beach race meetings. In South Carolina he came across the Thunderbird Motel, which had in its grounds a giant, eagle-like bird mounted on a pole. It seemed such an appropriate name for the new model, especially with its North American connotations, that he adopted it immediately, along with a symbolic representation of the bird.

Tyrell Smith and Ernie Nott of the Experimental Department had both logged a considerable mileage on 650cc prototypes. Their racing experience confirmed a Thunderbird was quite capable of covering 500 miles at an average speed of 90mph, which gave Edward the idea of staging a high performance display as the basis for its launch. Not only would it demonstrate the Thunderbird's performance capabilities in a most convincing manner, but also underline its reliability, on the assumption that there were no breakdowns. Even though Tyrell Smith and Ernie Nott had given Edward their assurances that such a feat was well within the new model's ability, he was not prepared to leave anything to chance.

In July that year, he set off for Montlhéry, the banked race track near Paris, which he intended to hire for the Thunderbird's launch . Driving the factory's Austin 16, he was accompanied by Tyrell Smith and Ernie Nott, with Alex Scobie following on one of the new models. After Alex had completed 25 laps at the track, a connecting rod broke and punched a hole in the machine's crankcase.

A month later, Alex and Ernie Nott returned, this time with two bikes, with the aim of completing 500 miles at an average speed of 90mph. All went well on the first day until the clutch on one of the machines burnt out as a result of neglecting to check the oil level in the primary chaincase. After replacing the burnt-out inserts with bottle corks cut to size, the test resumed the following day, only to be halted at the 375 mile mark. The French Dunlop representative had been horrified to see how much the tread on the left-hand side of the rear tyres had worn down, right through to the canvas. The second test had also to be aborted, but, as time was running short, it was decided to go ahead with the launch as planned on the assumption that the lessons learned would be used to good effect. Needless to

Clad in white overalls, three of the riders of the new 6T 649cc Thunderbird (left to right: Alex Scobie, Len Bayliss and Bob Manns), talk to Edward at the conclusion of the very impressive, high speed launch at Montlhéry. (Vida Wickes)

say, none of the problems encountered during these early 'dummy runs' was ever revealed to the Press.

Final arrangements for the launch were left to Neale Shilton. To make the planned high speed display even more dramatic, Edward decided it should comprise three and not just one of the new models. Furthermore, as a safeguard against any accusations that the high speed test might have been 'rigged', he stipulated it should be strictly supervised throughout by an ACU observer.

In this day and age, it may well be assumed that the whole circus of riders, their machines, all the necessary equipment and the back-up staff would be packed into a large vehicle emblazoned with the Triumph logo and driven to Dover to meet the cross-channel ferry. The reality could not have been more different: four Thunderbirds (one spare) were fitted with panniers and ridden to Montlhéry by Neale Shilton, Tyrell Smith, Alex Scobie and Len Bayliss, the last two of whom were to ride them on the track. They carried with them all the spares likely to be needed, including the tyres. When they landed in France they followed instructions to make their way to Paris, where

Neale had to report to Edward, who was staying with friends in Paris and would make his own way to the track.

When they arrived at Montlhéry, the riders met up with the other three - Allan Jefferies, Jim Alves and Bob Manns - who were to ride with them in the high speed display. They had made their way direct to the track from the International Six Days Trial in Italy. Ernie Nott was the odd man out; he too should have ridden, but was unfit to travel on two wheels. Recovering from a damaged shoulder he made his way to France in a more leisurely manner, and provided invaluable service in the pits.

The ACU's observer was Harold Taylor, a highly experienced and very successfull sidecar driver, seemingly not disadvantaged by the loss of a leg. He was manager of Britain's International Motocross Team and another who had ridden in the ISDT.

Needless to say, Triumph's team of riders had impeccable credentials and were well balanced. Allan Jefferies and Jim Alves were Triumph's well-known and considerably talented 'works' riders, the former having been Captain of Britain's ISDT Team before his recent retirement from competition riding. Alex Scobie was the company's foremost test development rider and Len Bayliss a member of the test staff, as well as a grass track rider of considerable repute. Bob Manns was also a Triumph test development rider who worked in the Competition Shop. He too had ridden for Triumph in the ISDT and had won a gold medal in the recently held event as a member of Britain's Vase Team. After a day of testing at the track, tyre wear was checked by Dunlop's M. Deleport and new racing tyres fitted before each machine had a thorough service. All was now set up for the morning of the following day's demonstration.

Sharp on 9.00am, Alex Scobie set off, followed by Bob Manns and Jim Alves. They were so well matched that their lap times were consistent and the distance between them hardly varied. Some anxiety was felt when one machine developed a leaking petrol tank, which called for an unscheduled pit stop, whilst another stopped briefly for a rear chainguard to be removed that had worked loose. The tank was exchanged for the one from the spare machine and the rider was on his way again in less than fifteen minutes. The riders were called in after being in the saddle for an hour so that his partner could take over. Everything went according to plan and, at the end of the fifth hour, the timekeepers confirmed that all three machines had maintained an average speed of over 90mph throughout the duration of the test.

To celebrate the occasion and dramatise the event for the benefit of press photographers, each of the three machines were taken out on to the track again, one after the other, after lowering the handlebars so that the riders could adopt a racing crouch. Each then completed a lap at over 100mph. News of the success of the venture was phoned back to Ivor Davies in his Meriden office, along with all the relevant data so that he could issue a press release to the media. Like the efficient Publicity Manager he was, most of it had been pre-prepared so that he had only to add in the figures. As he said afterwards, he found it very exciting, even though he had to work very hard to get out the good news as soon as possible. When the machines and their riders returned to Meriden the following day, the entire factory turned out to welcome them.

It had indeed been a remarkable achievement, bearing in mind that the Thunderbirds had to run on 'pool' petrol, which restricted their compression ratio to 7:1 and gave a power output of 34bhp. A great deal of publicity resulted, not only in the two motorcycling weeklies but also on the BBC when Edward was interviewed by David Martin. All three machines were subsequently stripped for examination by Harold Taylor; apart from a slack primary chain on one of them due to lack of oil, all were considered capable of an immediate repeat performance.

It would be expected that, in view of such a highly successful test, the Thunderbird would enjoy a rapturous reception in the USA, and possibly it would have received this had it not been finished in a disastrous slate blue colour and fitted with an underize carburetter that restricted performance. American dealers were amazed that a much-needed model should have been handicapped by such inept judgement, and it was largely as the result of their complaints that the colour scheme and carburetter size were changed in time for the 1951 season. Large orders had certainly been anticipated in home and overseasas markets as something like 2500 Thunderbirds were awaiting despatch from Meriden at the time of the Montlhéry launch.

The Thunderbird enjoyed a long and successful production run, with many changes in specification along the way, until it eventually ceased production at the end of the 1966 season. During its life, it had had rear enclosure and a change to a unit-construction engine and gearbox in 1963. Even after 1966 it continued in the form of a specially-modified version for law enforcement duties, fitted out with special equipment to police specification, at a time when criminals were using high performance get-away vehicles such as Jaguars. It was known unofficially as the Saint, a name coined by Neale Shilton who was then in charge of sales to police forces. It was an acronym of the machine's capabilities - Stops Anything In No Time!

From a dealer's point of view, especially in the USA, arrival of the Thunderbird was good news. Quite apart from the advantage of having a larger capacity Triumph with improved performance characteritics, stocking spares for it did not create any serious problems. The Speed Twin already had a good reliability record, and the Thunderbird looked as though it would follow suit, so the need for spares was unlikely to increase. Furthermore, many parts were interchangeable between the models so there was no need to carry a complete stock of spares for each. Perhaps of even more importance from a dealer's viewpoint was that availability of a larger capacity model meant greater profitability.

Back-up support from Meriden, in the form of advertising and promotional material, gave little cause for complaint and, as previously mentioned, a considerable number of new models were available for immediate delivery at the time of the Thunderbird's launch.

Sales of Triumph motorcycles to various police forces also benefited from introduction of the Thunderbird, as many were already equipped with Speed Twins for law enforcement duties. When the time came for existing machines to be replaced, it made sense to do so with the larger capacity

On arrival back at Meriden, Alex Scobie listens intently to a question, whilst Edward appears pensive. Len Bayliss quietly looks on. (Vida Wickes)

Thunderbird. Police forces at home and abroad tended to favour a Triumph built to police specification with an on-board radio transmitter/receiver, flashing lights, a loud-hailer and, later, a fairing. In the fullness of time, Neale Shilton had responsibility for liaising with various police forces all over the world, to help ensure their allegiance to Triumph remained unshaken. A considerable volume of business was had from this area alone. In early 1949, the Toronto police, for example, was the latest force to be supplied with Tiger 100s.

An unexpected spin-off to the Thunderbird was that, on overseas flights, factory employees wearing ties sporting the Thunderbird logo found, to their surprise and delight, that they received priority treatment when on a British Overseas Airways flight. Amongst other things, they were offered a visit to the flight deck when the aircraft was airborne. The Thunderbird logo was very similar to that of BOAC's Speedbird motif and it had been mistakenly assumed that they were BOAC staff. Few bothered to explain!

Triumph was already selling every motorcycle it could make, and serious thought had to be given to its advertising campaign. Whilst the Triumph name had to be kept to the forefront, there was little point in creating a demand that could not be fulfilled. The problem was subtly overcome by commissioning a series of cartoon-type advertisements from Alex Oxley, well known for his regular contributions to *Motor Cycling*. Each cartoon portrayed a highly improbable, but very amusing, motorcycling incident, bearing the common theme 'It's Easy on a Triumph'. The campaign proved a great success and succeeded in its objective.

Edward took a keen interest in all of the company's promotional activities, right from Triumph Engineering's first advertising leaflet, TE101 of April 1936. It was he who had enlivened the pre-war Triumph catalogues by printing them in two colours, black and blue, which made it possible to reproduce the silver, black and blue finish of the Tiger model range with acceptable accuracy. He had also restyled the Triumph logo in which the 'R' of Triumph was linked with the final 'H'. This had first appeared on the 1934 models and his subtle reworking gave it a more modern image. It was his preference to have the catalogues printed in 8 inch by 10 inch landscape format so that each machine was shown in full side view. He also insisted that most of the machine's control and electrical cables be artworked out so that the overall appearance was not unnecessarily untidy, and that the tyre valve was always at the bottom of the wheel, directly under the wheel spindle.

After the war, full colour reproduction was used to show to advantage the Speed Twin's amaranth red colour. Colour photography was not widely in use at this time, and there would have been difficulties in retouching or reworking last minute production changes in design, to say nothing of the added production cost. Catalogue design was handled by an outside advertising agency, after Ivor Davies, the company's Publicity Manager, had provided them with an initial brief. Like many companies, Triumph made a practice of changing its advertising agency from time to time, so that the designs and ideas submitted were never in danger of becoming stereotyped to please the client. Ivor's briefs to the agencies were based on his earlier discussions with Edward, which often ended with the words

"I will rely on your consummate ability to produce a proper Triumph job". Edward always had the final say and decided what was, and wasn't, acceptable and Ivor was likely to be the recipient of his wrath if he disapproved of the advertising agency's initial artwork. He would throw it around his office whilst he ranted and raved, but when eventually he regained his composure, he had the uncanny (and infuriating!) knack of coming up with exactly what was needed. A classic example was when he completely re-designed from scratch an exhibition stand for the 1949 Motor Cycle Show at Earls Court in about half an hour!

In those days catalogues were printed by letterpress and took three months to produce, a month for preparation of the artwork, photography and copy writing to be completed, a month for blockmaking, typesetting and proof-reading, and a further month for printing. Printing by offset litho had yet to become acceptable, otherwise the printing schedule could have been halved. Printing in colour required a whole week to lay down correctly, with precise registration, each of the four individual primary colours: computer-controlled, four colour presses were still a long way off. The average print run was 200,000 copies and all had to be ready for the annual

The Triumph stand at the 1949 Motor Cycle Show, which Edward designed in thirty minutes!

Motor Cycle Show, at which the next season's models would make their debut. All of this happened against a background of paper shortages, when art paper was particularly difficult to obtain. If anything threatened to delay the supply of either the paper or the catalogues, Ivor inevitably found himself in deep trouble again.

Detail modifications were again the order of the day when Triumph announced its programme for the 1950 season. The range of twins had expanded to six with the introduction of the Thunderbird, priced at £194. 6s. 3d., inclusive of Purchase Tax. One of the modifications to the range (excluding the Trophy Twin) was superimposing the Triumph logo on four chromium-plated parallel lines that extended from the nose of the petrol tank to the knee grips. This same theme formed the basis of Triumph's stand design at the 1949 Earls Court Motor Cycle Show, the design orignated by Edward after he had been so disparaging about the advertising agency's submission.

It had been decided that, henceforth, all Triumph petrol tanks would be finished entirely in enamel, without any chromium-plating apart from on the tank badges, and excluding the Trophy Twin competition models. Internal rusting, mostly on the export models, had been traced to plating problems, and was responsible for recurring warranty claims. The Speed Twin and the Thunderbird already complied with this ruling and, quite by coincidence, it appears to have been made at just the right time. It was not long before a shortage of copper, tin and zinc used in the plating processes became evident, which meant that, during 1951-2, more enamelled parts began to appear on British motorcycles - even wheel rims. The petrol tanks of the Trophy Twins also lost their chromium-plating for similar reasons, a point often overlooked when models built at this time are being restored to original specification.

The Thunderbird continued for the present in its slate blue colour; Edward's choice of colour. He liked to feel he had involved members of the staff in making decisions about the colour scheme for a new model, and would gather them together to do so. Unfortunately, these meetings were usually prefaced by the words " I have gathered you together to discuss the colour for next season's models and I have decided ...!" He liked to include some ladies in this 'decision making' because he believed women had good colour sense.

Externally, the 1950 Thunderbird differed little from its predecessor, although the sharp eyed would have noticed the extra finning of the cylinder head and barrel. These were precautionary moves to help offset any stresses that may have arisen from the more powerful engine. Internally, alloy connecting rods, similar to those used on the Grand Prix model, were fitted, and the combustion chambers of the cylinder head re-profiled to improve efficiency. With this latter modification went a pair of pistons of matching design. The clutch benefited from the addition of an extra plate, and the engine shaft shock absorber cam was re-profiled to apply a more progressive spring loading. An improved four-speed gearbox was now fitted across the range, which made gear selection even easier and gave the internals a longer life. A welcome improvement - again, applicable to all models - was adoption of an oil pump with an improved flow rate. Many believed the original design had been unable to cope with demand at high engine speeds and had been responsible for elimination of the entire Triumph entry in the 1948 Senior TT. There may well have been some truth in this, as the engine problems that caused the retirements related mostly to the big ends and the crankshaft assembly.

Early in 1950 came news of a useful Triumph accessory, the Twinseat, a stylish dualseat weighing no more than the combined weight of the saddle and pillion seat it was to replace. Available for £2. 4s. 6d. inclusive of Purchase Tax, it took the form of a shaped steel pan on which was laid an airfoam latex cushion, covered by black Vynide PVC leathercloth. Designed specifically for a Triumph twin, its underpan had two strip steel legs positioned midway, which located with the frame lugs to which the saddle springs had previously been bolted. Henceforth, the Tiger 100 model would be supplied with the Twinseat as standard, and soon after the other Triumph models would follow suit - with the exception of the competition models. This was very much the age of the dualseat, with a variety of proprietary designs readily available. Without any doubt the seats offered a good deal of extra comfort, especially for the pillion rider who otherwise would have been perched on a leathercloth-covered sorbo rubber pad bolted to the rear mudguard. Fittingly referred to as an 'upholstered brick', many a promising romance must have ended after a lengthy journey on one of these instruments of torture. Admittedly, more comfortable and spacious designs were available, but as the basic pad-type was invariably supplied with most motorcycles (as an optional extra), few wanted to scrap it and purchase a more expensive one, having already paid for the one fitted. If a different design was fitted, it often meant having to drill another set of mounting holes in the rear mudguard. For a machine with some form of rear suspension the dualseat was ideal. Not only did it provide both rider and passenger with a more comfortable ride, it was also much better-looking than a separate saddle and pillion seat.

However, such was the desire to have one that many were fitted to rigid frame machines without so much as a thought. Without any saddle springs to absorb the bumps and jolts, the rider soon found that he too had to endure an uncomfortable ride.

In May the Mark II version of the spring wheel was announced, and was a considerable improvement on the original design in several respects. Although Edward's basic design concept remained unchanged, the only really noticeable external difference was that the brake back plate now moved in relation to the hub centre, and the offside end plate had been ribbed. Internally, improvements had been made to the wheel bearings, which were now ball races, and the way in which wheel movement was controlled. The longer life of the wheel bearings and the way in which the rear wheel spindle moved within the hub meant that the wheel was less likely to tilt in the frame and affect handling. Even so, the wheel was still rather heavy and difficult to remove from the frame in the event of a rear tyre puncture, especially if the wheel was fitted to a Trophy Twin, which did not have a quickly detachable rear mudguard. The warning about dismantling the spring boxes without the correct equipment still held good. Under considerable pressure the springs could be lethal if the dismantler released them without adequate safeguards and happened to be in the firing line. The very least that could happen would be their rapid exit, often leaving a substantial hole in a garage or workshop roof!

A faithful few - just seven - pinned their hopes still on the Grand Prix racer for the 1950 Senior TT. Never intended to compete on level terms with the AJS and Norton 'works' racers - or, for that matter, a standard production Manx Norton - it is hardly surprising that the Grand Prix Triumph was now completely outclassed. After adopting the 'featherbed' frame designed by Rex McCandless, Nortons enjoyed a definite handling advantage. Under racing conditions, the Grand Prix Triumph could be tricky to navigate, especially with spring wheel rear suspension. One had only to stand close to Woodcote Corner at Silverstone to pick out the Triumphs from the rest of the pack. To ride one in anger on a short circuit could prove quite challenging to an aspiring road racer who might not be aware of how differently other machines handled at racing speeds. Tommy McEwan brought the first

mark, whereas Austria, the runner-up, lost 133. Bert Gaymer, riding in the British Vase 'A' Team on a similar mount to Alves, did not lose a single mark either. The third member of the Triumph Team this year was Peter Hammond, replacing Bob Manns who had left Triumph, he also qualified for a gold medal. As for the Manufacturers' Team Award, Triumph qualified for that, too, in common with Ariel, one of the two BSA teams, and Matchless. None of them dropped a single mark.

The Motor Cycle Show did not take place in 1950 as British manufacturers considered they were too busy working flat out to meet demand, and could not afford to spend time making anything other than essential minor modifications to their model ranges.

Triumph announced its range for the 1951 season, which had fallen to just four twins following the decision to discontinue the Grand Prix racer and the 3T twin. 175 of the racers had been produced in total yet, today, something like 200 seem to have survived! The reason for this apparent anomaly is that it is easy to construct a Grand Prix lookalike from a miscellany of Triumph parts, taken mostly from a Tiger 100. Some of these replicas are so well constructed that they have fooled even the experts. The bona fide Grand Prix models were always supplied with an individual

Triumph home into thirteenth place, but the best David Whitworth could do was finish nineteenth. Both were outside silver replica time. Last year's fifth place man, Sid Jensen, fared even worse, as he had to retire after completing his first lap.

Sadly, the Belgian Grand Prix that followed soon afterwards was David Whitworth's last race. Riding a Velocette in the Junior race, he came off and was hit by a following rider and killed.

Triumphs acquitted themselves much better in the Clubman's TT, which, if anything, justified Edward's belief in limiting any venture into road racing to the stock machine classes. A. Hill finished second at 75.30mph on a Tiger 100 (0.2mph slower than the race winner), with three more Triumphs in sixth, seventh and eighth places. Furthermore, Ivan Wicksteed set the fastest lap at 79.51mph before he was forced to retire. A total of twenty nine Triumphs took part in the race, the largest one-make entry.

The International Six Days Trial was again held in Wales: Britain had won it the previous year and had earned the right to run the event on home ground. It was yet another success for Britain's Trophy Team, of which Jim Alves, riding a Trophy Twin, was a member. The team did not lose a single

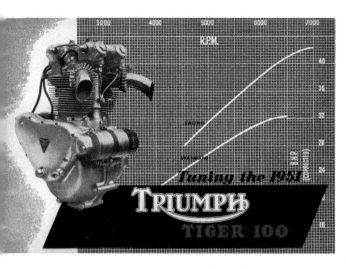

The booklet supplied with Triumph's Racing Kit for converting a standard Tiger 100 to racing specification. It contained full instructions for fitting the kit.

dynamometer test curve showing the power output, and they were claimed to be capable of reaching a maximum speed of 120mph when running on 'pool' petrol; no mean feat. Bearing in mind that Edward had always considered them to be "a means of enabling the non-professional rider to compete on level terms with all types of long and short circuit racing" (to quote the catalogue; no doubt Edward's words), they did surprisingly well under the circumstances. For what was essentially little more than a specially tuned standard production model, two Manx Grands Prix wins was not bad going by any standard.

As for the 3T twin, it was a very different story. This model had never sold particularly well, and it had a number of major components that were not compatable with the other models in the range. Although deciding to discontinue the Grand Prix racer, it was not Triumph's intention to abandon completely the tenuous connection with racing. Instead, it was decided to supply a complete racing conversion kit for a Tiger 100 at an all-in cost of £35. By offering it as an optional extra in kit form, it would not attract Purchase Tax as it would be fitted by the rider or his mechanic. With twin carburetters, high compression pistons, racing camshafts and valve springs, and many other parts, an engine assembled with care and modified according to the accompanying detailed instructions would find power output increased from 32 to about 43bhp. There would, of course, also be a reduction in the machine's overall weight of something like 25lbs when all the normal road-going and other superfluous parts were removed.

The new standard production Tiger

The component parts of the racing kit – everything necessary to complete the job.

100 had an even more appealing appearance, its cast iron cylinder head and cylinder block having been replaced by a close pitch fin diecast alloy head and barrel. This change in specification was also applied to the Trophy Twin, to replace its previous sandcast, square finned cylinder head and barrel that had originated from the wartime airborne generator unit. It meant that the latter's two-into-one, high level exhaust system had to be re-angled as the exhaust ports of the cylinder head were now splayed outwards.

It was during the early part of 1951 that Jack Sangster decided to make the final move in his protracted negotiations with BSA, and give it the opportunity to buy the Triumph Engineering Company. On this occasion, Edward was very much involved with this final stage of the sale of Jack Sangster's 'empire' to BSA, as his signature was on the agreement! An acceptable agreement with BSA was reached by mid-March. Only the broadest of details of the agreement were disclosed and in such a low key way that it was difficult to find anything at all about the takeover in either of the two motorcycle weeklies. Both conveyed the news to their readers in a terse statement which said, in effect, that Triumph's share capital had been acquired by BSA and that Triumph would continue to operate as a separate company with no changes in policy. Jack Sangster would continue as Triumph's Chairman and Edward as Managing Director. (Sangster was later appointed a director of the parent company, Birmingham Small Arms Co., Ltd. during 1953.)

It took some time for motorcycle enthusiasts to realise that Triumph was now part of the BSA Group. Each of the marques had fiercely loyal supporters, who were not to be upset at any cost. There was much speculation about how much BSA had paid to acquire Triumph, as the latter company was in a strong financial position at the time, with over £1 million in cash in the bank. BSA is understood to have paid £2,450,000, representing a sizeable return on what Jack Sangster had spent when he acquired the motorcycle side of the

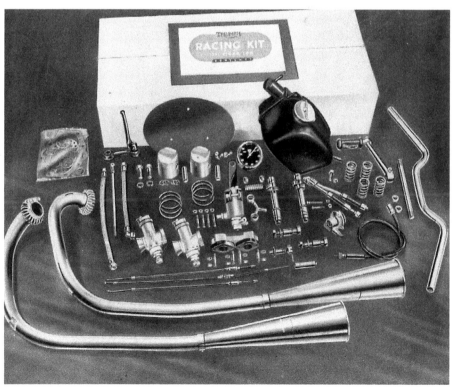

A standard production 1951 Tiger 100 before and after the racing kit had been fitted.

Triumph Cycle Company Limited in 1936. Even so, many years later, Sangster confessed that the sale of Triumph to BSA was the biggest mistake he ever made, surpassing that of his earlier sale of Ariel, a point on which Edward concurred. In fairness, however, it should be remembered that Sangster, in all probability, acted on sound professional advice. Had Triumph continued in business as a private company, his estate would have had to pay crippling death duties in the event of his demise. It has also been said that the transaction included the purchase of ET Developments, the company Edward had formed to protect the patentable rights of his own inventions.

For 1951, the TR5 Trophy Twin was also fitted with the new, close pitch fin engine, similar to that of the Tiger 100 but retaining the low compression characteristics of its predecessor. This is the author's 1952 model, with over 100,000 miles to its credit.

The question of whether or not the company that employed him should have had free access to these rights, under his terms of employment, had been a bone of contention between himself and Jack Sangster for some considerable time. By purchasing this company, the on-going situation would have been resolved satisfactorily - albeit at a price. It is believed that ET Developments was purchased for £250,000, which would have made Edward a wealthy man by motorcycle industry standards.

The 1951 International Six Days Trial was held in Italy, based at Varese, and once again Jim Alves was a member of Britain's Trophy Team. On this occasion he rode a 649cc Triumph; in effect, a Trophy Twin fitted with a 6T Thunderbird engine. Bert Gaymer, riding a 498cc Trophy Twin, represented Britain in the Vase A Team, the third member, John Giles, the Triumph Team's latest recruit, being similarly mounted. Yet again, Britain's Trophy Team emerged victorious, without losing a mark. The Vase A team also finished without penalty and Triumph was one of seven manufacturers that did not lose a mark. Both Alves and Gaymer received gold medals, and John Giles a silver, in recognition of their efforts. To have helped Britain win the prestigious Trophy four years in succession was no small achievement, and one which reflected well on Triumph. Henry Vale found he had some extra money in his weekly pay packet as an acknowledgement of Edward's gratitude - but only for that one week!

Reinstatement of the Motor Cycle Show in November 1951 marked the first appearance at Earl's Court of the new Tiger 100 and Trophy Twin models with the close pitch fin engine. On the night before the show opened, someone stole the magneto, carburetter and induction manifold from the Tiger 100 show model, which necessitated a rider leaving Meriden early the following morning with the replacement parts. When these shows were being held, this often became a daily routine, necessary to replace parts stolen the previous day. Exhibitions at Earl's Court were renowned for the many thefts, some of an amazingly brazen nature!

The annual show also provided manufacturers with an opportunity to entertain their overseas representatives in recognition of their services over the past year. In 1951, Triumph held a banquet at the Dorchester during show week, at which Edward and Jack Sangster played host to their overseas distributors. Their guests came from Colombo, Copenhagen, Dar-es-Salaam, Delhi, Helsingfors, Las Palmas, Los Angeles, Nova Scotia, Trondheim, Toronto, Valpariso and Vienna, and many other places, worldwide. There had been problems with some of the European dealers after the war; those in unoccupied countries having been accused of collaborating with the enemy. Fortunately, Edward was aware that these accusations may have been made by unscrupulous dealers who wished to acquire further dealerships. It was difficult for him to judge the situation from the British Isles and, as he said, "What do you do when soldiers enter your shop carrying machine guns?"

To mark the occasion of his parent's Golden Wedding Anniversary in 1951, Edward organised a party for them at the Savoy Hotel in London.

Bernard Hargreaves, winner of the 1952 Senior Clubman's TT on a 499cc Tiger 100. He led the race from start to finish, despite unknowingly losing a rear wheel retaining nut.

Triumph's long-awaited success in the Senior Clubman's TT came about in 1952, when Bernard Hargreaves led from start to finish on Tiger 100 at a race average of 82.45mph. Triumphs also took 5th, 6th and 9th places in a race that was otherwise dominated by Nortons. D. Tye was unfortunate enough to run out of petrol on the final lap when he was lying 6th, a fate shared by J. Bottomley who was laying 3rd. Bottomley was lucky enough to run out of fuel during his descent from the Mountain and was able to coast to the finish, losing only two places. In point of fact, Hargreaves was very lucky to finish at all, let alone win the race. When his engine was stripped for measurement after the race, it was found to be in excellent condition, both internally and externally, but when the machine itself was inspected, the offside rear wheel nut was found to be missing completely. Furthermore, the rev. counter bracket had fractured, leaving the instrument to dangle on the end of its drive cable. These problems had clearly caused Hargreaves little concern: at the prize-giving he claimed to have had "a nice ride" and wished to thank all who had helped him on the way to victory, ending his brief speech with the words "Now't else". At the lunch held to celebrate his Senior Clubman's TT win, Hargreaves was presented with a plaque on which was mounted a chromium-plated rear wheel retaining nut!

In early July, Triumph carried out a petrol economy test after fitting a Thunderbird with an SU carburetter. Although the carburetter was a standard MC2 type specified for motorcycle use, it was fitted with a type EB taper needle in place of the usual M9. This was to ensure that the machine ran on a weak mixture at low throttle openings. The Thunderbird itself had a slightly higher top gear than standard and the tyres were run at 35psi. The test comprised five laps of a 10 mile road circuit, and one of the five riders was Edward. The others were Tyrell Smith, the company's Experimental Engineer, 'Ginger' Wood, who represented the carburetter manufacturer, Dennis Hardwick of *Motor Cycling*, and Kevin Gover of *The Motor Cycle*. Each machine carried 300ccs of petrol in a glass container mounted on the tank top parcel grid.

The test was conducted in cool and breezy weather conditions, which would have affected the way in which the petrol vaporised and represented a ten percent loss in efficiency. The test results showed that a surprisingly low petrol consumption of 155mpg at 30mph had

As expected, a change of carburetter for the 1953 Thunderbird was confirmed. An SU type MC2 would indeed replace the Amal type 6.

Another change to the Thunderbird was the use of a more attractive polychromatic blue colour scheme to appease the American market.

The new addition to the range was the Tiger 100C, virtually a racing model supplied with silencers and full lighting equipment. Care was taken to advise prospective customers that it was not a high performance version of the standard Tiger 100, and, if used for touring, would give no particular advantage. In effect, it was a Tiger 100 modified by equipping it with all the bolt-on components from the Tiger 100 Racing Kit still available as an optional extra. It was competitively priced at £233.16s.8d., inclusive of Purchase Tax, just over £10 more than the standard Tiger 100.

All models (with the exception of the Trophy Twin) were now fitted with a new design Lucas 525 rear light, in which the lens was moulded in Diacon plastic. This was a move long overdue as the traditional 'fag end' rear light was virtually useless in fog and gave no warning of the rider's intention to brake. The new Lucas unit made it possible to incorporate a rear brake stop light, actuated from a simple pull switch attached to the rear brake pedal. All the other optional extras were still available, including the spring wheel, now provided as standard with the Thunderbird and the two Tiger 100 models. The only machines to which the dual seat was fitted as standard were the two Tiger 100s.

After the report on the 1953 Triumph range had been published in the 11th September issue of *The Motor Cycle*, Edward was concerned that the price reduction of the latest Speed Twin might be misinterpreted as a trend about to start within the industry. A statement from him was published in the following week's issue of the magazine, in which he explained it was solely due to production economies that Triumph's price reduction had been possible. In his opinion, it would be quite wrong to expect a general drop in prices. On the other hand, the price of British motorcycles had already reached the point at which export prospects would begin to suffer if they increased still further. Competition from German manufacturers in particular was a matter of growing concern, as they had the added advantage of modern, well-equipped factories financed by American lease-lend money. British manufacturers had to face facts: as raw material prices and production costs were unlikely to fall, and in all probability would increase, the only way in which even small price reductions could be made would be from internal economies.

The 1952 International Six Days Trial was held in Bad Aussee, Austria, and was anything but a success for the British entrants. The Trophy Team finished third, with a massive loss of 700 marks. Riders in the Vase teams fared no better either; the Vase 'B' team finishing 6th (501 marks lost) and the Vase 'A' team 8th (624 marks lost). The British teams were even out of the running for a Manufacturer's Team award, though, to be fair, the British entrants, irrespective of what

been achieved, even though a similar figure was unlikely to be attained by the average rider. Fuel economy tests were conducted under very special riding conditions, in which a machine was held at a steady 30mph with a constant throttle opening, and kept in top gear as far as possible. The brakes were not used unless absolutely necessary. The test begged the question - was Triumph intending to fit the Thunderbird with an SU carburetter in place of its Type 6 Amal?

During September, Triumph announced the range for 1953, which now comprised a total of five twins. Although the basic designs had remained unchanged, there were several noticeable differences. The Speed Twin had been reduced in price from £209.11s.2d. to £203.3s.4d., partly because the traditional dc lighting and ignition system had been replaced with a Lucas RM12 55 watt ac alternator. Since the alternator dispensed with the need for a dynamo and a magento, as well as a voltage regulator, this was an area in which savings had been made. However, it was not quite as straightforward as it seemed since other changes had also to be made. Fitting an alternator to the end of the crankshaft entailed having to modify the left-hand end to accept the rotor, and fit a new primary chaincase to accommodate the stator coils. The chaincase was fitted with a circular detachable cover so that the timing could be checked without having to remove the whole outer chaincase. As there was no longer an engine shaft shock absorber, the whole assembly had to be relocated within the clutch centre, taking the form of rubber buffers. The space previously occupied by the magneto now housed a Lucas distributor which was driven by the magneto's former drive pinion, with the ignition coil mounted above it.

A further modification related to the headlamp; the inclusion of an additional ignition switch with a key. It had an 'emergency start' position so that the engine could be started by diverting most of the output from the alternator if the battery was flat. The battery had, of course, to be kept charged whilst the engine was running, hence the need for a rectifier to change the alternator ac output to dc. It was fitted under the saddle in the area previously occupied by the old dc voltage regulator.

Other modifications included a new left-hand exhaust pipe to clear the new chaincase and an extension of the prop stand footpiece.

Triumph supplied sidecar outfits to the Automobile Association, finished in the colours of its 'road rescue' patrols. On what appears to be a very cold day in May 1951, Edward is present when the first batch is about to be driven away from Meriden by AA patrolmen.

make of machine they rode, were badly let down by the ancillary equipment manufacturers.

Things had started well when, after the first day's running, none of the British teams were penalised in any way. But on day two the abysmal weather began to take its toll. After the lunch check the machines had to stand outside in the pouring rain whilst their riders waited for six hours in a factory canteen before they could take part in the night run. Bob Mann's Matchless refused to start with a waterlogged magento, as did George Buck's Ariel sidecar outfit. Worse still, the distributor shaft had sheared on Harold Taylor's Royal Enfield outfit whilst he was on top of a mountain in the midst of a snowstorm. And so it went on, with even Jim Alves and Peter Hammond having to contend with ever worsening gearbox problems. Hammond went out on the fourth day and Alves on the fifth.

Interestingly, Alves was using what was, in effect, a prototype 649cc engine which, a year later, would be the power unit for a new T110 model. Triumph was remarkably adept at camouflaging changes in design so that they remained undetected by even the most zealous of sports reporters, as mentioned earlier. When the Trophy Twins first appeared, the works riders preferred to ride a 350cc twin in one-day events. As a result, some special 350cc cylinder blocks and heads were made that outwardly appeared identical to those of the 500cc twins. Although the riders seemed to be riding standard production models, nothing was further from the truth.

In the 9th October issue of *The Motor Cycle*, a further contribution from Edward appeared in print. Entitled 'Design and Development' and submitted at the request of the editor, it was intended to convey Edward's thoughts about the ways in which he expected design trends to change in the forseeable future. In reality, however, his comments were no more than the conclusions

many knowledgable enthusiasts would have drawn from their own observations. Edward confirmed that his earlier and oft expressed views about the ultra-fast international road racing models still held good, as none was likely to be produced as a commercially viable prospect. He expected that future development would concentrate on the four cylinder models, a fact which was already becoming evident. Most knew it was only a matter of time before the Italian fours achieved the standard of reliability that had so far held them back, after which the traditional British racing singles would no longer have the upper hand.

Next, came the continuing development of the clubman type racer so that it would appeal also to the more sporting rider who required much better than average road performance and was prepared to pay for it. Here. Edward believed that the vertical twin would continue to hold its own for a considerable period of time. This would, however, be at the expense of an ever-growing gap between this type of machine and those destined for little more than a daily commuting role. This was, in fact, also happening, or was about to happen, with the appearance of the Triumph and BSA 650cc twins and the higher performance variants that would follow them in due course. He foresaw the smaller capacity machines having a mainly commuting role, some of them being little more than a motorised attachment used to power a bicycle. Already significant strides had been made in this latter area and many were riding a powered bicycle who would never have considered buying a lightweight motorcycle. He saw particularly good prospects for the scooter, another area which was attracting a similar category of rider. Edward mentioned the Moto Guzzi Galletto as a particularly good example; it had all the attributes of a motorcycle, yet the convenience and appeal of a scooter. The German-made scooters had so far failed to make much of an impression on him as they were, in his opinion, overweight and more costly to purchase than a conventional lightweight motorcycle. These comments were hardly prophetic as the scooter 'boom' of the fifties had already started, and would continue for practically a decade.

Edward concluded by saying that nothing produced by the British motorcycle industry in the ten years since the war could be regarded as innovative, with the exception of the LE Velocette and the Sunbeam twin, although even the latter was little more than a BMW with the cylinders folded upwards. It was the LE's overall specification, and high level of silencing that had impressed him most, but as it was relatively expensive, he felt this would limit its appeal. He remained optimistic that, if lean times lay ahead, British ingenuity would succeed in maintaining progress, much as it had done in the 1920s - but without letting the customer do the development testing as had been a past failing.

This survey was not one of Edward's better efforts, as he himself admitted, and he apologised to the editor for the delay in submitting it. He confessed he had been preoccupied with other matters, including a world trip earlier in the year. The reason for this admission would soon become apparent.

Chapter 9: Triumph enters the lightweight market

It was not until the eve of the 1952 Motor Cycle Show that Triumph sprang a surprise, by unveiling an entirely new model that would take the 1953 range up to a total of six models. The newcomer was Edward's latest inspiration, a 149cc, overhead valve single with plunger-type rear suspension, the first 150cc Triumph since the XO5 series of 1934.

Since World War 2, two-stroke singles had enjoyed a virtual monopoly as far as the under 200cc market was concerned, only the 149cc LE Velocette offering any kind of token alternative. Even that was in a class of its own on account of its unconventional design, so the Triumph broke entirely new ground by offering the two-strokes a serious head-on challenge. Based on a loop frame with a single downtube and plunger rear suspension, the newcomer's cycle parts featured an undamped telescopic front fork, with an in-built nacelle that enclosed the headlamp - the by now familiar Triumph 'trade mark'. Interestingly, the frame incorporated a feature with which Edward had become obsessed in his determination to 'let the metal do the work'. It had only a single lower tank rail in place of the customary upper and lower tank rails, the petrol tank itself being internally stiffened. Not only did this save weight, it also helped reduce production costs. As there was no longer any need for the tank to have a central tunnel running lengthwise along its underside, it could be made from two pressings welded horizontally along the middle joint.

Further weight saving was accomplished by having the wheel spindle lugs of the rear suspension units made of light alloy.

An overhead valve engine of 149cc capacity had been chosen after much thought, as it was considered it would provide sufficient power to give a maximum speed of approximately 60mph and be capable of maintaining a cruising speed of 45-50mph. It would also be capable of carrying a pillion passenger without undue stress. For what was intended to be a high quality lightweight, it was believed that the extra cost of an overhead valve engine would be acceptable, especially in view of the benefits of better carburation and an efficient silencing system that would not result in a disproportionate loss of power. The use of a four-speed gearbox would maximise on the potential of the engine power output, as would the use of automatic ignition advance.

The engine was built on the unit-construction principle, with the four-speed gearbox forming part of the basic crankcase casting. The cylinder barrel was of cast iron, painted silver to match the light alloy diecast cylinder head. The oversquare bore and stroke dimensions of 57 x 58.5mm had been chosen to allow the use of generously sized valves, and to ensure the engine unit was as compact as possible and easy to remove from the frame. It was inclined forward at an angle of 25 degrees and had its two push rods enclosed within a single external chromium-plated tube. Each overhead rocker arm pivoted on a single spindle, and had an adjuster on its outer end. Covers retained by a single nut and washer ensured full enclosure of the valve gear, whilst allowing easy access for valve clearance adjustments.

Internally, a forged steel connecting rod ran on a roller bearing big end, the crankshaft assembly of which was supported on a roller main bearing at the primary drive end, and a plain bush on the timing side. The crankshaft pinion formed part of a male taper that pressed into the right-hand end of the crankshaft, and had a skew cut inside the timing pinion. The skew served a dual purpose as it drove a vertically-mounted distributor to the rear of the cylinder barrel and also a twin plunger oil pump which was linked to it by a short rod. The single camshaft was located directly above the crankshaft pinion, from which it took its drive. Primary drive was by an endless chain.

The electrics were powered by a crankshaft-mounted Lucas RM 13 six volt alternator, with a rectifier in the wiring circuit to convert the alternator's ac output to dc for charging the 10 amp hour battery. The headlamp switch had an 'emergency start' position to counter problems associated with a flat battery. An Amal 332 carburettor with a single float chamber supplied the correct mixture: the intake was connected by a long synthetic rubber tube to an air cleaner sandwiched between the two and a half pint oil tank and the toolbox. Both wheels were of 19 inch diameter, shod with 2.75 inch section studded tyres and mudguards of the close-fitting type. The brakes were both of 5.5 inch diameter.

Seating comprised a single saddle mounted on springs, and no pillion seat despite the claim that a passenger could be carried without imposing too much strain on performance. A centre stand was provided for parking purposes. Total weight was just 175lbs.

The overall specification included a 70mph Smiths speedometer (now included in the purchase price), and a horn enclosed within the headlamp nacelle, following customary Triumph practice. Finished in amaranth red lined with gold, with all the usual chrome-plated fittings that included the Triumph tank badge, the new model attracted no small amount of attention both at the show and in the motorcycling press.

Described in the 9.5 x 8.5 inch catalogue as "A Real Triumph in Miniature", the new model was depicted as an ideal mount for lady riders. Listed as the Model T15 Terrier and priced at £125. 4s. 6d, it cost only about £10-12 more than most of the less sophisticated two-strokes of similar capacity.

It has been said the Terrier owed some allegiance to a somewhat similar Terrot design, but, in all fairness, it must be emphasised that inventors and designers habitually study the designs of others. Not only does this avoid the possibility of patent infringement, it

Edward and Shirley Watts were married at St. George's Church, Hanover Square, London, on 19th July 1952. Wilfred Sutcliff (left), best man at Edward's first marriage, performed the same function again on this occasion.

also often helps to produce ideas that might suggest a new line of approach. For example, it has also been suggested that some design features in Edward's Triumph twin engine are similar to those found in the engine of the Riley car. However, this has also been said of Eugene Goodman's design of the Velocette 'M' series of engines! Bert Hopwood once readily admitted that when he was designing the engine for BSA's ill-fated MC1 racer, he derived inspiration from the valve gear layout of Val Page's dohc JAP engines of the mid-twenties. There are so many parallels like these, and not necessarily just within the same industry. The Gloster Aircraft Company was experimenting with a spring wheel in 1930 which was subsequently used in the undercarriage of the Gladiator biplane, although it did not require an arcuate movement. As Edward had often said to Jack Wickes "There's nothing new in the world, my boy".

Although the Terrier made the headlines towards the end of 1952, another earlier news item had not escaped the notice of the motorcycling press. When Edward returned from his latest overseas visit, he was accompanied by Miss Shirley Joan Watts, an Australian whom he had met in New Zealand where she was working as a waitress. She was working her way to Europe, taking various odd jobs along the way, and made quite an impression on him. He lost touch with her when he moved on and, when he tried to see her again, found to his dismay that she had left the place at which she was working. Thanks to his connections with the New Zealand police, he managed to track her down and sent her an air ticket to suggest they might meet in Rome. He proposed to her soon after her arrival and they married in St. George's Church, Hanover Square, London, W.1 on Saturday 19th July. Their reception was held in the Dorchester Hotel, Park Lane, after which they departed for a tour of Scotland.

On their return they settled initially at Woodside, Gibbet Hill, but this was only until Edward could find another larger house within reasonable travelling distance of Coventry. Woodside held for him too many memories of his earlier blissful days there with Marion.

Early in 1953, Jim Alves had the galling experience of having his Trophy Twin catch fire and burn out whilst he was on his way to the start of the Colmore Cup Trial. It was all the more irritating because this happened when he was within ten miles of the event start at the Saleyard, Shipston-on-Stour. Jim was only too aware of the Trophy Twin's shortcomings, particularly the need for pivoted fork rear suspension that was making life easier for his contemporaries in scramble-type events. By early March he had built a very purposeful-looking 'special' in his own workshop, using a Trophy Twin engine and gearbox in his own design of frame. Made from one inch diameter 14 gauge tubing with a 1.25 inch 10 gauge spine, Feridax McCandless suspension units pivoting on Silentbloc bushes provided the rear suspension. The pivot mounting was particularly sturdy, taking the form of a bridge piece fabricated from steel plate. The front end used a Triumph 'A' pattern steering head and a Triumph telescopic fork. Weighing only 305lbs it represented the efforts of Alves alone, and had not been works inspired. It would, of course, have been used in events that were not trade supported because it was company policy that the works riders use only machines that - outwardly, at least - closely resembled the current over-the-counter production models.

On 21st April 1953, the first of Edward's and Shirley's two daughters was born. Edward was now aged 52 and, as will be seen subsequently, proved to be a very caring and devoted father who adored his children, his only regret being that they had arrived so late in his life. It was a strange coincidence that 1953 was not only the Coronation year of Her Majesty Queen Elizabeth II, but also that April 21st happened to be the Queen's birthday. Edward had been born on the day that Edward VII was proclaimed King. The pair named their daughter Shirley after her mother, Elizabeth because her date of birth coincided with that of the Queen in her Coronation year, and Jane because Marion's father had always called her Jane. Of these three names, Jane became the one that was used.

The post-World War 2 motorcycle scene was now changing rapidly from the way it had been in the thirties. One problem of increasing urgency was the need to reduce the ever-growing number of fatalities and accidents involving motorcyclists, which could be attributed to a variety of reasons. A high incidence of head injuries was especially disturbing, and attempts were being made to encourage riders and their passengers to wear safety helmets without having to invoke legislation to make it compulsory. Lord Lucas, Parliamentary Secretary to the Ministry of Transport, hinted that legal means would have to be introduced if this was the only way to resolve the problem.

The motorcycle industry took heed by improving the standard of lighting on motorcycles. Already the widespread use of rear suspension, telescopic front forks, more efficient brakes and better tyres had helped to offset problems arising from Britain's deteriorating roads, which had suffered from neglect during the war years. Campaigns to encourage the wearing of safety helmets were already taking effect. The police set a precedent by ensuring that helmets would be worn at all times by motorcycle patrolmen, and the AA and RAC motorcycle patrols followed suit, as did the motorcycling press. The need to have some form of head protection seems also to have registered with Edward, who was wont to disappear down the Meriden mile at racing speeds whilst trying a bike on impulse, with only his homberg hat on his head. A few months later when he, his Work's Director and his Service Manager, took part in an extended ACU observed endurance run described later, all three set a good example by wearing safety helmets.

On the occasion of Her Majesty Queen Elizabeth II's Coronation on 2nd June, the Metropolitan Police provided her escort, all riding Triumph Speed Twins. Ironically, sales to the police, although prestigious, were not profitable due to the changes in specification that had to be made. These included fitting a radio transmitter and receiver, a loud-hailer, legshields and a handlebar screen, a single seat and a larger capacity battery.

A road test of the latest Speed Twin appeared in the 13th August issue of *Motor Cycling*, a test of some significance as it was fitted with the new ac/dc electrical system. The test concluded with a very favourable comment, suggesting that anyone who purchased the latest model would have every reason to be more than satisfied. It had yet to be discovered that when the emergency start system was activated it was not infallible. Because most of the output from the alternator was directed to the ignition system, unless the ignition timing and position of the alternator rotor were exactly matched, the engine was unlikely to run satisfactorily. It was a shortlived problem, resolved by the equipment suppliers - but not before it had attracted unfavourable comment.

The 1953 International Six Days Trial was held during mid-September in Gottwaldov, Czechoslovakia. On this occasion the British Trophy Team gave an impressive performance, winning the event with no loss of marks and ensuring it would be staged in Britain the following year. Jim Alves was again a member of the British Trophy Team with his 646cc-engined Trophy Twin, and John Giles was a member of Britain's Vase B Team riding a 498cc Trophy Twin. The Vase B Team was out of the running for the Vase, having lost a total of 17 marks. The Vase was won by Czechoslovakia.

Prior to the 1953 Paris Motorcycle Salon, the equivalent of Britain's annual Motor Cycle Show Show, Neale Shilton had been appointed Sales Manager of Triumph. Since 1950, he had been helping Harry Holland, the Export Manager, develop new export markets in addition to his duties as a sales representative. It came as a pleasant surprise to be given responsibility for UK sales.

At the Paris Show an entirely new Triumph twin made its debut, the Tiger 110, the first Triumph to have pivoted fork rear suspension. It marked the beginning of the end of the spring wheel, the new frame being only three quarters of an inch longer than its rigid counterpart. Its 649cc engine was similar to that of the prototype engine Jim Alves had been using in his ISDT twin, differing from the Thunderbird engine in several respects. It had a heavier crankshaft assembly running on larger diameter main bearings, identified by the bulge in the right-hand bearing housing of the crankcase, high compression pistons, enlarged inlet valves and ports, and a larger bore carburetter. It produced 42bhp with an air cleaner and silencers fitted to give a maximum speed in excess of 110mph, which necessitating a larger diameter front brake of eight inch diameter. Finished in an attractive shell blue sheen, and

with a two-level dualseat, the Tiger 110 could also be supplied with an optional quickly detachable rear wheel. The UK price was later confirmed at £240, inclusive of Purchase Tax.

According to Jack Wickes, the drawing office staff was made aware of the need for a frame with pivoted fork rear suspension when Edward told them exactly how it was to be designed. He was insistent that the front half of the old frame should be retained, essential to uphold his maxim of the greatest effort for minimum cost. About to depart on one of his visits to America, he made it clear he expected a prototype to be ready upon his return.

Built exactly as Edward had laid down, the prototype frame was a backward step: Triumphs had never been renowned for roadholding, but when Tyrell Smith and the others rode the machine to which the frame had been fitted, they found its indifferent handing, due to twisting of the unbraced rear fork, gave real cause for concern. Tyrell Smith decided there was only one thing to be done; fit a near vertical seat tube and re-position the engine and gearbox as close together as possible. Assisted by Ron Hazlehurst, these modifications were made to give the Triumph a pivoted fork frame that was to set a pattern for the years to follow. It was not the first time that one of Edward's designs had been surreptitiously modified, later meeting with his grudging approval.

Ironically, it was the Terrier that brought about Tyrell Smith's downfall only a short while after. When the prototypes were being tested, they were plagued by seemingly endless electrical failures, which meant the required number of development miles were not being covered. Inevitably, someone had to take the blame, and Tyrell Smith was the unfortunate recipient. Summoned to Edward's office by way of John Nelson, he knew what lay in store and came out with a few choice words! Unfortunately, Edward happened to be right behind John Nelson. Smith got his marching orders and left to join Jaguar's Racing Department. Ultimately, he returned to the motorcycle trade when he became a technical representative for Girling, manufacturer of hydraulically-damped suspension units.

On Monday 5th October, Edward left Meriden riding one of the new 149cc T15 Terrier models, accompanied by Bob Fearon, Works Director and Alec Masters, Service Manager, on similar models. Immaculately clad in new Barbour suits and wearing safety helmets, the trio was heading for the Imperial Hotel in Exeter, where they would stay overnight before setting out for Land's End the following morning. Following in a car, their escorts must have wondered whether an unexpected incident within the first hour of departure could be interpreted as a bad omen: as the riders swept around a bend, in line astern, they suddenly disappeared from sight. All the escorts could see was a huge white cloud that looked like cement dust. It was, in fact, liquid fertiliser which had been shed by a lorry. This so-called 'fertilisation ceremony' later provided scope for no end of jocular comment!

The following morning the riders made their way to the starting point, the Victoria Inn at Roche, where Alan Maclachlan, former RAC Motorcycle Manager, was the landlord. Then it was off to Land's End. The escorts included John McNulty, the ACU's observer, and Eric Headlam, who supervised the trio's itinerary and ensured they maintained an average speed of 38mph to keep to their planned schedule. A third member, Colin Swaisland of Esso Petroleum, was riding a Speed Twin. He was the cameraman, making a cine film in colour of the observed test. After covering the first 180 miles they again stayed overnight at the Imperial Hotel, Exeter, from where they set out the following morning for Leamington Spa via Honiton, Shepton Mallet and Bath, pausing for lunch at Malmsbury. Then it was on to Cirencester, Stow-on-the Wold and Warwick.

When the new Tiger 110 made its debut at the Paris Salon Show, it was the first Triumph to have pivoted fork rear suspension. A high performance 650cc model, it was well received by the American market.

Edward had been looking forward to this trip which, to use his own words after they had arrived at the Regent Hotel, was "Just the job - I needed it to jerk me out of a groove". Pleased by the way in which the next 263 miles had gone, he later went on to say "Speaking purely as a rider, I think this little Terrier has got something that's going to appeal to quite a lot of people". Bob Fearon was just as enthusiastic, claiming he had forgotten what good fun motorcycling could be. He realised how much better he could see the countryside than from the inside of a car, and, for that matter, smell it too!

On Thursday they arrived in Carlisle, having travelled via Leicester, Doncaster, Scotch Corner and Penrith, with a pause for lunch at Boroughbridge. Although they had covered 246 miles, the longest leg of the run so far, they arrived an hour before schedule, which prompted Edward to ask "why aren't we scheduled to do more miles in a day? This is so easy it's just plain silly." The answer, of course, is that it was prudent to make allowance for rain, fog and other poor weather conditions that could have slowed them up considerably.

As Friday dawned they headed for Inverness, another long leg of 263 miles which took them through Lanark and Stirling with lunch taken in Perth. The route then continued through Pitlochrie and Kingussie to their hotel in Inverness.

Although it was easy to become complacent as the journey thus far had been so easy, when they started out early on the Saturday morning the weather forecast was not so good. Now they had only 158 miles to cover, which included a return to Wick after they had reached John O'Groats. Sure enough, it wasn't long before rain began to fall. Bob Fearon ran out of road whilst negotiating one of Scotland's never-ending bends, giving cause for real anxiety. Rather than drop the bike and risk jeopardising the run, Bob clung on and ran wide onto the grass verge, hitting a hidden culvert that caused his bike to leap into the air. Still in command he managed to rejoin the road to everyone's relief after what must have been a heart-stopping moment.

A mile further on his bike started to misfire, probably as a result of his off-road excursion. A frayed strand in the throttle cable was removed and the sparking plug changed, without any sign of improvement. A more thorough check revealed a chafed battery lead. Rather than lose more time effecting a repair, it was decided the final 50 miles would be covered with the ignition switch in the emergency start position. And so all three riders arrived safely at John O'Groats by midday, with time to enjoy a cup of coffee before returning to Wick to officially complete the mileage. It mattered little that it was now raining hard.

When the results were analysed it was found they had covered 1008 miles in a total running time of 27 hours, 29 minutes, which represented an average speed of 36.68mph. Fuel consumption had averaged an incredibly low 108.6mpg, despite a higher average speed than the estimated 30mph. Worthy of special note was the weight of the individual riders: Alec Masters tipped the scales at 13 stone, 7 pounds, Edward at 14 stone, 3 pounds, and Bob Fearon 16 stone, 7 pounds. It had been a memorable journey from the riders' point of view, and as a public relations exercise had given Triumph's new lightweight a considerable boost. The motorcycling press dubbed the event the 'Gaffers' Gallop' and each rider was presented with a specially bound album containing photographs taken during the trip. How many other Managing Directors would have taken the opportunity to demonstrate the reliability of one of their own products in such a positive manner?

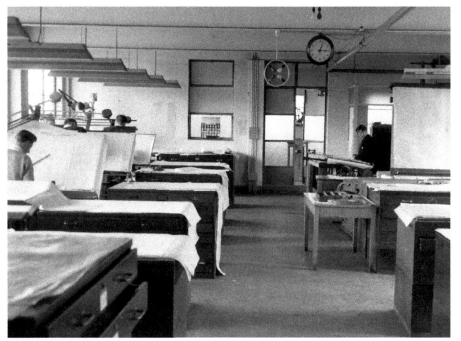

The drawing office at Meriden, date unknown. (Vida Wickes)

The 1953 Motor Cycle Show at Earls Court followed soon afterwards, opening its doors in mid-November, and Triumph used the occasion to spring yet another surprise. Apart from the new Tiger 110, on display in Britain for the first time, there was also an enlarged version of the Terrier, the T20 Tiger Cub with an engine of 199cc capacity, also featuring plunger rear suspension. It cost £127.4s, approximately £10 more than its 149cc counterpart, and would be available in the traditional Triumph Tiger colour scheme, now changed to what was officially described as a shell blue sheen.

The new season's 6T Thunderbird followed in the footsteps of the 5T Speed Twin, having been converted to alternator electrics and coil ignition. The Tiger 100C had been dropped, the standard model now sporting a frame with pivoted fork rear suspension similar to that of the T110. The spring wheel was reserved for only two of the remaining rigid frame models, the 5T Speed Twin and the Trophy Twin. Still listed as an optional extra, it cost £20.8s.11d., inclusive of Purchase Tax.

To round off the year, Triumph 'works' riders Johnny Giles and Jack Wicken tied to win the Southern Trial, a trade-supported event held on 31st October. When Jim Alves' score was added, Triumph secured the Manufacturers Team Award.

As the year drew to a close, Jim Alves saw potential in the diminutive Terrier as a lightweight trials model, and set about modifying one for off-road use. As will be seen in the following chapter, his foresight was soon rewarded.

Three of Triumph's executives set off from Land's End on a proving run, riding the new 149cc Terrier model. Left to right: Bob Fearon (Works Director), Edward and Alec Masters (Service Manager). In the background are Eric Headlam (Triumph) and John McNulty (ACU Observer), third and fourth from the left. Only towards the end of the run did the riders' new Barbour suits get tested when it rained.

Smiles all round on having arrived safely at John O'Groats. Edward now appears to have been convinced of the need to wear a safety helmet. How many other Managing Directors of British motorcycle manufacturing companies would have been prepared to test their latest model in this way?

Chapter 10: Johnny Allen's record-breaking saga

Introduction of the 199cc Tiger Cub provided the company with another lightweight of slightly larger capacity, more suitable for carrying a rider and pillion passenger at a respectable cruising speed, with good fuel consumption. It would also compete more successfully with the lightweight two-strokes available from Triumph's contemporaries which dominated the lower end of the market.

The 149cc Terrier was to continue in production; the engine big end assembly changing to one of the shell bearing type to fall in line with that of the new Tiger Cub. Many regarded this as a retrograde step, believing that a shell bearing would not be as forgiving in the event of oil pressure fluctuation, a belief that subsequently proved correct. The Terrier continued in production for a further three years with only a few minor modifications, and was dropped from the range in August 1956.

The Tiger Cub engine was an enlarged version of the Terrier unit, with a revised big end assembly as mentioned above. The engine had bore and stroke dimensions of 63 x 64mm compared to the Terrier's 57 x 58.5mm, its integral four-speed gearbox having different gear ratios. A larger bore Amal carburetter was needed and a larger section (19 x 3.00 inch) tyre, with the option of an upswept exhaust system. In common with other models in the Tiger range, the frame and cycle parts were painted black and the petrol tank and mudguards finished in the new shell blue sheen colour that would

The T20 Tiger Cub was an enlarged version of the Terrier, accomplished by increasing both the bore and stroke to give a capacity of 199cc. It was finished in the 'Tiger' colours of that time, officially known as shell blue and black. Like the Terrier from which it was derived, it, too, had plunger-type rear suspension initially.

The trials version of the Terrier, built by Jim Alves in the workshop adjoining his motorcycle business in Glastonbury, Somerset. He modified a second-hand model bought in from a customer in a part-exchange deal. Meriden was not associated with this project in any way and had no intention of making a similar model.

henceforth apply to all machines. The frame and cycle parts were identical to those of the Terrier.

As may be expected of such an expert, Jim Alves had given the construction of a trials version of the Terrier a lot of thought, and this was apparent when, riding it, he won the Colmore Cup Trial held on 6th February 1954 with a loss of only six marks. His win aroused sufficient interest for John Thorpe of *Motor Cycling* to try out the machine under Jim's supervision on one of the local trials hills. Being much less experienced than the bike's constructor, Thorpe found it to be very forgiving when, quite unintentionally, he veered off course and disappeared over a six foot drop! It demonstrated good traction over the abundant notoriously wet Somerset clay. In short, Thorpe found it difficult to believe that a converted, road-going model could perform so well when ridden off-road in totally different conditions.

The surprising fact was that the engine and gearbox of Jim's Terrier - which was not new when Jim set about modifying it - had not been touched. It was a machine he had acquired from one of his customers, presumably having taken it in part-exchange for another model at his motorcycle shop in the Somerset town of Glastonbury. It had taken him just under a month to complete the conversion. Basically, he repositioned the rear fork bridges of the frame to provide sufficient clearance for a 400 x 19 inch section rear trials tyre and used competition-type aluminimum alloy mudguards to replace the originals. The front fork nacelle had been removed, together with all the lighting equipment, and ignition was by battery only, which meant disconnecting it when the engine was not running. A 21 inch front wheel, also shod with a trials tyre, helped provide extra ground clearance. Trials handlebars, a rubber competition saddle, and an exhaust pipe with an upswept end were also considered necessary. By fitting a larger diameter rear wheel sprocket, the bottom gear ratio was lowered to something like 34:1. Jim had stood a good chance of winning the earlier St. David's Trial held on January 16th, had not a failed condenser in the ignition circuit caused his retirement.

It was made quite clear to readers of *Motor Cycling* that there was no possibility of the Triumph factory manufacturing a trials version of the Terrier. It was Jim alone who had taken the initiative to carry out such a conversion and it was he, no doubt, who had a hand in the construction by Peter Hammond, a fellow works-supported rider, of a similar model. Edward had always been adamant that if a 'works' machine was to compete in competition events, it had to appear virtually identical in outward appearance to the 'over the counter' production model. That is, assuming one which could be bought at a local Triumph dealership was available.

Television trials and scrambles, organised by the ACU in conjunction with the BBC, were now becoming popular, providing excellent unpaid publicity for the manufacturers invited to take part, especially those whose machines were in the winning team. They also helped generate a wider interest in motorcycle sport and, within a very short period of time, the rider's names became familiar nationwide.

In the second trial of the series, held during early March on a pocket-sized course near Wendover, Bucks, Triumph riders

The Turner family moved to Bericote House, Blackdown, near Leamington Spa, in 1954. Much larger than Woodside and with more spacious grounds, it was also more isolated.

representing the team from the west scored a convincing win. Jim Alves, remaining faithful to his Terrier, lost not a single mark, whilst Peter Hammond, on a Trophy Twin, lost only three. The other two members of the west team were both Ariel riders: 'Nipper' Parsons and Bob Ray. Jim Alves tied with John Giles to put up the best individual performance, both of them with a clean sheet. John Giles, mounted on another Triumph Trophy Twin, had ridden for the south team.

In the Kickham Trial, held in the Wessex centre, Jim Alves' success with his 150cc Terrier continued when he won the Cross Cup for the best performance by a 150. He was only 8 marks adrift from the winner, David Tye, a works-supported BSA rider. This was no small accomplishment, considering that the small capacity trials two-strokes were now becoming a force to be reckoned with, offering a serious challenge to the previously dominant four-strokes.

Whilst much of this had been going on, Edward was away from Meriden. During January he had taken Shirley and their young daughter, Jane, on a sight-seeing visit to Australia which included a visit to Shirley's mother. By this time the family had moved from Edward's old home at Gibbet Hill, in Coventry, to Bericote House at Blackdown, near Leamington Spa.

Soon after Edward's return Triumph lost another valuable member of the Experimental Department through the death of Ernie Nott. In his day Ernie had been a very successful road racer for Rudge and Husqvarna, after which he became a member of Rudge's Racing Experimental Department. He joined Triumph in 1947, bringing with him a wealth of experience in engine building and tuning.

In the 1954 Scottish Six Days Trial, Jim Alves' name again appeared in the awards list. In this event he rode a works-prepared 199cc Tiger Cub competition model, similar in many respects to his home-built, off-road version of the Terrier. He won the 151-200cc award, with an overall loss of 32 marks.

Returning during August from one of his frequent business trips to the USA, Edward invited the Press to the Meriden factory to introduce the 1955 model range. It had been expected he would begin by referring to business matters, and in particular the way in which Triumph was continuing to make significant progress in the North American market. Much to everyone's surprise, he launched

The machine that became known in America as the' Trophybird 650', at first a Trophy Twin fitted with a 6T Thunderbird cast iron engine, and later with the newer Tiger 110 all-alloy engine.

straight into a tirade about the inadequacy of Britain's roads and the ever-increasing volume of traffic that was impeding the rapid transportation of goods destined for export. He had seen for himself how America had dealt with a similar problem, where first-class roads made motoring a pleasure and not the nightmare that had confronted him on his arrival home. He left no uncertainty in anyone's mind that this steadily deteriorating situation could be attributed directly to the government of the day, which was taking something like £400,000,000 a year from the so-called Road Fund which originally had been introduced to help finance the building of new roads and the upkeep of those already in use. The money in it had been syphoned off and used for other purposes, which is why the accident rate was rising as the roads fell into disrepair, and the expected improvements to help relieve congestion had failed to materialise. Each year more than 5000 people were killed and 211,000 injured in road accidents.

In Edward's opinion it said much about the skill of the average British driver that the figures quoted were not ten times higher. Having driven in virtually every country in the world during the past 35 years, he considered Britain to be the most dangerous country of all for motorists and pedestrians alike. Something had to be done in the form of an enormous capital expenditure programme for road-making plant and machinery, as an economic necessity of the very highest priority.

After this bitter diatribe about Britain's roads, Edward then introduced the Triumph range for the 1955 season. He confirmed Triumph had sold 50% more motorcycles to the USA in 1954 than it had the previous year, and, to use his own description of the company, it was: "a merry little business in a thriving industry". Production at this time is believed to have been running at a rate of over 30,000 machines a year, more than Norton or AJS and Matchless.

Since Triumph had introduced two new models the previous year, there were only detail modifications to the existing model range for 1955, with one exception. That related to the TR5 Trophy Twin, the alloy 498cc engine of which would be modified to more closely resemble the specification of the 649cc T110 engine. In the main, this meant a higher compression ratio of 8:1 and use of the T110's camshafts. Some tended to think of this as a retrograde step as it would boost the power output to 33bhp at 6500rpm and take away the charm of the original 'soft', low compression engine.

Other changes included fitting a Lucas K2FT magneto because the original BTH component was no longer in production, and revised gear ratios more in keeping with the increased power output of the engine. As the 1955 model would also feature the new frame with pivoted fork rear suspension, it would be correspondingly heavier, with an overall weight of 365lbs, a significant increase of 65lbs on that of its predecessor.

Apart from the aforementioned colour change to the 'Tiger' models (and the Trophy Twin), the alloy-engined Tiger 100 would henceforth be fitted with a Lucas 'wader' magneto, whilst the T110 model would benefit from a more robust forged centre stand. The SU carburetter, fitted exclusively to the 6T Thunderbird, was to be replaced by an Amal 376 Monobloc type, and the machine's colour scheme changed to a polychromatic blue. These were long-awaited changes requested by the American market, which would be pleased to see them. The alternator of the 5T Speed Twin was upgraded by fitting a Lucas RM12 unit, and repositioning its stator so that it was no longer attached to the primary chaincase cover.

A change in engine specification had already been made to the Terrier, as mentioned earlier, with regard to the big end bearing assembly. Other detail modifications made to both the T15 Terrier and T20 Tiger Cub included fitting a Lucas RM13 alternator and a new Sentercel rectifier. A new wiring harness with connecting plugs would now permit disconnection of the engine and headlamp electrical components during maintenance, if required.

In the International Six Days Trial that followed just over a couple of months later, Jim Alves - as a member of Britain's Trophy Team - had to revert as a matter of necessity to a 649cc Triumph Twin. The ability to maintain a strict time schedule was the overriding factor, as it was essential to enter the best possible machine available in this important event when national prestige was at stake. A works-prepared, large capacity twin of the type that had been so successful in the past was obviously the best available option.

Jim's machine was similar to the one he had ridden the previous year in Czechoslovakia; basically, a Trophy Twin fitted with a 649cc T110 engine. John Giles rode a similar machine as a member of Britain's Vase B Team. Both machines featured a new frame fitted with pivoted fork rear suspension. One of the Army's ISDT teams was similarly equipped, but its rear sprung models were fitted with a standard 498cc Trophy engine. Although the British Trophy Team finished with a clean sheet, the Czechoslovakian team did so, too. As the Czech team had shown the greatest improvement over the previous year's speed schedules, it received the Trophy. Although Britain's Vase B Team had also finished unpenalised, Holland had put up the better performance to win the Vase. The British A Team's loss of 100 marks put Triumph out of the running for the Manufacturer's Team Award.

When a T110 model was made available for *Motor Cycling* to road test only a few days before the 1954 ISDT, it was allocated to Bernal Osborne, who used it to cover the event for the magazine. Barely run in, the T110 was pressed into use almost immediately and ridden to Llandrindod Wells. Once there, it provided a vital service in getting the photographer's plates and his own copy about the first day of the trial from Llandovery to the railway station at Abergavenny in record time, for despatch to London. Not only did it demonstrate its high speed characteristics, but also its flexibility and good handling. When the opportunity presented itself later, a number of high speed runs were made against the stopwatch. The highest speed recorded was 114 mph, in an 18-20mph side wind. After the standard carburetter jet had been removed and replaced by one a size 20 larger, a flash reading of 117.2mph was achieved.

Surprisingly, petrol consumption averaged out around the 93 to 96mpg mark when speeds were held within the 65-70mph range, yet the latest Amal 376 Monobloc carburetter, only recently announced, had yet to be fitted. With such good available performance, the rider had to use the ignition advance lever intelligently to prevent the engine from pinking. Braking was in keeping with performance levels, and the angle of the handlebars in relation to the dualseat provided a comfortable riding position. During the hours of darkness the headlamp gave a good beam but, if high speed riding was required, the headlamp had to be set up to throw the main beam as far forward as possible.

In short, the new T110 model looked as though it could be a real winner, especially in the USA where above-average performance was a major selling point. Only the Gold Star BSA single had a higher maximum speed than the T110.

Early in October British motorcycle manufacturers held a celebratory luncheon at Grosvenor House, London, to pay tribute to Graham Walker for all the work he had done on behalf of the industry. Jack Sangster took the Chair as President of the British Motorcycle Manufacturers' Union, and Edward was amongst the 47 in attendance, to represent Triumph. Graham Walker had played a major role in progressing the aims and interests of the industry from 1938 to 1954, during which time he had been editor of *Motor Cycling*. Edward had gone out of his way to maintain a very close personal relationship with the editors of both weekly motorcycling magazines, his other contact being Arthur Bourne of *The Motor Cycle*. He welcomed their visits and relied on their observations to help keep him up-to-date with news of what was going on within the industry, as well as their views on how trends seemed likely to develop. Their regular meetings supplied much that he might otherwise have missed when he was away on his regular overseas visits. He could rely on them implicitly when confidential matters were discussed, and often referred to Arthur Bourne as the 'high lama of motorcycling'.

On St. Patrick's Day, 17th March 1955, Edward and Shirley Turner were blessed with the birth of a second daughter, Charmian Marion. Her first Christian name came from a Jeffrey Farnol novel, in which the heroine was Charmian, Lady Vibart. Her second Christian name was obviously associated with Edward's first wife, Marion, who had enjoyed this novel, and always remained in Edward's thoughts.

Late in May the Triumph Owners' MCC staged its first ever rally, and members were entertained by factory staff at the Triumph factory. Something like 2000 members and friends made their way to Meriden to present an impressive line-up of machines on the lawn in front of the factory. D.R. Foskett's immaculate 1951 Thunderbird attracted much attention in the Concours D'Elegance, many finding it difficult to believe it had covered 17,400 miles. Allan Jefferies, Club President at that time, described it in his inimitable manner as a cross between a canary and a Thunderbird! Its cream-coloured tank

This 'retro' model made by Kawasaki in 1999 closely resembles a Triumph twin, but has a 675cc four valve dohc engine. It is a model Triumph should have made, and it is unfortunate that the company did not proceed with its own earlier prototypes. (Kawasaki Motors (UK) Ltd)

and mudguards, and chromium-plated or highly polished component parts undoubtedly gave that impression.

The afternoon's entertainment centred around a Moto Ball match on the lawn, and a display by the Royal Signals. John Giles and Jack Wicken looked in on their return from the Welsh Two Days Trial. They had won the Welsh Trophy and the Metropole Cup for the best 500 respectively.

Whilst Edward was away on one of his overseas visits, Frank Baker took it upon himself to build a very special racing twin. Based on the Tiger 100, Baker's objective was to run it by participating in some unofficial practise prior to the 1955 Senior TT. All might have gone according to plan had not a rider from New Zealand, M.E. Lowe, been left without a bike. He managed to persuade Frank to lend him the 'special'.

Unfortunately, Edward happened to be in the Isle of Man that year. The Triumph caught his eye as Stan Truslove, Baker's assistant, was wheeling it about the paddock. After commenting on what a beautiful machine it was, Edward asked Stan who it belonged to, and Stan had to admit "It's ours, Sir!", whereupon Edward blew his top, because of his oft-stated comments about it being Triumph policy not to support racing. Although Lowe did well, running within silver replica time at one point in the race, a blocked carburettor jet caused his retirement after the fourth lap.

Needless to say, Frank got a roasting back at Meriden and found himself 'posted' to the Middle East. There was a need to sort out some problems with a consignment of Tiger 100s with oil pump problems that had been dispatched to the Saudi Arabian army. Frank departed with Edward's words ringing in his ears: "We will talk about your future at a later date!" He had to work hard, too, as when he arrived at the army compound in Saudi Arabia all the machines were buried under a huge mound of sand! Fortunately, the TT incident had been forgotten by the time he returned home.

Edward had his own way of showing displeasure whenever his orders were disobeyed, and John Nelson recalls an occasion when a prototype dohc camshaft twin was being set up for a test bed run in Triumph's Experimental Department. Edward happened to look in as the engine was being prepared and leaned heavily on the test staff to get it started as quickly as possible. In the ensuing rush it was set up too hastily and produced less power than a standard Tiger 100. Unimpressed, Edward ordered it to be put in the cellar and forgotten, as he had done with other projects that fell short of promise.

Anxious to find out why the engine had proved so disappointing, John took another look at it and found that the valve timing had slipped. Put back on test, it gave a power output that bettered 45bhp before any further attempts to improve on this had been made. Hearing the noise, Edward returned and gave John another of his roastings! If an engine failed to meet expectations immediately, it was enough to damn it for good as far as Edward was concerned.

The Senior Clubman's TT attracted some attention this year from the Triumph enthusiast's point of view. Run over the Clypse circuit for the first time, its entry list included John Griffiths, a *Motor Cycling* staffman who was riding a race-equipped Tiger 100. It was not expected that John would emerge the winner or, for that matter, even be well placed, so it was much to his credit that he finished 13th at a race average of 63.55mph. On his eighth and best lap, he went around the course in just under ten minutes. His machine had been supplied originally with full race kit for a forthcoming road test, but early in 1954 it had been converted to standard road specification, which gave it a maximum speed of 100mph on the level under favourable conditions. For Griffiths' TT debut it was re-converted to race specification by fitting twin carburetters, high

compression pistons, sports camshafts and close ratio gears. This raised maximum speed to 116mph, and gave it Jekyll and Hyde characteristics.

The 1955 International Six Days Trial was another debacle for the British entry. As on previous occasions, Jim Alves was a member of the Trophy Team, this time on a 498cc Trophy Twin, and John Giles, on a similar mount, was in the Vase 'A' Team. Again held at Gottwaldov, Czechoslovakia, a rear wheel spindle problem with Ted Usher's Matchless put Britain's Trophy Team out of the running on the first day, whilst on the second day Jim Alves lost marks when he stopped to help Jack Wicken who had a sticking throttle slide. Bob Ray had a similar problem the following day and the Trophy Team ended up with an overall loss of 329 marks. The Vase 'A' Team had its share of troubles, too, and, by the end of the event, had lost 502 marks. Czechoslovakia again won the Trophy; it was becoming apparent that riders of small capacity two-strokes stood the best chance of success.

In the 29th September issue of *Motor Cycling*, a brief announcement stated that a Triumph held the World Motorcycle Speed Record when an average speed of 193.72mph was recorded over a two-way run at Bonneville. It had been achieved by Johnny Allen in a fully-enclosed shell propelled by an unsupercharged 6T Thunderbird engine, using AMA-certified timing equipment. Whether or not this record would be ratified by the FIM was open to question, as the AMA did not recognise the FIM and its timing equipment had not been approved by the FIM. The AMA went ahead and submitted a claim to the FIM for the record with an affidavit confirming the speed, to be followed by the completed FIM documents necessary to support the claim. At the time the record was provisionally held by Russell Wright, who had achieved a speed of 185mph on a streamlined Vincent twin in New Zealand two months earlier.

Edward was delighted by this achievement and took steps to ensure the record-breaker would be available for display on Triumph's stand at the Earls Court Motor Cycle Show, due to open in mid-November. This was agreed, on the understanding that Triumph would not dismantle the machine whilst it was in Britain. It arrived at Elmdon Airport, Birmingham, on 7th November, after the long journey from Fort Worth, Texas. On arrival it was met by the Lord Mayor and Lady Mayoress of Coventry, Alderman and Mrs. E.W. Dewis, Councellor McDonnell, Hugh Palin, Director of the British Cycle and Motor Cycle Manufacturers and Traders Union Ltd., directors and executives of Triumph Engineering, and representatives from Amal, Dunlop, Lodge, Lucas, Renolds and Smiths Motorcycle Accessories. Inevitably, there were problems with HM Customs, who were reluctant to release the machine unless they could be positively assured it would be returned to the USA when the show was over.

Edward was unable to be at Elmdon when the Triumph arrived as he was on his way to meet representatives of Johnson Motors of California. It was left to Neale Shilton, UK Sales Manager, to deputise for him and welcome the visitors. However, he was there in time to witness Johnny Allen, the bike's 'pilot' during the successful record-breaking attempt, sign the visitors book at the Mayor's Parlour in Coventry, in the presence of the assembled dignitaries. 'Stormy' Mangham, a 49 year old airways pilot who had designed and built the streamline shell, had accompanied Johnny, to be with him during the show. The sponsor for the attempt, Bill Johnson of Johnson Motors, Pasadena, California, would also be present. He was one of those whom Edward had gone to meet.

Also on display at Earls Court, on the Avon Tyres stand, was Russell Wright and Robert Burns' Vincent twin, timed at 185mph over the flying kilometre. Wright's record had not been officially recognised either, and to have two record-breakers at the same show was quite an achievement.

An interview with Johnny Allen, giving a full account of his record-breaking run and the run-up to it, was published a week later in *Motor Cycling*. Allen paid credit to Jack Wilson, a Triumph dealer in his home town, who had been responsible for preparing the record-breaker and tuning its engine.

The first ever road test of a Tiger Cub was published during October, which showed it had a maximum speed of fractionally below 58mph. Favourable comment was made about the mechanically-operated gear indicator incorporated in the headlamp, along with the switchgear and an 80mph Smiths speedometer. The Amal Type 332/3 carburetter permitted easy starting, although it had been set a shade on the rich side on the test machine. The riding position was good and could accommodate a six foot rider, although its nose tapered somewhat abruptly, creating a tendency for the rider to slide forward. The 16 inch diameter tyres and combination of the telescopic front fork and plunger rear suspension meant a cruising speed of 50mph could easily be maintained, even when less-than-perfect road surfaces were encountered. Fuel consumption averaged out at around the 100mpg mark during give-and-take riding, and the brakes came up to expectation.

For night riding the five and a half inch diameter headlamp provided adequate illumination, and it was noted that unsightly wiring connections had been done away with. The contact breaker points behind the cylinder barrel were readily accessible for maintenance, as was the ohv rocker gear. At the end of the test, the engine/gear unit remained commendably oil-tight.

Priced at £131.8s., the conclusion was that the Tiger Cub was excellent value for money, and compared favourably with many two-strokes of similar capacity.

When the Triumph range for 1956 was announced in late October, there was one more addition to the range, a 649cc TR6 version of the TR5 Trophy Twin. Its engine was close to the specification of that of the T110 model, the overall specification of the complete machine being similar to that of the 498cc Trophy Twin, and sharing the same lighting equipment. It was another model that attracted a good deal of attention in North America, and in no time at all it had acquired the unofficial name of 'Trophybird'. The other models in the Triumph range continued much as before, with only detail modifications to update them. The most significant difference in the twin cylinder engines was that the white metal big end cap and crankshaft bearings were discarded in favour of Vandervell shell bearings. which made replacement much easier and obviated the need for a skilled fitter.

As the year ended, the FIM was no nearer to confirming whether or not Triumph's claim to the World Motorcycle Speed Record would be accepted. Already the FIM was at the centre of a great deal of controversy following its suspension of Geoff Duke's racing license,

Abbotsvale, in Crayfield Grange Road, Coventry, a large house built during the thirties with a landscaped garden and four and a half acres of land. It was less isolated than Bericote House.

Edward with his two young daughters at Abbotsvale: Charmian (left) and Jane.

Shirley with the two girls in the grounds of Abbotsvale.

after he had taken part in a riders' strike as a protest against race organisers providing such poor prize and start money.

In 1956 the Turners' domestic life underwent a further change. Shirley felt lonely and isolated at Bericote House, a large Tudor-syle house set in extensive grounds that included a small farm, where she spent so much time with two young children. Whilst here, Edward seemed to live in the past: away from home for long periods, especially when travelling abroad, and very set in his ways when he returned, it was beginning to put a strain on his second marriage. Something needed to be done, so a compromise was agreed that resulted in a move to Moor Park, near Rickmansworth. The house was near a golf course and within easy reach of London, which meant Shirley's longing for the bright lights of the City could at last be realised.

From Edward's point of view, however, it turned out to be a retrograde step that placed him at a disadvantage. He was now isolated from his wife and young family throughout the week and had to take up residence in the Leofric Hotel, Coventry. No matter how good the hotel, it still had that impersonal atmosphere about it, to remind him of his 'double life'; with his working colleagues during the week, and with his wife and children at weekends. Furthermore, his outgoings had increased as he now had hotel bills to pay. With his chauffeur, Frank Griffiths, driving him to and from Moor Park, he began to feel a stranger in his own house, especially as he did not receive the welcome he might have expected at weekends. There was only one answer: admit the arrangement had been a failure and

move back to the Coventry area. He found another Tudor-style house not far from his old home at Gibbet Hill, and the move to Abbotsvale, Cryfield Grange Road, Coventry, took place about a year later. It was a big house, built during the thirties, with a landscaped garden that needed a full-time gardener. In total, there was about four and a half acres of land which included a small wood, the remains of an old quarry, and a pond. Located about midway between Coventry and Kenilworth, it was one of several large houses interspersed amongst the local farming community. Well separated from its neighbours, it was less isolated than Berricote House and made quite an impression on Jane, their eldest daughter, who can still recall its layout and that of its grounds in graphic detail.

Edward's children adored him and considered him a wonderful father, despite the fact that he was 52 when Jane was born and 54 when Charmian came along. He was quite adamant that they should make their own way in life and that there would be no distinction between them. He also wanted them to have the educational opportunities that would enable them to earn their own livings, and have careers independent of their future husbands, should they so wish. He had a wonderful eye for clothes and would buy his children grand party dresses whilst he was in America, as well as swimsuits for Shirley. He knew exactly what size was required, without having to be told. One February he taped a whole series of stories for his children before he went off to America, one for every day of his absence. The one they enjoyed most was a particularly gruesome one about a donkey who was killed when a boa-constrictor coiled itself around its stomach and squeezed it to death, after which the snake swallowed it whole. Like all such stories it had a happy ending because the donkey had not really died at all and was rescued alive and well after someone cut off the snake's head! These few glimpses into Edward's private life show a side of him not seen by those who have written about his lack of humility, and the way in which he distanced himself from others around him.

It has been said that the books a person reads give an insight into their character, so it's interesting to note the books that could be found on the shelves of the two bookcases in Edward's study at that time. A few were novels, but, in the main, they were mostly historic works or biographies. Included amongst them was Winston Churchill's My Early Life and a complete set of his History of the English Speaking Peoples, both volumes of T.E. Lawrence's Seven Pillars of Wisdom, Carola Oman's

Nelson and Arthur Bryant's histories of England. Very much a patriot at heart, Edward had great admiration for Winston Churchill and enjoyed reading about some of the great men of the past.

His study is where he would have his supper in the evening, sitting in front of the television, finding it a good way in which to unwind and relax by watching some of his favourite Westerns. Understandably, Shirley found this difficult to accept and on at least one occasion declared almost in despair "All I seem to do is sit here and watch the newscasters grow older". Any personal letters were handwritten here, too; his characteristic fine slanting script derived from the copper-plate handwriting taught at school.

On Sundays, when the weather permitted, Edward would follow a set routine by taking the two girls for a mid-morning walk, whilst Shirley prepared their Sunday lunch. He always took the same route, turning right at the gates to the house. Here, they would stop to pat

Four riders from what was known as the Beat System Crime Squad Motorcycle Patrol, on their rigid rear end Speed Twins. The transmitter/ receivers were of the valve type, and were both heavy and power-consuming, which necessitated heavy-duty batteries slung each side like panniers, and a high output dynamo. The radius of transmission/reception covered the Metropolitan Police area.

'Old George', a retired carthorse that would come ambling up for sugar or an apple as they made their way to the farm that was almost at the bottom of the hill. Had they turned left it would have been only a short walk before they reached the junction with the busy Coventry to Kenilworth road. They continued over a small, humped back bridge that spanned a small stream and continued up the next hill, which at first was quite an expedition when the two children were very small. There was another pause to look at an ancient oak tree which would often prompt Edward to tell the girls about the great battles of British naval history when ships had hearts of oak and how they had progressed to ironclads, so that fine old oak trees such as this were no longer at risk. Then they would turn around and head for home, where Edward would leave them and go and visit friends in the neighbourhood for pre-Sunday lunch drinks and a chat.

If the weather prevented them from taking a walk, drinks before lunch were served from the cocktail cabinet in his study. Its colourful bottles and labels seemed to fascinate the youngsters. Also to be found in the study were several pictures hanging on the wall, one of which was a small portrait of Edward in his naval uniform. Another of him as a younger man, holding a cigarette, hung in the main part of the upstairs hall, both of them having been painted in oil by his sister Maud. A third portrait, also bearing Maud's signature, hung in one of the guest bedrooms. That one was of Marion, Edward's first wife, who had died so tragically in the road accident described earlier. Almost opposite the doorway of this room was a high window sill on which rested another memento of hers, a silver teapot, always afforded great respect by the girls. It was as though Edward could never get her out of his mind.

The first half of 1956 was relatively quiet as far as Triumph was concerned, although in April the Advertising and Publicity

The police were always good customers, but, by the time all the special equipment had been fitted, the profit from these sales was marginal, if any. Police-equipped Triumphs were displayed at the Whitehall 1212 exhibition (Whitehall 1212 was Scotland Yard's telephone number at that time). Here, Sir Harold Scott, the Commissioner of Police, tries one of the two-way radio telephones.

Manager, Ivor Davies, announced successful experiments had been completed with Triumph motorcycles equipped with two-way radio, which had been sold to the police. The equipment, made by British Communications Corporation Limited, of Wembley, Middlsex, represented a considerable breakthrough. Triumph was selling considerable numbers of the Speed Twin model to the police, especially those in the Metropolitan Division.

In the area usually occupied by the parcel-carrying grid, a container shaped like an inverted triangle contained a microphone and earpiece in the form of a telephone handset, which could be lifted out on a flexible cord. The transmitter/receiver unit was mounted at the rear of the machine, where one would normally expect to find a rear carrier. It was sixteen inches long, measured eight inches at its widest point, and was five and a half inches deep. It weighed 35lbs and necessitated fitting a single padded seat in place of the customary dualseat. From the unit an aerial extended to about an inch higher than the rider's head; hung on the left-hand side of the handlebars

Also included in the equipment was a loud-hailer for crowd control. Note the fire extinguisher strapped to the left-hand legshield.

was a loud-hailer for making public announcements. A Lucas RM14 crankshaft-mounted alternator was sufficient to cope with the power demand from the machine's valve-operated transmitter/receiver, working in conjunction with a 21 amp hour battery. *Motor Cycling* carried out testing in the Cotswolds over a distance of some 20 miles; they were very convincing.

A few weeks later, during mid-April, Triumph held its annual staff party at the Leofric Hotel in Coventry. Edward and Shirley acted as host and hostess and many well-known Triumph agents were included in the invitations list. Speaking on behalf of the Triumph Board and executives, Edward made his guests very welcome, after which there was a buffet supper followed by a first-class cabaret. It was a memorable evening that continued into the small hours.

Much has been written about Sir Bernard Docker, Chairman of BSA, and the ostentatious lifestyle that he and Lady Nora Docker enjoyed. By the mid-fifties, Sir Bernard found himself in an increasingly insecure position because, not only was the Daimler part of the group in serious financial trouble, but the range of cars was generally unexciting, with an air of staidness about them. There was growing dissent amongst the majority shareholders, especially the Prudential Assurance Company, which had expressed concern about the way in which Sir Bernard flaunted his extravagances at the very time when the company was incurring losses in its car and motorcycling activities. It had not gone unnoticed that Sir Bernard had spent a small fortune on his gold-plated Daimler, and on his yacht, the Shemara, whilst Lady Nora had purchased expensive designer dresses on the company expense account, allegedly for publicity purposes at the Motor Show.

Jack Sangster led a coup to depose him. Although Sir Bernard managed to retain his seat longer than expected (sometimes using his casting vote as Chairman to his advantage), he finally lost the battle on 1st August 1956 at an acrimonious meeting when over 1000 shareholders were present. Jack Sangster replaced him on the BSA board, knowing he was likely to do so for only a short period. Coincidental with this, Edward was given a seat on Daimler's board to assist his mentor set the company on the road to recovery and profitability as soon as possible.

Although Daimler had supplied cars to King George V and Queen Mary, and was entitled to display the Royal Warrant, it had been suggested in some quarters that the Royal Family vehicles were in danger of being upstaged by some of the more flamboyant Docker Daimlers. Sir Bernard claimed his cars had brought the company the equivalent of £500,000 in publicity, and on this score alone their cost could be justified.

Jack Sangster's immediate problem was to find a replacement for James Leek, BSA's Managing Director, who was suffering poor health and had announced his intention to retire at the end of September. A legendary and highly-respected member of the BSA board, who had done much to put BSA Motor Cycles Limited on a firm footing, it would clearly be very difficult to find someone of similar calibre to replace him. Within a few days of James' departure, Edward was appointed his successor as Managing Director of BSA's Automotive Division. Whilst retaining his existing Managing Directorship of Triumph, his area of responsibility now encompassed Daimler cars and Ariel, BSA, Sunbeam and Triumph motorcycles.

Soon after his new appointment, Edward was asked by the Daimler board to design an entirely new V8-engined car to give the company the modern image it so desperately needeed. Back in his office at Meriden, he mentioned this request to Jack Wickes and asked him how he would set about such a project. After some thought, Jack suggested a Cadillac engine would be as good a starting point as any, whereupon

Whilst designing the new Daimler sports car, the SP250, Edward also drew up a four and a half litre vee-eight engine for use in Daimler saloons. (Barry Pladdys)

Edward, with a smile, produced a Cadillac manual and spare parts list from a drawer in his desk. He was already one jump ahead and had decided the engine would have its valve gear operated by push rods rather than by overhead camshafts! By following this route the engine would be cheaper to manufacture and he could introduce motorcycle engine practice when designing the cylinder head, drawing on the experience acquired from his Thunderbird engine.

All of this led to what eventually became the Daimler Dart, a 2.5 litre sports car with a lightweight fibreglass bodywork. Unfortunately, the car's name was shortlived as a result of the threat of litigation by Chrysler, which had already registered this name for a car to be made by Dodge. Instead, Daimler adopted the now familiar SP250 designation, the official project number allocated to the car.

Although Edward's involvement with the SP250 and other Daimler car projects was of relatively short duration, spanning a period of four years, he nevertheless made his mark. Apart from the design of the 2.5 litre V8 engine for the SP250, he also originated a 4.5 litre engine of the same configuration for a limousine. His flair for styling was evident in the SP250, for which Jack Wickes produced a

magnificent eighth scale clay model on which the final bodywork was based. It represented an entirely new and up-to-date concept for Daimler. Interestingly, he did not involve his own small design unit at Triumph with the Daimler projects as it was already fully committed to Triumph's forward planning. Instead, he utilised Daimler's own drawing office and engineers, for whom he later expressed great admiration for their skills and ability to solve problems as and when they arose. He went as far as to say that he regarded them as: "one of the finest set-ups I have ever seen - far better, I may say, than I've ever been used to in motorcycles".

Some SP250s were purchased by a division of the Metropolitan Police as pursuit cars, and it is ironic that they were often involved in chasing errant motorcyclists of the cafe racer cult riding high performance Triumph twins! The SP250 was one of the very few police vehicles able to catch them.

A dinner was held in Jack Sangster's honour during June by members of The British Cycle and Motor Cycle Industries Association to mark his retirement as Chairman of the Motor Cycle Industries section. He was presented with an engraved silver Georgian tankard

It's ironic that the Metropolitan Police purchased some SP250s, the only police cars capable at that time of out-running the high performance twins being used on public highways by the café racers. Many of the racers' machines were Triumphs, designed by Edward, and now he had provided a car capable of catching them! Interestingly, the police also purchased some Tigress scooters for use by their WPCs.

THE BEST MOTORCYCLE IN THE WORLD

A new 'mouth organ' tank badge was the most noticeable feature on the 1957 twins.

by Donald Heather, the new section Chairman, who was Managing Director of Associated Motor Cycles.

During the early part of August, record breaking at Bonneville again made the news when NSU arrived to make its bid for the world motorcycle speed record. It is alleged it cost NSU something like £50,000 to contest nine different capacity classes, ranging from 50 to 1000cc. NSU was so confident of success that it produced a booklet with the quaint title Let Us Dare It! When Wilhelm Herz set a new record with a mean speed of 210.64mph on a fully-enclosed supercharged 500cc NSU twin, and NSU was on the way home with its objective achieved, it was learnt that Johnny Allen had made a further record attempt after NSU's departure, and had raised the newly-set record to 214.72mph. To make matters worse, Johnny had done so with the same cigar-shaped Triumph powered by a 650cc Thunderbird unsupercharged engine that had taken the record to 193.72mph the previous year! He had again been sponsored by Bill Johnson, President of Johnson Motors Inc.

Due to procrastination bordering on intransigence from FIM,

the international body that governs motorcycle sport, Johnny Allen's previous record had not yet been ratified. Now it paled into insignificance as his latest bid had snatched back NSU's newly-achieved record in a matter of days! Edward saw this as vindication of Triumph's earlier claim and was confident the new record would be ratified. Precautions had been taken to have the AMA timing equipment FIM approved before Johnny's latest attempt. A certificate confirming this had been issued and signed by none other than FIM Secretary General, Tom Loughborough. Neale Shilton, Triumph's Sales Manager, who had done much behind the scenes to make sure everything went smoothly, claimed his correspondence file devoted entirely to Johnny Allen was now three inches thick!

The 1956 International Six Days Trial was held in Garmisch Partenkirchen in Bavaria. The 31st in the series, it was claimed to be the biggest ever held, with 320 competitors. John Giles on a 650cc Triumph was a member of the British Trophy Team, and in the British Vase A and B teams it was interesting to note that George Fisher and Ken Heanes had been entered on 175cc sleeved down Tiger

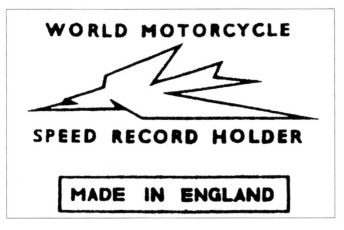

The specially-prepared World Record Holder transfer which Edward decreed should henceforth be applied to all new Triumph models, without waiting for the FIM to ratify Triumph's record. Appropriately, it incorporated the Thunderbird logo.

Cubs, and Peter Hammond on a 500cc Trophy Twin. The two factory-prepared Cubs featured pivoted fork rear suspension, an indication of what was to come when Triumph announced the 1957 model programme.

Czechoslovakia emerged the winner of the prestigious International Trophy yet again, with no marks lost. The British team lost 380 marks, which relegated it to third place. In the Vase contest, the British B team lost 100 marks to finish 7th, and the A team 704 marks, which left it in 17th place. Triumph was also unable to secure one of the Manufacturers' Team awards. If it was any consolation, John Giles, Jack Wicken, and Ken Heanes all completed the trial without any loss of marks, to each receive a gold medal.

At the FIM Autumn Conference it transpired that NSU had queried whether Johnny Allen's latest record-breaking attempt had complied with the rules, because the FIM-appointed timekeeper had left Bonneville before the attempt on the record had been made. Although he had handed over authority to a well qualified AMA official, this had been seized upon by NSU as a possible breach of FIM regulations. A telegram sent by NSU to the President of the CSI, Piet Nortier, had requested further unspecified information about Johnny Allen's record-breaking attempt and, as a result, Nortier had notified the FIM of his intention to hold an inquiry. It meant that any decision to ratify Triumph's latest record would be further deferred until the CSI's meeting at Milan in December.

The publication of a report on the FIM Conference in the 11th October issue of *Motor Cycling* elicited a response from Neale Shilton on behalf of Triumph, in an effort to clarify the situation. Shilton confirmed he was in possession of documentary evidence which proved beyond any shadow of a doubt the validity of Johnny Allen's record-breaking attempt. A subsequent statement from NSU stoutly denied an unsportsmanlike attitude. To reinforce Triumph's conviction of a rightful claim to the record, Neale Shilton responded with a further statement. It set out in very clear detail why there could be no question of a breach in the regulations governing the timing and supervision of the Triumph record, and ended with the following: "The Triumph Engineering Company has sent a frankly worded telegram to the ACU for transmission to the FIM, demanding immediate action to remove any doubts cast upon the validity of

the Triumph record by events in Paris (the FIM headquarters). It is imperative that this action is taken at once as it is not a situation that can wait until the next meeting of the CSI in Paris."

Whilst the FIM continued to defer a decision, other more urgent matters had to be dealt with at Meriden, not least of which was release of details about the 1957 model range. Information about the new models was released much later than usual, only a month before the 1956 Motor Cycle Show opened. As far as the twins were concerned it was a case of technical improvement. The most noticeable feature was a new 'mouth organ' petrol tank badge, which had a chromium plated, grille-type background. Other refinements included full-width wheel hubs (including the TR5 and TR6 Trophy Twins), a quickly detachable rear wheel, and - as an optional extra on the Tiger 100 - a new splayed inlet port cylinder head for twin carburetters. This had been tested by Johnny Allen during some of his record-breaking attempts on the Bonneville salt flats.

Creating the most interest was the restyled Tiger Cub model with pivoted fork rear suspension. The fin area of the cylinder head was increased in size, and there was a restyled dualseat with deeper side valances. A froth tower had been added to the oil tank to prevent leakage through the breather, and the chainguard over the final drive chain had been deepened. Internally, the shell bearings used in the big end assembly and the timing side main bearing were of an improved, high load type.

A competition version of the Tiger Cub was also now available: the T20C was based on the works models that had been entered in the recently-held ISDT. Main essentials were a 3 x 19 inch tyre and a 3.50 x 18 inch rear tyre, both of them of the Dunlop Trials Universal type. The wheels were built with butted spokes and there was also a crankcase undershield. Other necessities included an upswept exhaust system and a Trophy Twin type front mudguard with an external bridge between the front fork legs. Good ground clearance had been achieved by replacing the centre stand with an extended prop stand.

During early November, Johnny Allen and Jack Wilson returned to Britain to be present on the Triumph stand at the 1956 Motor Cycle Show, where once again the record-breaker was on display. At the very least there could be no doubt that it provisionally held the motorcycle world speed record, and there were few who doubted its claim. The machine arrived about a week later, and, on this occasion Triumph was prevailed upon by BBC Television to let it film some demonstration runs. The Commandant at RAF Wellesbourne, near Warwick, gave his permission for one of the runways to be used, so the streamliner was transported there whilst en route to London.

Ivor Davies admitted to having some qualms about this. A deposit had been paid to Customs and Excise which would be returned when the machine was sent back to the USA, on the assumption that the Triumph would be used only for display at the show. But the opportunity for it to be seen on national TV in the BBC's evening Sportsview programme was too good to miss, so Neale Shilton decided to go ahead and argue with Customs officials afterwards. After the BBC had filmed several bottom gear runs, both the machine and Johnny Allen departed for the BBC studios in Shepherds Bush, to appear live in that evening's Sportsview programme.

It was hardly likely that exposure on national TV would escape the attention of Customs and Excise and, sure enough, a letter from them arrived at Meriden a couple of days later, advising Triumph that the deposit had been forfeited. Neale Shilton replied that he would be forwarding the letter to the local member of Parliament, accompanied by details of all the orders received as a direct result of the record achieved by the machine. A subsequent telephone call from Customs and Excise confirmed the deposit would be refunded after all, and would Neale please refrain from forwarding the letter.

The second appearance of the Triumph at the Earls Court Show, where stand attendants wore specially made lapel badges bearing the legend Triumph 214, was a tremendous success. Johnny Allen was the guest at a number of receptions that followed, and was presented with a water-colour of the run by the First Secretary of the US Embassy. An especially nice gesture was the presentation of a Certificate of Appreciation to Neale Shilton for his part in helping Johnny achieve his 214.72mph record on 6th September 1956.

A full two-page account of the preparation of the machine for the record-breaking run, and an account of the successful attempt, was published in the 15th November issue of *Motor Cycling*. Although the Triumph was returned to the USA, many years later it came back to Britain for permanent display in the National Motorcycle Museum, close to the National Exhibition Centre, Birmingham.

The air of uncertainty surrounding the Triumph record took a further twist in December when Piet Nortier refused to ratify the record. He claimed the decisive factor was that Tom Loughborough had no authority to issue the certificate which verified that the AMA's timing equipment fully met the requirements of the FIM. Yet Tom was the FIM's Secretary General and had sent a congratulatory telegram on behalf of the FIM after the record had been broken!

This refusal really incensed Edward and provoked him into threatening legal action unless he could have a face-to-face meeting with Piet Nortier to bring the matter to a satisfactory conclusion. At the subsequent meeting in Paris, Nortier asked for their discussion to be conducted on camera and stuck resolutely to his opinion that the AMA timing equipment had not been officially recognised by the FIM. The meeting resulted in a complete impasse.

Since all available evidence seemed heavily in favour of Triumph, the general consensus of opinion was that Triumph had every reason to claim the motorcycle world speed record. Early in the New Year, Edward decided to jump the gun and capitalise on this by instructiing that Triumph's advertising literature be superimposed with the words 'Holder of the World Motorcycle Speed Record 214mph'. He also ordered that, henceforth, all new Triumph motorcycles should have an extra transfer on the top of the headlamp nacelle, featuring the Thunderbird motif, with the words 'world motorcycle speed record holder'.

The record-breaking saga appeared to come to a conclusion in April 1957. At its Vienna Conference, the FIM announced its intention to disallow Johnny Allen's record and also, for that matter, the record set by Bob Burns' Vincent at the same venue. However, it was not the end of the story as far as Edward was concerned. As threatened earlier, he intended to engage a QC to fight Triumph's case, convinced there was sufficient positive evidence to confirm Johnny Allen's record had conformed, to the letter, with all the stipulations which had to be met. The British motorcycling press seemed to think so, too, and the question of whether or not a Triumph had broken the record still remained a contentious issue.

It was at the FIM's Conference in Paris, held during late October 1957, that a final, unequivocal 'no' was given, confirming its refusal to ratify Johnny Allen's record. As Norman Sharpe, editor of *Motor Cycling*, put in his report on the conference, it was the day: "the ideals of motorcycle sport died".

Still determined not to concede, Edward called a press conference at the RAC Club in London during March 1958, to consider commencing court proceedings on the world record issue. He intended to make known the opinion of an eminent QC, who had examined all the evidence on behalf of the British Manufacturers' Association. The President of the FIM, M. Augustin Perouse, had been advised by the Association that if the record had not been ratified within a month, a legal assessment of the FIM's behaviour would be made public. Legally, there was no valid reason why the record should not have been ratified, irrespective of the side issues raised, which the FIM regarded as irrelevant. The Manufacturers' Association maintained there could be no doubt that Johnny Allen's speed of 214.72mph was the official World Speed Record for a solo motorcycle, and all that remained was for the FIM to accept it. This approach to M. Perouse represented the last attempt to persuade the FIM to accept the fact and reach fairly amicable agreement: if this didn't work, the only other option would be the courts.

Sadly, the stalemate continued, and eventually it became apparent that the chances of overturning the FIM's decision were very slim; with reluctance, the threat of legal action was quietly dropped.

Several more years were to pass before a Triumph speed record made in the USA was officially recognised by the FIM. If anyone suffered loss of face from this unfortunate incident it was the FIM.

A competition version of the T20 Tiger Cub was also available in 1957, as shown in this catalogue illustration.

Chapter 11: Unit-construction twins

By the mid-fifties motorcycle production at Meriden was running at a rate of over 30,000 machines a year. Edward ran a very tightly controlled production programme in which output never completely kept pace with demand. The production output figure represented the optimum necessary to ensure maximum profitability, which may explain why Jack Sangster was quite happy to leave Edward to run the Triumph Engineering Company with almost complete autonomy. This Edward did as if it was his own business, keeping an ever-watchful eye on any extravagances.

Despite his other directorships, Edward was rarely seen outside of Meriden. He tended to regard BSA with what amounted to almost total antipathy and once claimed he could never hope to get the Small Heath plant into profitability. Neale Shilton recalls one occasion when Edward's desk had been moved, which elicited the comment: "I am now sitting seven yards closer to Small Heath and I do not intend to get any closer!" Edward's office was on the first floor of the main administration building. Large and rectangular in shape, its walls were painted pale blue and there was a dark blue covering on the floor. On one wall hung a gold 'sunburst' clock. On entering his office there was seating on the left, his desk and chair occupying the right-hand corner but not directly facing the door. His secretary, Nan Plant, had her chair on the other side of his desk, and also a small office of her own. A table - with a selection of motorcycle magazines - helped break up the expanse of space between the door and desk.

Occasionally, on a Saturday morning, Edward would take his two young daughters to the factory, where they would sit patiently in his office whilst he dictated a few letters to his secretary. There was one occasion when he bawled her out, which took them both by surprise. Nan went very red-faced but gave as good as she got. Asked about this incident many years later, she said that Edward did not "necessarily shout at her all the time", but admitted she used to save up difficult jobs for Saturdays as she knew the staff in the Drawing Office and the other white collar staff on that floor did not come in that day. Edward could then shout at her as much as he liked and have time to cool off before Monday! She did a lot to protect the staff - and even Edward - from himself. A secretary of the old school, Nan was very efficient and gave the outward impression of being strict, yet she could be very diplomatic in the way she went about things.

1957 was an important year in the history of the Triumph Engineering Company because it marked the occasion of its 21st Anniversary. The inaugural luncheon to commemorate its foundation had been held on 27th January 1936, but, unfortunately, it was no longer possible to hold the commemorative dinner at the original location, the King's Head. It had been razed to the ground on 14th November 1940 at the height of the Luftwaffe's blitz on Coventry, along with the old Triumph works in Dale Street and the Cathedral. Instead, the

A luncheon was held in the Leofric Hotel, Coventry on 17th January 1957 to mark the 21st anniversary of the founding of the Triumph Engineering Co. Ltd. Here, Jack Sangster welcomes the guests. On his left is the Lord Mayor of Coventry, Alderman W.I. Thompson, J.P. On Edward's left is Hugh Palin, President of the Association of British Cycle & Motor Cycle Manufacturers Union. On the extreme right, Harry Louis, editor of The Motor Cycle, *listens with cupped ear. Next to him is Allan Jefferies.*

directors, staff and works executives gathered in the Leofric Hotel, Coventry, on 17th January, to entertain 45 guests to dinner. In his opening speech to welcome them, Jack Sangster noted that 30 of those present had also attended the original luncheon 21 years ago.

The Lord Mayor, Alderman W.I. Thompson, J.P., responded on behalf of the guests but, before he sat down, Edward presented him with a framed photograph. After Allan Jefferies had made his usual witty speech, which paid trubute to Triumph's 21 years from a dealer's viewpoint, Edward was able to mention Triumph's latest success in the USA in his reply. Bud Ekins had won the Big Bear Run on a Triumph and sales to the USA had reached the point where they equalled the entire output from the Triumph factory during 1936-7. Edward would be visiting the USA and Australia the following day, on a sales promotion tour.

Whilst Edward was away a display of Triumph, BSA and Ariel motorcycles at Mallory Park race circuit had been arranged by Jack Sangster. It was to be followed by a lunch at which he would introduce the BSA Group's new Vice-Chairman, Eric Turner, who had been recruited from the Blackburn and General Aircraft Group to fulfil this role. His background was that of an accountant and, in 1955, he had become the Blackburn Group's Managing Director and Chairman. Although he shared the same surname as Edward, he was not related to him, and furthermore had no previous experience with the motorcycle industry.

After the lunch at Mallory Park, Eric Turner addressed the gathering, having been invited to give his impression of the array of machines laid out for inspection. According to Neale Shilton, one of those present, Turner's comments were not at all well received. In his opening remarks he made it clear he did not like motorcycles and, having come from the aircraft industry, was at a loss to understand why three separate manufacturers within the Group were all making different models. He would have expected a commonalisation of parts so that by using a standardised range of engine units, the differences between the various models would be largely those of colour and tank badges. In point of fact, Edward was already one jump ahead as, on his return from his overseas tour, he was to take on an additional responsibility.

As from 1st May 1957, the Power Unit Division of BSA came under his control following some reorganisation at Small Heath. Already he had designed and laid plans for the production of two different types of scooter, identical versions of which would be sold under the BSA or Triumph names, and differ only in colour scheme and the badge that identified the maker! All production would be in BSA's Waverley Street factory.

It had been widely expected that Edward would be Jack Sangster's obvious choice as Chairman elect, to take over from him when he stood down. There was much speculation about why this had not occurred, and it is Bert Hopwood's biography that seems to offer the most plausible explanation. When Edward approached Bert during early 1961 to persuade him to re-join Triumph in an executive capacity, he did so in the knowledge that the AMC Group was experiencing difficulties at boardroom level. Edward was now a diabetic and genuinely anxious to retire at the age of 65, the more so as he no longer ran a private company but was answerable to shareholders through a Board of Directors. The BSA Board had accepted this and was pressing him very hard to appoint a Director and General Manager who would eventually succeed him as Managing Director. Bert had the impression that Edward had already committed himself to retirement at the age of 65, and genuinely wanted Bert to

return to Triumph, even asking Bert's wife Margery to 'work on him'.

Reverting to Triumph's 21st Anniversary, it was unusual for Triumph to announce a new model earlier than a few weeks prior to the annual Motor Cycle Show, at which it would make its first appearance. However, 1957 was an exception to the rule, and for very good reason. Edward had added an entirely new 350cc twin to the range to commemorate Triumph's 21st Anniversary and, in any case, there would not be a 1957 Show. Appropriately, the new model had been designated the Twenty-one and was described as a sports roadster featuring unit-construction and semi-enclosure. Triumph had needed a 350cc twin for some time to replace the 3T twin that had been withdrawn from production at the end of the 1950 season. The 350cc class was popular amongst motorcyclists, as this capacity rating attracted a more favourable insurance rate and a lower road tax payment than a 500. A 350 was more than capable of carrying a pillion passenger at a satisfactory sustained cruising speed, without any marked decrease in performance, and return a good mileage per gallon figure.

The new twin differed in that its engine unit had been designed on unit-construction principles. The concept itself was anything but new as New Imperial had started making unit-construction singles in 1932, and was, by no means the first either. Even the old Triumph company had produced a unit-construction single in 1922, the 346cc lightweight Model LS. Edward had, of course, already adopted this trend when he designed the Terrier and the Tiger Cub, but they were only singles. Having applied the same principle to a twin, he could later extend this mode of construction to the other twins in the range. BSA would follow suit.

The engine and gearbox were combined in one compact unit. Whilst the engine was still readily recognisable as a Triumph, it nonetheless had several distinctive features, which included a new design of rocker box which sat on a close pitch fin aluminium alloy cylinder head. Short tubular steel inserts screwed into the exhaust ports, over which the inch and a half diameter exhaust pipes fitted. The cylinder block was also close pitch finned but of cast iron. The internals of the crankcase followed normal Triumph practice, with the exception of the connecting rods, which took the form of steel stampings, with shell big end bearings. The drive side of the crankcase was extended to form the inner chaincase and end wall of the gearbox. Although the gearbox shell was integral with the main crankcase casting, its internals - complete with gearchange mechanism - could be withdrawn with its polished end cover after the primary and final drive transmission had been removed. The primary drive was by a duplex chain, the clutch having a shock absorber in its centre, as the alternator rotor was mounted on the end of the crankshaft.

The frame followed a practice originated by Edward some while ago in having no upper tank rail, the internally stiffened petrol tank doubling as a stressed member. Of the cradle type, the frame had a single front downtube, with twin tubes below the engine/gear unit. At its rear end it featured pivoted fork suspension controlled by hydraulic suspension units, in accord with current practice. Where it broke away from convention was that its rear end was enclosed within a steel pressing that served also as the rear mudguard, its sides extending below the top run of the wheel. The front mudguard had also been heavily valanced with the same objective - to give better protection. The use of 17 inch diameter wheels lowered the level of the dualseat to 28.5 inches, the front wheel having a full width hub. The machine's overall weight was 317lbs.

It will be recalled that, on an earlier occasion, Edward had foreseen the need for better protection for both rider and passenger from wet roads and road debris in general, as well as providing a motorcycle with a much cleaner image. Now he was practicing what he had preached. In profile, the pressing resembled an upturned Victorian bath tub which, within a very short period of time, was exactly how the enclosure was described by motorcyclists! A nice touch was the tool carrier under the hinged dualseat which carried all the tools supplied with the machine in a foam rubber pad, with cut-outs to match up with the tools. The whole machine was finished in an attractive polychromatic silver grey, with a plated Twenty-one legend in script mounted at an angle on the left-hand side of the rear enclosure.

In point of fact, the Twenty-one represented yet another attempt by a motorcycle manufacturer to tempt those who previously would never have considered a motorcycle as a cheap and convenient form of transport. The public in general tended to associate motorcycles with noise, danger, broken, dirty fingernails, and the need to dress up like someone from Mars. The industry must have spent millions of pounds trying to perfect a motorcycle that projected a completely different image in order to capture a hitherto untapped section of the market. Some got close, with designs like the Royal Enfield Cycar and the LE Velocette, but not close enough to achieve their objective. The solution eventually came from an unexpected quarter, with the scooter boom of the fifties, which was at its peak for a decade. The Twenty-one represented a half-way stage to the utopian situation and went some way towards dispelling the illusion of a motorcycle as being filthy dirty. It was a superbly styled and extremely attractive motorcycle, which undoubtedly inspired many partisan riders to change allegiance in favour of Triumph.

The UK retail price of Triumph's new model was £175, £217 with Purchase Tax. It seemed unlikely that there would be much demand for the Twenty-one in the USA, Triumph's main export market, on account of its small capacity. Even if Twenty-one did conveniently translate engine capacity into cubic inches, the way engine capacity

The first Triumph unit-construction twin, the 348cc Twenty-one, was launched during the company's 21st anniversary year, hence the name. It was finished in a polychromatic silver grey and later catalogued as the 3TA model.

s measured in the USA, it is a country where big is always best and large capacity Harley-Davidson twins rule the roads. There was also as yet no reason to suspect that enclosure in any form would be scorned by American enthusiasts, as became apparent later.

Prior to launch, much of the road testing of the model Twenty-one had been carried out by Charles Grandfield, Triumph's Chief Engineer, previously employed by Rolls-Royce. Also closely associated with the project were Harry Summers, Project Draughtsman, and the inimitable Jack Wickes who had a hand in its styling. A road test conducted by Bernal Osborne, the Midland editor of *Motor Cycling*, indicated that the new model was capable of well over 80mph; not that he was able to confirm this with an engine that had not been run in. This figure came from Percy Tait who had used maximum performance to escape from those who showed an interest in the prototype whilst it was still under wraps. Bernal had the bike for only thirty minutes and limited his criticisms to the longer than necessary gearchange lever and positioning of an out-of-sight gear indicator on the top of the gearbox casting. This, however, seemed unfair as all the other Triumph twins had it in a similar position, where it had been for years! Only the Terrier and Tiger Cub had the cable-operated indicator in the nacelle, which was, admittedly, a much more convenient location if such a device was really necessary.

A road test of the latest Tiger 100 was published in the 18th April issue of *Motor Cycling*. It was interesting because the test machine had been fitted with the optional twin carburetter cylinder head, which produced another 13mph. A maximum speed of 105mph was achieved at the MIRA Test Track near Nuneaton, yet, surprisingly, fuel consumption of 80mpg was recorded at an average speed of 40mph. The machine was in full road trim which included lighting equipment and silencers.

As Triumph riders had enjoyed very little success in the ISDT during recent years, John Giles must have felt some trepidation when his entry was submitted for the three-day Tatra Trial in Czechoslovakia. Riding a factory-prepared 498cc Triumph Trophy Twin as usual, the Sidcup and District MCC Team - of which he was a member - was awarded The International Club Trophy. Giles also won the Best Individual Trophy and a Gold medal. The Sidcup Team totally outclassed the opposition and was the only team to finish complete, with no marks lost on time. Described as a cross between the ISDT and the Scottish Six Days Trial, the event was regarded as the toughest reliability trial in the world. No wonder, therefore, that the Sidcup Team's trials models had all been fitted with knobbly tyres, which was acceptable in the regulations.

The less said about the 1957 ISDT the better, as there were no official British entries this year. British manufacturers had agreed to abstain from the event, so the sole rider of British nationality who took part did so as a private entrant. Held yet again in Czechoslovakia, Germany won the International Trophy, whilst the Czechoslovakian 'A' Team won the International Silver Vase. Britain's sole representative, Eric Chilton, riding a 650cc Triumph TR6 Trophy Twin, did well to qualify for a Bronze Award.

Details of Triumph's model range for 1958 were announced during late October; it amounted to nine different models. Again, it was largely a question of detail modifications - eighteen in total - spread across the range. The Triumph T15 Terrier had now been dropped from the range, the Terrier and the original version of the Tiger Cub being the only two models ever to be made with plunger rear suspension by Triumph. Now the standard 199cc T20 Tiger Cub and its competition variant, the 199cc T20C, were Triumph's two smallest capacity models. Both benefited from a duplex primary chain, which necessitated redesigning the inner primary chaincase housing. The

sealing of the gearbox final drive had also been improved, and an anti-theft device included in the headstock. This enabled the machine to be immobilised with its front fork in the full left-lock position. Similar anti-theft provision had been made for the 500cc and 650cc twins, although, somewhat cheekily, the lock and key for the latter were listed as optional extras and had to be paid for!

The new Twenty-one, 350cc, unit-construction twin took pride of place in the Triumph range and was the subject of a four-page advertisement in the 28th February issue of *Motor Cycling*, as there would be no Motor Cycle Show in 1957 at which to introduce it to the general public. The Industries Association had decided to opt out from its annual showcase, although not all members had been in agreement with this decision. Henceforth, it would be held on alternate years, the next one to be staged in 1980. This decision showed a remarkable lack of foresight at the very time when foreign competition was beginning to increase and damage exports.

For 1958, the T21 would have a modified petrol tank with a raised centre seam covered by a chromium-plated strip, and also a parcel grid mounted on the tank top. A new frame had changed the steering head angle to 66.5 degrees, and provision had been made for fitting panniers. This was accomplished by including end lugs in the rear frame structure for use in conjunction with fixing points at the pillion footrest brackets. A prop stand was an optional extra.

The 649cc 6T Thunderbird had reverted to an SU carburetter rather than have an Amal 376 Monobloc carburetter like that fitted to all the other twins. It was claimed the SU 603 type was much more satisfactory for sidecar work.

A great deal of interest was created by a new type of gearbox for the 498cc and 649cc twins, which had an automatic clutch device included with its gearchange mechanism. It reduced gearchanging to just one operation, without the need to use the clutch lever on the handlebars. The clutch was momentarily disengaged by the mechanism whenever the gearchange pedal was moved to select another gear. Its automatic action could, however, be overridden if the clutch was cable-operated in the usual way. Registered under the name Slickshift (an Americanism if ever there was one), it was regarded with suspicion in some quarters, and never received the acclaim anticipated: motorcyclists were still very conservative in outlook.

So far, no mention has been made of the ninth model on Triumph's stand, a TRW military model, Triumph's 498cc side valve twin. It was there as a reminder that it was still in production for use by the armed forces and government services, home and overseas.

In early November, a T20C Tiger Cub competition model achieved an outstanding victory when Artie Ratcliffe won the Alfred A Scott Memorial Trophy in the Scott Trial. The Trophy was awarded for the best performance on time and observation, and Artie had performed so well that he was also received the Frank Fletcher Trophy for the best performance on observation alone. To even finish was no mean feat in this classic event, which was first held in 1913. Some idea of its challenging nature can be ascertained from the fact that, although Artie won, he lost 104 marks; 23 on time and 81 on observation!

It was a good way to round off a distinctly unremarkable year: petrol rationing had been in force again earlier in the year, there'd been no Motor Cycle Show at Earls Court, no support from the industry for the ISDT, and an announcement from British manufacturers that they would be withdrawing from international road racing! Triumph's problems with the FIM over recognition of Johnny Allen's 214mph speed record added to the general air of gloom and despondency.

For 1958 Triumph announced that all three members of the trials team - John Giles, Roy Peplow and Artie Ratcliffe - would be riding 199cc Tiger Cubs. In addition, 17 year old Colin Lambert of

a new achievement by ARIEL

Held on the longest day of the year for obvious reasons, the Thruxton 500 Mile Race - which had started as the Thruxton Nine Hour Race - was now in its fourth year. Open only to standard production motorcycles which had to conform to strict regulations, victory had so far eluded Triumph riders. This did not apply to the 1958 event however, as it was won by Mike Hailwood and Dan Shorey sharing a 649cc Triumph T110. They finished two laps ahead of the 692cc Super Meteor Royal Enfield twin piloted by Bob McIntyre and Derek Powell, who had offered stiff opposition and had the advantage of an extra 50ccs.

During July Ariel launched its latest model at Grosvenor House in London's Park Lane. It represented a complete breakaway from the four stroke models with which Ariel had so long been associated in the past, because the newcomer was a twin cylinder two-stroke. The 249cc Leader had arrived after four years of research and development, designed by Val Page. It was a revolutionary design in many respects, not least of which was the full enclosure. Just over 100 representatives of the national, technical and trade press were present at the launch, and one of the national dailies had purchased six Leaders to give away as competition prizes. The guests were first welcomed by Ken Whistance, Ariel's Director and General Manager, followed by a supporting speech from Edward in his capacity as Head of the Group, of which Ariel was a part. Edward described the Leader as "an ambitious machine and a precursor of fashion", for which he saw a big future. Geoff Duke was sufficiently impressed to agree to do a lap of the Oulton Park circuit on a Leader during the forthcoming August Bank Holiday weekend. Many journalists saw this model as an indication of the revival of British enterprise at a time when the industry had been accused of dragging its feet.

BSA was next to come up with some advance information about two entirely new British scooters. The scooter 'boom' was now nearing its peak and it seemed remarkable that none of the leading British motorcycle manufacturers had yet ventured into this burgeoning market. Vespa and Lambretta had already captured a sizeable portion of the market between them; the former having its design made under licence by Douglas (Sales and Service) Limited, of Bristol. The majority of scooters on the market at that time were of continental manufacture, usually sold through an offshoot of their manufacturer or concessionaire. It had not been fully realised that, by adopting this approach, scooter manufacturers gained a foothold in the UK market and would use this to their advantage in later years by introducing motorcycles from the same manufacturer.

Although many believed the scooter to be of Italian origin, this was far from the truth. The scooter was a British invention conceived before the 1914-18 war, which had failed to make much impression at that time due to the way in which it had been marketed.

British riders were again evident in the 1958 ISDT, held in Garmisch Partenkirchen. Triumph was represented by John Giles and Ken Heanes (649cc Triumphs) in Britain's Trophy Team and Roy Peplow (498cc Triumph) in the Vase A Team. Although the British contingent had high hopes of doing better than on previous occasions, the results of the event followed an all too-familiar pattern: Czechoslovakia won both the International Trophy and the Vase, with Britain well out of the running. Britain did not even qualify for a Manufacturer's Team

Bournemouth would receive a limited amount of factory support following his recent string of successes in trials. As far as scrambles were concerned, Triumph would be represented by John Giles, Ken Heanes and Brian and Triss Sharp.

Always on the spot when there was something of interest at Meriden, *Motor Cycling's* Midlands representative, Bernal Osborne, had a chance to try out a standard T20 Tiger Cub fitted with the latest Zenith carburetter. Zenith's 17MX model made starting easy and gave a good tick-over, whilst responding readily to the throttle. Bernal found the machine on test would actually continue to tick-over when lying on its side. It would return just over 100mpg when the speed was maintained at a steady 50mph.

The Triumph trials team showed it was likely to prove difficult to beat this year when Artie Ratcliffe won the Bemrose Trial with a best solo performance. Roy Peplow won the Lapidosa Cup as runner-up, and the Fred Craner Cup for the best one-make team was shared between John Giles, Roy Peplow and Artie Ratcliffe - all Tiger Cub mounted, of course.

Award. There was, however, some consolation for both John Giles and Ken Heanes who lost no marks and were awarded a Gold medal. Roy Peplow had suffered a broken gearbox, which put him out of the running. His enforced retirement cost the Vase A team, of which he was a member, 100 marks a day.

The controversy over Johnny Allen's bid for the World Motorcycle Speed Record had barely died down when, early in September, came the news that a Triumph had taken it even higher! Towards the end of Bonneville's Speed Week, 18 year old Jess Thomas completed two runs with the streamliner previously ridden by Johnny Allen, to raise the AMA Class A record for 500cc machines to 212.288mph. For these runs the bike had been fitted with a 498cc Triumph engine prepared by Jack Wilson, the man responsible for the engine used in the previous record-breaking attempt. After the successful runs by Jess, a 650cc engine was installed, but there were problems and it was not possible to repeat a promising one-way run at 221.811mph in further record-breaking bids.

On the same day, Bill Johnson (unrelated to Bill Johnson of Johnson Motors) broke the AMA's class C record for standard machines on a T100 Triumph. His engine had been prepared by Joe Dudek and a mean speed of 147.32mph was achieved over two runs; quite remarkable for what looked like a standard production model.

This new record set by Jess Thomas was comfortably in excess of the 210.64mph recorded by NSU, in the eyes of the FIM the official World Record holder. It is understood that this was not another attempt to regain the record for Triumph, but merely to see whether it was possible to replicate the record denied Triumph using the same timing equipment.

In the 4th September issue of *Motor Cycling* was an announcement from BSA about the C15 Star, a new 250cc, unit-construction, ohv single. Although the engine was mounted vertically in the frame, the immediate conclusion was that it had been influenced by Edward's Tiger Cub. It too had a single top tube frame, with a single downtube that branched into a twin tube cradle below the engine/gear unit. Rear suspension was of the pivoted fork type, now in almost universal use throughout the industry, its movement controlled by Girling suspension units. A Lucas alternator supplied the electrics and the ignition, with a Sentercel rectifier to convert the ac current to dc for battery charging. Both wheels were of 17 inch diameter, with 6 inch diameter brake drums in full-width hubs. Claimed to be capable of 70mph, the C15 Star was a distinct breakaway from BSA's earlier designs. It was for sale at £172, inclusive of Purchase Tax, and would be available in several optional colours, fuchsia and turquoise being the most predominant.

Roy Peplow was in the news again when he won the Mitchell Trial on his 199cc Tiger Cub for the second year in succession. Held in the Ponytypool area, Roy lost only 12 marks, and was well ahead of the runner-up.

News that British motorcycle enthusiasts would relish today came during October, when American Bill Hunt, of the All Japan Motor Cycle Club, won the first Mount Asama International Clubman's Race riding a Triumph of unspecified capacity. The 500cc five-lap race was won by K. Honda, also on a Triumph, at 46.98mph. The event was run on an unpaved surface which, having been swept by a typhoon before the meeting began, was very muddy.

The course of the 1958 John Douglas Trial was also in a very muddy condition, but did not prevent Roy Peplow winning on his 199cc Tiger Cub, with a loss of 35 marks. John Giles, on a similar mount, won a First Class Award. A few weeks later he was a member of the Midland Team that won the ACU Inter-Centre Team Trial with 23 marks lost, less than any other member of the team.

For 1959 the Triumph programme comprised eight models; the 498cc TR5 Trophy Twin had been dropped from production, and only its larger brother, the 649cc TR6, was still made. As the anniversary year would have passed by the beginning of 1959, the 350cc unit-construction model Twenty-one henceforth would be catalogued as the 3TA. This model had now been joined by a similar unit-construction version of the Speed Twin, the 5TA, which would retain the Speed Twin name. Its capacity was now 490cc and it had 17 inch diameter wheels. The change in specification resulted in a welcome price reduction.

In its latest guise, the T20 Tiger Cub had a quickly detachable, but stylish, centre fairing. To enhance appearance, the petrol rank had been restyled and was visibly deeper. The engine was more distinctive, too, with an increased finning area and a Zenith carburetter to replace the Amal type fitted previously. The T20C competition model continued virtually unchanged, apart from a narrower petrol tank, twin seals on the gearbox final drive shaft, and provision for fitting a larger gearbox final drive sprocket.

Despite what had been said the previous year, the 6T Thunderbird lost its SU carburetter in favour of an Amal instrument, and was to be available in a charcoal grey and black finish. It would also have the latest Lucas RM15 alternator. The new Tiger 100 had a different finish, too, of two-tone black and white. Other modifications had been made throughout the Triumph range as part of the regular updating programme. Amongst them - although not visible - was a new, one-piece, forged flywheel assembly with a bolt-on outer ring for the higher performance twins. All of these models retained magneto ignition and a dc dynamo, and the recently introduced Slickshift gearbox continued to be fitted.

A sensational new model in the range, the 649cc Bonneville, was the one that attracted the most attention. Selectively assembled and bench tested, the new model, with its twin carburetter cylinder head and inch and a half diameter exhaust pipes, had a power output of 45bhp and an impressive maximum speed of 120mph. It marked the birth of what was to be the most outstanding production model ever to leave Meriden. Impressive in its original pearl grey, tangerine and black finish, it sold for £294.8s.3d inclusive of Purchase Tax.

This year, Triumph's customary presentation of its new models to the press had taken on a quite different format. Instead of holding it at Meriden, Edward decided to take a complete range of the new models to the Long Mynd Hotel at Church Stretton, Shropshire, where the press would assemble for dinner on the Friday evening, before being let loose on the bikes the following morning. Edward would be present with Mr W. Winters, the recently-appointed Works Director, Neale Shilton, Charles Parker, Ivor Davies, Charles Grandfield, Alec Masters and Jack Wickes. Hugh Palin had also been invited, as Director of the Industries Association.

Edward had intended to set off on the Bonneville but, instead, took the Twenty-one. The write-up in *Motor Cycling* suggested the Bonneville had been 'taken out of service because it was unsuitable for the terrain', when, in fact, the real reason was quite different and had been discretely overlooked by the press. What actually happened was that when Edward took the Bonneville to set off for the run around the test route, he could not get it to start. None too amused, he took Neale Shilton's Twenty-one and set off, leaving Neale with the offending machine. It had no compression on one cylinder and, when Neale got it to start, it would fire on the good cylinder only. He wheeled it away surreptitiously, knowing it would have to be taken apart at Meriden on the Monday to find out exactly what was wrong. One question remained - how could have this have happened?

Neale recalled the machine had previously been lent to

STAR Model C15.

for TRIALS and SCRAMBLES

❋
FOR TRIALS

The launch of BSA's new 249cc ohv C15 Star single in September 1958 suggested that, if competition variants became available, they would pose a serious threat to the already successful off-road Tiger Cubs.

Barry Ryerson of the Volunteer Emergency Service, a group of motorcyclists which provided an emergency service to rush urgently needed blood supplies and drugs to hospitals. He implored Barry to be honest when asked if anything had gone awry whilst the bike was in his hands. The future of the Bonneville depended on his reply as production could be delayed or even jeopardised. Barry owned up and said that, as he was approaching Shreswbury along the A5, he had missed top gear when changing up from third, which caused the rev counter to soar beyond the red line. A valve must have touched a piston and bent so that it no longer seated and put that cylinder out of action.

Knowing Edward would ask him to report to his office immediately he arrived at Meriden on Monday morning, Neale laid out the damaged parts on a tray to take to him. Annoyed that the embarrassing incident had occurred in front of the press, it took Edward some time to calm down and look at the problem objectively from an engineer's viewpoint, when the evidence of the damage and

the way in which it had occurred was all too obvious. Much to Neale's relief, Edward could see no reason why production of the Bonneville should be delayed, but as a safety precaution he stipulated that stronger valve springs were to be fitted forthwith.

Some confusion appears to exist about how the Bonneville model came into being. In Neale Shilton's biography *A Million Miles Ago*, he alleges he suggested to Edward that a new model was needed to replace the T110, and had the temerity to suggest a high performance version fitted with twin carburetters. He went on to recommend it should be called the Bonneville and be finished in a two-tone sky blue and white to reflect the blue and white of the Bonneville salt flats. Yet, in the same paragraph, Neale says that the only time one could make a technical recommendation to Edward was when asked to do so. To add to the confusion, several different sources have said Edward claimed that fitting twin carburetters would lead the company to Carey Street (the location of the bankruptcy court!), and would create a problem with fitting air cleaners. Yet, by

Triumph's 649cc TR6 Trophy model generated no small amount of interest when it made its debut in 1956, despite use of the 'Slickshift' gearbox which never met with the level of enthusiasm that had been anticipated. Lord Brabazon of Tara seemed enthusiastic enough about the TR6 when he sat on one at an Earls Court Motor Cycle Show.

this time, Triumph was already marketing a twin carburetter set-up for the Tiger 100 as an optional extra!

It is difficult to come to a firm conclusion about this matter, except to say that the project could not have gone ahead without Edward's consent, and it seems more likely that it was his idea in the first place. Edward would have had the satisfaction of marketing a high performance model with the Bonneville name as a reminder of the FIM's refusal to acknowledge Johnny Allen's World Motorcycle Speed Record against overwhelming evidence to the contrary!

On the eve of the 1958 Motor Cycle Show, BSA's Automotive Division released details of the new 172cc and 249cc scooters. The announcement took the trade by surprise because the scooters were to be marketed under the Triumph name as well as that of BSA. Until now, the two companies had continued to market their individual models. The Triumph versions would be sold as the TS1 (173cc) and the TS2 (249cc) Tigress, and the equivalent BSA models as the B1 and B2 Sunbeams, resurrecting the old Sunbeam name owned by BSA. The 173cc models had a single cylinder, two-stroke engine, and the 249cc models an ohv, in-line, twin cylinder engine with the option of an electric starter at extra cost. The electric starter models were denoted by an additional 'S' appended to the model designation. The Triumph and BSA scooters were identical, apart from the badge on the bodywork, and all were made at BSA's Waverley Street factory. Although not mentioned at the time of launch, Edward was responsible for their design.

All shared a common cradle frame made of one and a half inch tubing, with the headstock attached to the twin front downtubes where they came together. The tubes splayed out to support the floor structure and were adequately cross-braced. They then swept upward in a vertical position to meet a loop to which the seat was

attached. Of the single blade type, the front fork had its centre section offset to the left with a stub axle for the 10 inch diameter front wheel. It carried a compression spring and was hydraulically damped. Both solid centre wheels were quickly detachable and interchangeable.

The engine/gear unit was located below the seat and connected to the 10 inch diameter rear wheel on the left-hand side by a fully-enclosed gear drive within an aluminium casing. The drive formed an integral part of the pivoted rear fork assembly, its movement controlled by hydraulic rear suspension units. The bodywork had the customary scooter-type apron at the front on which was mounted a single headlamp. It provided the rider with good weather protection and carried a small instrument panel with a speedometer, lighting switch, and, in the case of the 250cc 'S' models, an electric starter button below. The front wheel had a deeply valanced mudguard in keeping with the scooter-type body. The floor area of the scooter was covered by a rubber mat, with foot boards running each side.

The engine/gear unit was enclosed within detachable, all-enveloping bodywork, which had air intakes in its lower portion. A lockable dualseat hinged to the left, to give access to oil and petrol tanks and battery; the tool kit was contained within an underseat tray. Gearchanging was accomplished by a pedal on the right-hand side of the floor pan with a rod-operated linkage to its motorcycle type selector. There were four gear ratios. The rear brake pedal was on the left. The front brake and clutch levers were on the handlebars, in conventional positions, along with the headlamp dip switch.

The two-stroke engine was of conventional piston port design, with a flat top piston. It had a cast iron cylinder barrel and an aluminium alloy cylinder head, and was lubricated by petroil. Blades set into the external flywheel generator rotor provided fan cooling via ducting. A rectifier in the system ensured the generator's ac output was converted to dc, to keep the 6 volt battery fully charged. Provision was made for a direct oil feed to the casing that contained the gears which provided the final drive to the rear wheel. As the 173cc, two-stroke model did not have provision for an electric starter, a kickstarter was mounted on the right-hand footboard.

The 249cc, in-line, ohv, vertical twin engine was of a much more sophisticated design and quite unique. A single alloy casting formed the crankcase, gearbox shell and cylinder block, the cylinders having cast-in iron liners. The pistons were carried on forged manganese-steel connecting rods and conformed to current Triumph practice in having plain, shell-type big-end bearings. The two-throw crankshaft was of forged steel, running on one and one eighth inch diameter journal bearings. Good balance was achieved by the use of bob weights, the crankshaft being ported to provide a high pressure feed to the big ends. A three-plate clutch took the drive to the gearbox off one end, the other end having an external flywheel fan with a toothed ring around its circumference for the starter motor drive, if fitted. It also contained the ac generator, its rotor bolted to the crankcase casting. The contact breaker took the form of a double assembly driven from the camshaft, connected to twin HT coils. If an electric starter was fitted, the machine had a 12 volt electrical system and the alternator a higher output.

The camshaft was high-mounted behind the cylinder block, flat base tappets linked to the rocker arms by short duralumin push rods

The 649cc Bonneville is widely regarded as the most prestigious model ever made by the old Triumph Engineering Company, and second-hand prices reflect this. First introduced in late 1958, and made with the American market very much in mind, the T120 Bonneville met with instant acclaim. Selectively assembled and fitted with a twin carburetter cylinder head, one of these models, ridden by Percy Tait, a works tester, was electronically timed at 128mph on MIRA's test track. This early 1959 model has a nacelle headlamp, which was soon abandoned for one more in keeping with the model's capabilities. (John Nelson)

with steel capped ends. The oil pump drive was taken from the end of this camshaft. The lubrication system was of the wet sump type, following normal car practice. The cylinder head was cast in light alloy with vertical valves in cast iron guides and straight thrust rocker arms on a common spindle. The two exhaust valves, however, required cranked rockers. All were enclosed within a car-type rocker cover. The engine 'ran backwards' and transferred drive to the four-speed gearbox via a 2:1 reduction gear. The four-speed gearbox followed motorcycle practice and had a neutral finder. It also had a kickstart if the electric starter option had not been taken up.

The Triumph scooters were available in a shell blue sheen finish, and the BSA Sunbeams in a bright polychromatic green. Prices for the 173cc models were £164.19s.8d., the the standard 249cc models £187.2s.6d., or, if the latter was supplied with an electric starter, £200.17s., all inclusive of Purchase Tax. At the show, Edward managed to get Harold Watkinson, then Minister of Transport, who had been invited to open the show, to sit on one of the bikes to have his photograph taken.

Unfortunately, the scooters arrived far too late on the scene; within a year, the scooter 'boom' in Britain had reached its peak and was on the decline. From the industry's point of view it was 'too little, too late'. With Vespa and Lambretta having held the lion's share of

the market almost from the beginning, it will come as no surprise that sales of the BSA and Triumph scooters fell far short of expectation. Production came quietly to an end in September 1963.

As the year closed, there was news of a special competition version of BSA's 250cc Star, a prototype of which had been entered in the British Experts Trial to be ridden by Brian Martin, who had already used it successfully to win the Holoway Cup in the National Knut Trial. Although his luck was out in the British Experts, Brian did sufficiently well to merit a First Class Award . Early indications were that the Tiger Cub might have to face up to some keen competition in the near future from BSA's bigger capacity challenger.

The scooter display on Triumph's stand at Earls Court was simple but impressive.

Chapter 12: Japan's threat to the British motorcycle industry

At the end of May 1959 Edward filed a patent under the joint names of the Triumph Engineering Company and ET Developments Limited. British Patent No. 809,968 related to an automatic transmission system suitable for lightweight motorcycles and scooters. It was basically a belt drive between the engine and countershaft, running on variable pulleys, with provision for a centrifugal clutch and a final fixed ratio drive to the rear wheel. It also took into account a means of by-passing the clutch in favour of a free wheel device that would give the option of coasting or override braking. It was, in fact, an inkling of what was going on behind the scenes as the patent had been taken out to protect the automatic transmission Edward had designed for what was to be the Tina scooter, due for launch during 1962.

A road test of the 249cc BSA Sunbeam B2 scooter was published in the 9th April issue of *Motor Cycling*. It was the first of the magazine's prolonged mileage tests in which the scooter acquitted itself well. Overall appearance received favourable comment, even though the stylish panels were not quite as easy to remove when access to the engine unit was required as those of its contemporaries. It was easy to raise on its centre stand and could be easily started by the side-mounted kickstarter (this was the model that did not have the optional electric starter). Maximum speed was 63mph and it would cruise at 50-55mph, thanks to a high-revving, twin cylinder engine. The rocking pedal gearchange lever was very positive in action and there was a handy separate neutral selector. Transmission was smooth and the exhaust well silenced.

Both brakes would stop the machine within 30 feet from 30mph, and lighting was adequate for the night crusing speeds of which the scooter was capable. Roadholding, always open to criticism on account of the small diameter of most scooter wheels, led to it being described as the 'Daimler of the scooter world'. The conclusion was that at £187.2s.6d. inclusive of Purchase Tax, the Sunbeam B2 should have a brilliant future.

It was widely acknowledged that Triumph made the best twin cylinder engines, so it was a natural choice of power unit when Don and Derek Rickman of New Milton, Hampshire, produced their Metisse scrambler. Using their own design of frame, and sometimes fitting a Matchless or a BSA single cylinder engine, they scored countless wins by riding their machines in scrambles events. Other popular 'specials' - such as the Triton, based on a Norton 'featherbed' frame - also made use of a Triumph twin engine, and the Tribsa, which used a BSA frame. Many examples of these were made by different manufacturers, the most prominent manufacturer of the Triton being Dave Degens: a surplus of Norton 'featherbed' frames had been available, having been 'robbed' of their 499cc dohc Manx engines and gearboxes for use in Formula 3 racing cars.

A road test of the Triumph Twenty-one published in the 30th April issue of *Motor Cycling* was prefaced by the words "A Very Fast and Economical Medium-capacity Roadster", and very complimentary it was, too. According to the tester, Bernal Osborne, one of the bike's greatest virtues was its ability to return an overall fuel consumption of 85mpg during 'give and take riding at fairly high cruising speeds'. Suspension and roadholding were good and the engine quiet, with an unobtrusive exhaust note. The gearbox was well up to Triumph standards, and it was said that the bugbear of all unbalanced vertical twins - vibration - was not evident until 7000rpm when a 'perceptible tremor at the knee grips could be felt'. It should, of course, be remembered that road tests at that time were described with a certain amount of licence by the writer: a bad report might well result in the magazine losing the manufacturer's advertising revenue. If the machine under test was obviously below standard, a 'gentleman's agreement' was activated: the test would be abandoned and the manufacturer given the opportunity to rectify any faults before a re-test took place.

Roy Peplow put up a quite outstanding performance in the 1959 Scottish Six Days Trial, winning the event outright on his 199cc Tiger Cub with a loss of only 18 marks. He finished with two marks less than the legendary Gordon Jackson riding a 348cc AJS. Roy had, in fact, made history as he was the first rider of a machine of under 250cc capacity to take the premier award in this prestigious event. On the penultimate day it had become a fiercely contested, three-cornered fight to the finish between Peplow, Jackson and the mercurial Sammy Miller.

The 1959 International Six Days Trial was another complete farce as far as Great Britain was concerned, as the British Trophy Team finished 7th, one from last, losing a massive 1301 marks. Two 649cc Triumph twins were in the Trophy Team, ridden by Ken Heanes and Eric Chilton, and there was some confusion about whether or not Eric had qualified for a Gold medal. By way of compensation, Roy Peplow won the Cambrian Trial on his Tiger Cub, way ahead of all the others, forfeiting just three marks. His was a near-perfect performance.

Towards the end of September, an Anglo-French tie-up was announced in which Terrot, now part of the Peugeot Group, would take over sales, distribution and servicing of Triumph motorcycles in France. The agreement would also cover the French African countries, with the exception of Algeria. Triumph motorcycles would henceforth be sold alongside Terrot lightweight motorcycles and scooters, but for the time being the arrangement would not include Triumph scooters. Phelon and Moore, of Cleckheaton, held the licence to make Terrot scooters in Britain under its own name.

At the West of England Trial, Roy Peplow again carried off the premier award, whilst Artie Ratcliffe, similarly mounted on a 199cc Tiger Cub, took the 200cc award. Ray Sayer was also well in the running, riding a Tiger Cub, and their combined efforts ensured Triumph received the Best Manufacturer's Team Award. In the Perce Simon Trial that followed soon after, Roy Peplow came within an inch of winning that, too, only to have Jeff Smith just beat him on his 249cc BSA. Jeff's front wheel spindle was an inch from the Section Ends card at the Badgers Holt Section, so he lost two less marks! All was not totally lost as Roy had the satisfaction of winning the Vale Cup as runner-up.

For the 1960 season the Tiger 100 was the next in the line to join the models having a unit-construction engine and 'bath tub' rear enclosure. Now catalogued as the Tiger 100A, it was about 50lbs lighter than its predecessor and cost £12 less. All the unit-construction twins would henceforth have an adjustable Weller-type chain tensioner incorporated within the primary chaincase, to ensure primary chain tension could be correctly maintained.

The 649cc twins benefited from a new frame, instantly recognisable by its twin down tubes that formed the cradle below the engine. Any single tubes used in the frame's construction were of heavier gauge, and there was a massive malleable iron lug at the base of the vertical saddle tube. The Thunderbird also profited by having the new frame, to take advantage of its improved steering geometry, whilst other improvements included a new front mudguard and fork similar to that of the 5TA model. As the rear end was now enclosed in the same way as the unit-construction models, the wheel sizes were reduced to 18 inch diameter and the petrol tank made easier to remove. A Lucas RM13/15 alternator dispensed with the need for the separate, front-mounted dc dynamo fitted previously.

Unfortunately, the design of the new duplex tube frame was flawed. Edward still advocated 'letting the metal do its work' and the new frame differed from some of Edward's earlier designs in which the top frame rail had been omitted. Instead, it dispensed with the lower frame stiffening member which acted as an additional brace to the steering head. It was soon apparent that it did not handle as well as had been envisaged, a problem soon exacerbated when it was learnt that one of these frames had broken below the headstock. It had happened in the USA during the Big Bear Run, an off-road desert racing event held in California's Mojave Desert. According to contemporary reports, the breakage occurred when the rider hit a series of ruts at high speed and was thrown off, sadly, to die from his injuries. Edward was there at the time and initiated an immediate investigation at Meriden. Extensive tests were carried out at the Motor Industry Research Association's track at Nuneaton, where a frame broke after four days. It was confirmed that even at moderate speeds similar breakages could occur when the machines were ridden over pave. There was only one answer; modify the design by reinstating the missing stiffening member and provide the headstock with the additional bracing it needed at its lower end. Inadequate bracing had caused the headstock to flex sufficiently to fracture the twin front downtubes at the point where they joined the lower end.

The 1963 649cc models benefited from this modification, although, as will be seen in a later road test report, handling characteristics of the T120 Bonneville at high speed could still give rise to anxiety.

All the twins were now available with the option of a quickly detachable rear wheel, and there was wider - but not yet exclusive - adoption of the energy transfer system for ignition and lighting. The latter did not initially provide the advantage that Triumph's new model announcement suggested. It worked well if the ignition timing had been set up accurately, but if not the likelihood was that the

Roy Peplow put up some impressive performances on 199cc competition Tiger Cubs. He won the 1959 Scottish Six Days Trial with a loss of only 18 marks, and the Cambrian Trial that followed soon afterwards. Here he is seen in the 1959 British Experts Trial, where he finished 6th. (B.R. Nicholls)

engine would start but fail to run properly. It was a problem the electrical equipment suppliers had to address with some urgency.

The 649cc Bonneville was another model that adopted the new frame and the same front fork as the Thunderbird and its three gallon petrol tank was made easier to remove. It retained sports-type mudguards, however, and had a quickly detachable headlamp, dispensing with the nacelle. All of the high performance twins were now fitted with a five-plate clutch.

The Tiger Cub was the model that benefited most from the update viewpoint, profiting from Roy Peplow's Scottish Six Days Trial winning machine. Production of the old T20C competition model had ceased during June, and it was replaced by a new T20S version. Most noticeable was its heavy-duty front fork based on the model Twenty-one design. At the rear end the swinging fork had been widened to accept a 4 inch section rear tyre. Both wheel sizes had been increased to 19 inch diameter. This was another of those models or

Continued page 109

Colour gallery

Taken soon after his appointment as designer and engineer, Edward is seen seated at his desk in Ariel's Selly Oak factory.

ARIEL

The 1932 Ariel catalogue cover featured the prestigious Square Four model. Top of the range and expensive, it sold in small numbers.

Although the Square Four was redesigned in 1935 and its capacity increased to 997cc, it was still expensive and continued to sell in relatively small numbers. It stayed in production until August 1959, a commendably long run.

Some of the 3HW models were used by the RAF, as was this 1945 model restored by Ken Middleditch. The 3HW models differed from their pre-war predecessors by having the rocker box cast integrally with the cast iron cylinder head. (Author photo)

The 349cc 3T de luxe model was the only pre-unit 350cc Triumph twin to go into production after the war, and then only from 1946 until 1951. From all accounts it was a very sweet-running machine, with reasonable performance, but the engine differed in some ways to that used for the bigger twins, and did not help the commonality of parts policy.

Above (both photos): Another engine that bore allegiance to the wartime generator unit was that of the 499cc TR5 Trophy Twin, also introduced at the 1948 Motor Cycle Show. Britain had won the prestigious International Six Days Trial that year, to which the Triumph works team had contributed by finishing unpenalised. One of the team, Allan Jefferies, had been riding what amounted to a prototype version. The Trophy twins had a single carburetter, and a 'soft', low compression version of the Grand Prix engine. The machine shown is a 1949 model that has been restored by Ken Middleditch. (Author photos)

The new 6T Thunderbird in its original slate grey finish and with SU carburetter.

The Terrier, Triumph's first lightweight since 1934. Despite the single cylinder engine, it was very much a 'real Triumph in miniature', with the characteristic headlamp nacelle and finish in Amaranth Red. It was also the first Triumph to have plunger-type rear suspension.

The TRIUMPH Terrier
150 OHV

TRIUMPH NACELLE TYPE HEADLAMP

2⅜ GALLON PETROL TANK

TRIUMPH TELESCOPIC FORKS

DEEP SECTION MUDGUARDS

LARGE DIAMETER BRAKES

EFFICIENT SPRING FRAME

O.H.V. ENGINE and 4-SPEED GEARBOX

PRICE
Retail £98 plus Purchase Tax of £27 - 4 - 6
TOTAL
£125 - 4 - 6

For 1957 the T20 Tiger Cub had pivoted fork rear suspension, and several other advantageous detail changes.

TRIUMPH

THE HIGHEST SPEEDS EVER ACHIEVED ON A MOTORCYCLE

Triumph's successful record-breaking bid at Bonneville was just what the company needed to help boost sales still further in America. Sadly, after a long, drawn out saga, the record was never ratified by the FIM because the AMA was not a member of the FIM, even though all the requirements had been met.

The Sleekest Smoothest Scooter Ever!

This is the " Tigress "— a magnificent new scooter by Triumph. Choose your engine—simple two-stroke or lively o.h.v. twin, both with 4 speed gearbox.

Controls ? Simpler than any car. Styling ? Look at the beautiful lines. Comfort ? Hydraulically controlled suspension front and rear and a supple full length latex filled seat. Safety ? Powerful 5 inch brakes and hairline steering. Efficient in design, efficient in operation, the Triumph " Tigress " will give you a completely new conception of scooter performance.

Tigress

TRIUMPH

BRIEF SPECIFICATION

ENGINE TS1. 173 c.c. single cylinder two-stroke fan cooled. Flywheel magneto. Petroil lubrication.
ENGINE TW2. 249 c.c. o.h.v. vertical twin. Alloy cylinder head. Car type lubrication. Fan cooling. A.C. Alternator.
TW2/S. As TW2 but with self starter.
GEARBOX. 4 speeds. Neutral finder. Positive footchange. Gear

primary drive. Duplex chain final drive in aluminium oil bath case.

WHEELS. Pressed steel, quickly detachable and interchangeable.

BODY. Beautifully styled, pressed steel. Spacious flat platform and front apron. Latex foam twinseat hinged for access to engine and fuel tanks. Duplex tubular frame.

ELECTRICAL EQUIPMENT. TS1 6 volt flywheel magneto with A.C. lighting coils. TW2 6 volt with A.C. Alternator. Twin contact breakers and coils. TW2/S 12 volt with car type starter. All models have powerful headlamp, horn and combined tail/stop lamp.
SUSPENSION. Double plunger type telescopic fork. Swinging arm rear with combined suspension/damper unit.

TECHNICAL DATA	T S I		TW2 and TW2/s	
Engine Type	2 stroke		OHV	
Number of Cylinders	1		2	
Bore/Stroke mm.	61.5 × 58		56 × 50.62	
Bore/Stroke ins.	2.4 × 2.3		2.2 × 2	
Cylinder Capacity ccs	173		249	
cu. ins.	10.6		15.2	
Compression ratio	7.5 : 1		6.5 : 1	
BHP at RPM	7.5 HP @ 5,000 r.p.m.		10 HP @ 5,500 r.p.m.	
Primary drive	Gear 2.27 : 1 Ratio		2.0 : 1 Ratio	
Rear Drive	Duplex Chain		Duplex Chain	
	with Tensioner		with Tensioner	
RPM 10 m.p.h. Top Gear	948		834	
Gear Ratios	Top 4.55 : 1 3rd 5.8 : 1		Top 4.0 : 1 3rd 5.2 : 1	
	2nd 9.1 : 1 1st 13.6 : 1		2nd 8.0 : 1 1st 12.0 : 1	
Carburetter	Zenith		Zenith 17MX	
Tyres—Front }	3.50 × 10	}	3.50 × 10	}
Rear }	Scooter tyre		Scooter tyre	
Brake diameter	5″ dia. × 1″ wide		5″ dia. × 1″ wide	
Finish	Blue		Blue	
Seat Height	28″	71 cm.	28″	71 cm.
Wheelbase	48″	122 cm.	48″	122 cm.
Length	72″	183 cm.	72″	183 cm.
Width	24″	61 cm.	24″	61 cm.
Ground Clearance	5″	12.7 cm.	5″	12.7 cm.
Weight	220 lbs.	100 Kg.	240 lbs.	109 Kg.
Petrol capacity	1½ gallons	6.8 litre	1½ gallons	6.8 litre
Lubrication	Petroil		2½ pints oil	142 cc.

ACCESSORIES—A full range of accessories has been designed for the Triumph Tigress including windscreen, spare wheel and cover, luggage racks, wheel discs, etc. Details on request.

TRIUMPH ENGINEERING COMPANY LIMITED

SCOOTER DIVISION

Waverley Works   **Birmingham 10**

Ref. 446/58   Printed by W. W. Curtis Ltd., Coventry, England

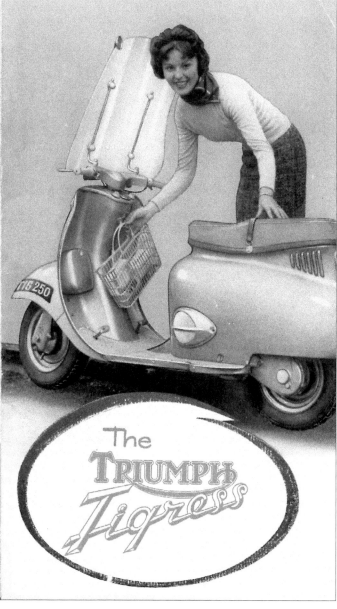

Above and opposite: Although Triumph (and BSA) entered the scooter market far too late, when the 'boom' in their sales was coming to an end, the twin cylinder models were unique in having in line cylinders. The question was, did the potential purchaser have sufficient interest in the technical specification for it to influence his or her choice?

The 350 c.c. Twenty-one maintains the immense popularity which marked its first introduction to the medium-weight range. Quiet and flexible with a sparkling performance this machine has created its own individual appeal. Light alloy cylinder head, unit construction four-speed gearbox and semi rear enclosure make this model the automatic choice of the rider who demands the best in the 350 c.c. class.

Twenty-one

350 c.c.

THE CLUTCH OPERATING MECHANISM ON ALL 350 c.c. AND 650 c.c. MACHINES IS DESIGNED TO FACILITATE EASY REMOVAL, AND SERVICING.

SPEED TWIN

500 c.c.

Identical specification to the Twenty-one, but with the added power and liveliness of a 500 c.c. engine, the Speed Twin enjoys the virtues of lightweight ease of handling, ultra modern design and exciting performance. This famous sporting roadster, which set the pattern of twin cylinder design, offers that extra power for livelier performance and more effortless travel.

The new
BSA SUNBEAM

The 'bathtub' rear enclosures on the unit-construction models had been so disliked, especially in America, that a compromise was reached by replacing them with a 'bikini' fairing on the later models, as on the Twenty-one and 5TA Speed Twin models pictured in a 1964 brochure.

All the scooters were made at BSA's Waverley Street factory, and were identical apart from colour scheme and the badge on the front apron. BSA resurrected the old Sunbeam name as it had acquired this company some years previously.

designed in the Ariel manner

The 50 c.c. Ariel Pixie is something entirely new in ultra-lightweight motor cycles. Like the famous Ariel Leader and Arrow motor cycles it is of very advanced design. The engine is an overhead valve design for complete reliability and great economy.
This is combined with a four-speed gearbox and mounted in a unique and most attractive pressed steel "chassis". Revolutionary rubber suspension front and rear provides comfort under all conditions. The "PIXIE" is low in first cost, light and easy to handle and is ideal for personal everyday transport.

modern, clean, stylish

The 50 c.c. o.h.v. **Pixie**

The engine unit of the 49.9cc Ariel Pixie was a smaller version of that used for the 74.8cc BSA Beagle. Earlier, both companies had been working on their ultra-lightweights independently, until Edward intervened. To bring the two designs closer together in accord with BSA Group policy, Ariel's original ohc engine was replaced by a scaled-down version of BSA's engine. The cycle parts, however, still differed.

no gears!
no clutch!

...it couldn't be easier

As the Tina Automatic Scooter catalogue shows, it had been designed primarily with lady users in mind. Note the combined right and left foot brake pedal, and left-hand kick starter.

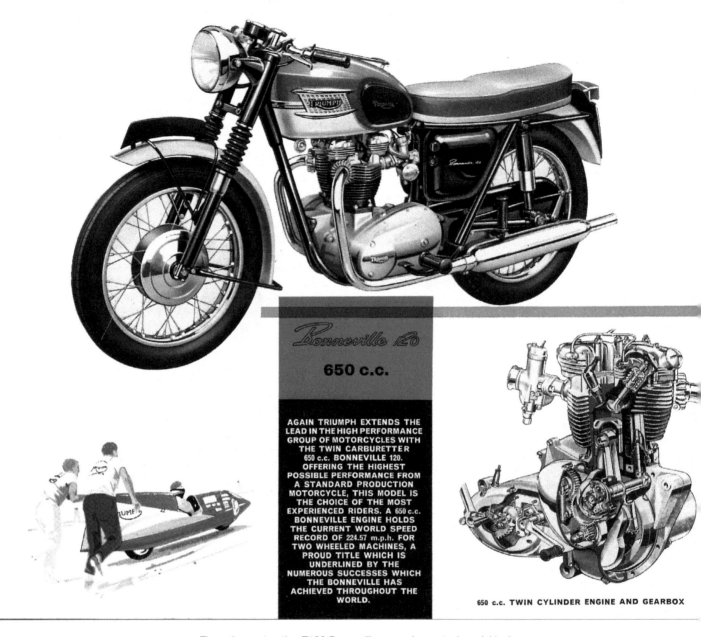

Bonneville 120

650 c.c.

AGAIN TRIUMPH EXTENDS THE LEAD IN THE HIGH PERFORMANCE GROUP OF MOTORCYCLES WITH THE TWIN CARBURETTER 650 c.c. BONNEVILLE 120. OFFERING THE HIGHEST POSSIBLE PERFORMANCE FROM A STANDARD PRODUCTION MOTORCYCLE, THIS MODEL IS THE CHOICE OF THE MOST EXPERIENCED RIDERS. A 650 c.c. BONNEVILLE ENGINE HOLDS THE CURRENT WORLD SPEED RECORD OF 224.57 m.p.h. FOR TWO WHEELED MACHINES, A PROUD TITLE WHICH IS UNDERLINED BY THE NUMEROUS SUCCESSES WHICH THE BONNEVILLE HAS ACHIEVED THROUGHOUT THE WORLD.

650 c.c. TWIN CYLINDER ENGINE AND GEARBOX

The unit-construction T120 Bonneville, a much coveted model today.

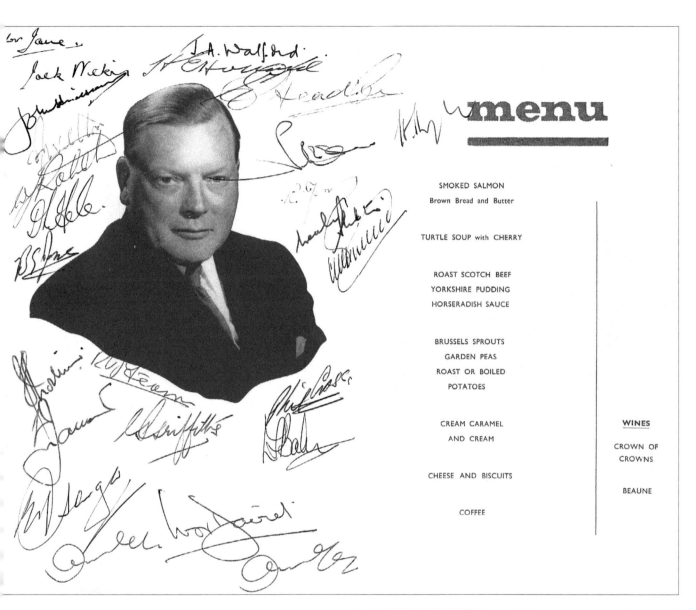

menu

SMOKED SALMON
Brown Bread and Butter

TURTLE SOUP with CHERRY

ROAST SCOTCH BEEF
YORKSHIRE PUDDING
HORSERADISH SAUCE

BRUSSELS SPROUTS
GARDEN PEAS
ROAST OR BOILED
POTATOES

CREAM CARAMEL
AND CREAM

CHEESE AND BISCUITS

COFFEE

WINES

CROWN OF
CROWNS

BEAUNE

On 12th May 1966, the senior staff entertained Edward at the George Hotel, Solihull, at what, in effect, amounted to a farewell dinner. Whoever organised it was thoughtful enough to send a signed copy of the menu to each of Edward's children, a much appreciated gesture. This is the centre of the copy that was sent to Jane, showing all the signatures.

A very fine photograph of Edward in later life aboard the Charane, *confidently in charge, as usual.*

The new home in the Bahamas, on Tarrytowr Drive, near Freeport, Grand Bahama Island. Brit Eriksen accepted Edward's invitation to join them and they remained there for a couple of years. Edward's worsening diabetes, and the need to find a suitable school for young Edward, eventually necessitated their return to England.

A last, sad look at the deserted factory that once made "The World's Best Motorcycle".

Charmian took it upon herself to visit the now deserted Triumph factory at Meriden on the eve of its demolition.

losing only three marks on his first lap, then a further four on his second. It put him well ahead of runner-up Eric Adcock, who lost 21 marks riding a 246cc DOT. In the Southern Experts Trial that followed shortly afterwards, John Giles took the solo award under particularly difficult conditions following several days' rain. He lost 64 marks against Peter Stirland's 67, which gives an idea of what sort of conditions the entry of 102 solo riders had to content with.

At the end of the year a brief announcement in the motorcycling press confirmed that, with effect from 1st January 1960, Eric Turner would be joining the board of BSA as Chief Executive of the Group. He also became Deputy Chairman of the parent company, succeeding Lewis Chapman C.B.E. who was voluntarily retiring from this position but remaining a director.

Early in 1960, it was becoming obvious that the 249cc BSA Star was becoming a serious threat to Roy Peplow's runaway trials wins. John Draper won the Victory Trial on a C15T trials version of this model, and with Jeff Smith and Brian Martin on similar mounts, BSA was awarded the Team Prize. On yet another C15T, Brian Povey won the Walter Hackett Cup. It was unusual for Roy to come away with only a first class award.

A road test of the latest version of Triumph's Tiger 100, the T100A unit-cnstruction model, showed it lived up to the reputation of its predecessor with a near-identical performance. A maximum

Artie Ratcliffe finished tenth in the 1959 British Experts Trial, to win the 200cc award on his Tiger Cub. (B.R. Nicholls)

which energy transfer ignition and lighting had been specified, where it could be used to better advantage as it would provide direct lighting without need for a battery. The headlamp was detachable and fitted with push-type switches for the main beam and dip settings.

Other important modifications to the Tiger Cubs in general included a modified cylinder head with an enlarged inlet valve, and an 18mm Zenith carburetter. In common with the other models, the Tiger Cubs had a muted exhaust system that took the staccato bark out of the exhaust note. The standard road-going T20 Tiger Cub also had the wheel diameter increased; in this instance, to accommodate 17 x 3.25 inch section tyres.

As *Motor Cycling* reported in its 17th December issue, there had been a decisiveness about Roy Peplow's success in the Northern Experts Trial. Riding his 199cc Tiger Cub as usual, he had set the pace by

John Giles had brought Triumph considerable success over the years, and was as much at home on a Tiger Cub as he was on a twin. His confident, yet relaxed riding style is clearly evident here aboard a 499cc twin in a 5th May 1959 scramble at Brands Hatch. (B.R. Nicholls)

speed of 104mph was recorded and fuel consumption of 78mpg at a constant speed of 50mph, despite the fact that the engine now had a cast iron cylinder barrel. The tester appeared to hedge his bets about replacement of the magneto with the energy transfer system, hinting that starting from cold required two or three kicks. There was also an unidentified bottom end 'rumble' from the engine on the test machine, and a third gear that tended to whine, whilst the exhaust had what was described as 'a sharp edge' when the power was wound on. Road-holding at high speeds had improved, although it was advisable to make use of the steering damper as speed increased. The brakes were good and the gearbox of the standard one would expect from a Triumph. Lighting had definitely improved due to the new electrical system, and maintenance was easy to carry out with the toolkit provided.

No mention had been made of the 'bath tub' rear enclosure, about which opinion seemed to vary. Particularly good points of the new model were its lower riding position and two-tone ivory and black finish, a radical departure from the traditional blue and silver of the Tiger range. In all, a worthy successor to the original Tiger 100, which made the headlines when it was launched way back at the 1938 Motor Cycle Show.

The first ever 100 mile motorcycle scramble was organised by the Twickenham and District MCC towards the end of April on a one and a half mile course at Tunnel Hill, Pirbright. It was won by Ken Heanes on a 498cc Triumph, who finished two minutes ahead of runner-up, Brian Leask. Heanes

had been riding for three hours, interrupted only by a pit stop and a pause for a drink. By the time he crossed the finishing line, he was totally exhausted and had earned every penny of his £70 prize money.

Further changes in the structure of the BSA board were announced in mid-July. Eric Turner now had a seat on the Triumph and Ariel boards as part of a plan to make all the companies in the Group function autonomously, each with their own board of directors. In some of the other companies additional directors had been appointed.

Many of Triumph's employees had given long and loyal service, and it is unfortunate it's not possible to mention them all. At the risk of making an exception, Sydney Tubb of Kenilworth deserves special mention as he joined the old Triumph Cycle Company in 1919 after demobilisation from the RAF, in which he had enlisted when it was known as the Royal Flying Corps. He was made foreman in charge of assembly in 1923 and was in charge of the Assembly Department when he retired during August 1960. He was given a fitting send-off as the Guest of Honour at a dinner party provided by the directors and many of his colleagues.

An unusual but highly successful test was staged during mid-September when two 249cc scooters, a Triumph Tigress and a BSA Sunbeam, completed a 1837 mile run under ACU observation. That

Riding a 199cc Tiger Cub, Giles took the solo award in the 1959 Southern Experts Trial, held under particularly difficult conditions following several days of heavy rain. Here he is in the 1962 Southern Experts Trial. (B.R. Nicholls)

Ken Heanes excelled in scrambles, although this was not the only branch of motorcycle sport at which he shone. He won the first ever 100 mile scramble organised by the Twickenham and District MCC in April 1960, after three hours of riding that ended in victory and total exhaustion. This photograph of him in action was taken at a Jewels Hill scramble on 31st January 1960. (B.R. Nicholls)

this test was carried out successfully in appalling weather conditions was much to the credit of the four riders involved: Derek Handy, John Harris, Brian Martin and Henry Vale. The test commenced at The Green, Meriden, where the riders were started by Geoff Duke and John Surtees on Sunday, 18th September. They set off for Edinburgh, which they reached by 8.00pm after stopping for lunch at Boroughbridge. By the evening of the following day, they arrived at John O'Groats after riding through some of the worst weather the Scottish Highlands could produce. The following day they retraced their steps to Edinburgh, and on the Wednesday Kidderminster was the destination. From there they rode to Penzance on the Thursday. Friday saw them back again at Meriden and glad to be there, too, as the West Country had provided weather similar to that encountered in the Scottish Highlands.

The scooters had run perfectly and, when stripped down for examination by an ACU engineer, were not only still oiltight but not even fully run-in! Throughout the test they did not exceed 45mph, averaging 35.1mph during their running time. The BSA Sunbeam had returned 102.05mpg and the Triumph Tigress 101.18mpg. It had never been the intention that the scooters achieve anything spectacular, only to demonstrate how well they would perform under average conditions whilst under strict impartial observation.

Triumph's subsequent advertisement showed how economical it was to run one of these scooters: it had cost just a half-penny a mile for the purchase of petrol and oil to travel such a long distance.

It was now becoming apparent that Japan was a growing threat to the very existence of the British motorcycle. Honda had made a sensational entry in the 1959 125cc Lightweight TT, when it entered four riders on dohc twins who had finished 6th, 7th, 8th and 11th, and won the Manufacturer's Team Prize. For 1960, Honda fielded six riders in the 125cc and 250cc Lightweight races, and there were also three 125cc Suzukis entered initially under the Colleda name. The Honda riders finished 6th, 7th, 8th, 9th and 10th in the 125cc race, each winning a silver replica. M. Kitano, who finished 19th, took the Overseas Newcomer's award. Three finished in the 250 race; Bob Brown gaining a silver replica and M. Kitano and N. Taniguchi a bronze replica. The Suzuki entrants were less fortunate, only two of them finished, one of which - T. Matsumoto - qualified for a bronze replica.

In terms of road-going models, Honda had already established a distributor in Britain, Maico (Great Britain) Limited, who was selling the 124cc twin cylinder Benly and Benly Super Sports, and the larger capacity 247cc twin cylinder Dream and Super Dream models. Although Suzuki and Yamaha had yet to be represented in

Britain, Jimmy Matsumiya, from a garage below his flat in London, was lending Suzukis to journalists and others interested in discovering what kind of an alternative they offered to the already well-established Honda range. With all this going on under their very noses, it is surprising that the leading British manufacturers failed to acknowledge the danger of their own markets being eroded by a flood of machines from the Far East which were of surprisingly good quality. Their's was a head-in-the-sand attitude, so convinced of their position that they could not conceive an outsider could possibly offer a better product. Cynics claimed the Japanese could offer competitively priced products because of low overheads, their workers' staple diet being just two bowls of rice a day. Some even believed that an electric starter was effeminate and that motorcyclists still enjoyed taking their machines to pieces at weekends! How wrong they were.

Despite all the disparaging comments being made by representatives of the British motorcycle industry, no-one had yet taken the initiative to visit Japan and see for themselves exactly what was going on. Edward had witnessed how the British Board of Trade had opened the floodgates to imports from Japan without much prior consultation with UK business interests. There had been no bargaining over the introduction of a corresponding quota for British products to be exported to Japan, which is something he regretted. So that he could see for himself the extent of the threat and just how it was likely to affect the British motorcycle industry, he took it upon himself to visit Japan on a fact-finding tour. By visiting the Japanese motorcycle manufacturers through an introduction made by Triumph's Jananese importer, he could draw his own conclusions and, on his return, present a detailed report of his findings to the industry. Although his report was reproduced in Ivor Davies' now out-of-print book It's a Triumph, few seem to be aware of its existence. By reproducing his report in full again it will leave little doubt that Britain's leading manufacturers were given fair warning of what to expect if they failed to take the threat from Japan seriously. It was dated 26th September 1960.

Edward seems to have had little difficulty seeking out a Triumph dealer in Japan!

During a visit to Honda, Edward was met by Benjiro Honda, the brother of Soiochiro Honda who founded, in October 1946, what was to become the Honda Motor Company.

REPORT ON JAPAN BY EDWARD TURNER

As a result of the tremendous growth of the Japanese motorcycle industry, and the worldwide repercussions on our industry, it was decided that I should pay a visit to Japan to see first-hand what is going on; to examine, if possible, their organisations, to visit the principal factories, to observe manufacturing methods, to discuss with Japanese managements their plans, particularly as regards exports, and to obtain as much information as possible on the Japanese motorcycle industry in order that we should be fully informed of the situation and be in a position to plan counter-measures to try and preserve our own share in motorcycle world markets.

I had previously examined one or two of the better Japanese products, such as the Yamaha, Honda and Suzuki, and formed a very high opinion of their design, finish and manufacturing accuracy, but no impression I had gained of the obvious upsurge of this important industry in Japan bore any relation to the shocks I received on closer examination of this situation on their home ground.

The revelations of Japan as a whole are truly shocking and I am amazed that more of this has not been published in those British newspapers purporting to keep the public of this country informed of world developments.

Japan has 90 million highly intelligent, very energetic, purposeful people, all geared to an economic machine with an avowed object of becoming great again, this time in the world of business and industry, and nothing apparently is going to stop them. Tokyo, with its population of 11 million, the largest city in the world, is entirely Western and the streets are crammed with well-dressed, well-behaved, busy people. Its traffic congestion, composed almost entirely of Japanese cars and motorcycles, is as bad as in any other city of the world but over a much greater area, and the shops and great stores are filled with an infinite variety of goods, all of the highest quality.

At the outset one must discard the old concept of Japanese manufacture being a cheap imitation of that of the West. Today, with Japanese manufactured goods of all types, the accent is on quality. They are fully aware of the reputation they have to live down and, for many years now, the finest machine tool equipment, techniques and scientific ability and keen commercial enterprise have been applied to this end.

Japan today is the largest manufacturer in the world of motorcycles, all of excellent quality. One company of this largest national producer of motorcycles produces more motorcycles than the whole of the British Industry put together, and this is only one of the 20 or more motorcycle companies in full operation. They are producing well over half a million motorcycles a year (against 140,000 British) of which Honda produces approaching a quarter of a million, with 5 other companies each producing more than 25,000 units a year.

The production of motorcycles has been accelerating so fast that it is very difficult to obtain up-to-date figures for the current output but, in every case, it can be assumed to be more rather than less than the figures stated in Appendix A. The reason for this tremendous upsurge in motorcycle manufacture (which, incidentally, has been occurring in the camera, radio and domestic appliance industries with equal intensity and similar rates of acceleration) is the very high standard of living enjoyed by the Japanese population today, brought about by the peculiar living conditions in Japan where personal overheads are low, and although wages, too, are low by our standards, the margin for spending is probably greater than in our own country. The motorcycle business is exactly suited to the improved conditions of young Japan and young Japan regards a motorcycle, purchased mainly on instalments, as being a desirable acquisition from the transportation point of view and gaining 'face'. Also, Japan has become, since the war, very much a mechanical and technical nation. The great wealth that poured into Japan as a result of the occupation, and the relatively small proportion of the budget being devoted to defence until recent times, together with the very liberal approach to industry of Japanese financiers, have been, of course, major causes for what can only be described as a phenomenon.

I see the Japanese today combining the intense conscientious thoroughness and meticulous attention to detail of the German, with the very open-handed uninhibited approach to sales of the most blatant American sales corporation. This combination, together with a restless energy and a national sense of purpose, has had spectacular results in the nation's economy. Of course, there have been casualties and in the motorcycle business many firms have gone under and many more are likely to follow. I see clearly the bigger fish swallowing the smaller ones and, although I would not be surprised to see less than 10 motorcycle companies in existence in three years' time, 4 or 5 of these would be immensely powerful.

The speed with which the Japanese motorcycle companies can produce new designs and properly tested and developed models is startling, and the very large scientific and technical staff maintained at the principal factories is, of course, out of all proportion to anything ever visualised in this country, or, for that matter, in the United States. Honda alone, the largest company, has an establishment of 400 technicians engaged in styling new manufacturing techniques, new designs, new developments and new approaches. The whole of the technical and scientific force of Japan, which enabled them, without help, to put up such a considerable show in the last war, and a whole new generation of scientists, seem to have flocked to the motorcycle, motor car and electronic industries, and, unlike our own country, there is an enormous pool of well-trained brains to be had at nominal cost.

Wages, of course, are, by our standards, very low. The Yamaha Company, for instance, which is an old-established, musical instrument firm making pianos, harmonicas, etc., were not in the motorcycle business five years ago and their progress is dramatic in that they have a well-equipped factory twice the size of Triumph with a first-class product, and are currently making over 80,000 units a year. They pay £10 a month, reckoning 1000 yens to the £. Honda pay rather more and would average £15 per month, but it should be borne in mind that the system is different from ours. The work-people live in company-owned houses and pay less than a dollar a month rent and buy food at cost.

On the other hand, there is no question in Japan of laying off work-people, When an industrial enterprise employs people, it keeps them on the payroll through good times and bad, but the disadvantage of this system for them will be apparent only in bad times. There are still two to three million unemployed in Japan, notwithstanding its very busy economy. The newspapers claim this figure but the Government only admits to 300,000, but all appear to be prosperous in the outlying cities through which I passed on the way to Hamamatsu, which is one of the big motorcycle centres some 250 miles from Tokyo. I noticed particularly people waiting on the railway stations as I passed through; they were well dressed in Western style and seemed to be more prosperous than the people of many provincial towns in this country today.

I visited Yamaha, Suzuki and Honda factories, was well received and shown anything I cared to see. My sponsor, the Triumph distributor Messrs. Mikuni Shoko, is a Japanese company with a hook-up with Amal in this country, and apart from the relatively unimportant side of the business of handling imported motorcycles, they are large carburetter manufacturers supplying carburetters to the motorcycle and motor car industry in quite a big way.

They assigned their Import Manager to look after me during my journey but, unfortunately, he spoke only very limited English and I, therefore, was at some disadvantage in going into real technicalities or any subtleties of polite conversation. On the other hand, I felt I had the advantage of better reception by being in the company of a Japanese.

During the time I was away from Tokyo on these visits, I stayed in Japanese style hotels, which, though elegant and interesting, are by Western standards not the most comfortable in the world.

Yamaha: At their factory I saw a shop floor scene not very dissimilar from Triumph but with far more movement, particularly of components, a certain amount of mechanisation and a high tempo of good quality and apparent enthusiastic effort. Machine tool equipment was first-class and new.

In common with the other two factories I visited, 85% of the machine tools were Japanese made and the odd 15% were split between German, Swiss and American. The only piece of British equipment I saw was Sykes gear cutters, of which they spoke very highly.

Suzuki: The Suzuki factory, reputed to be the second largest to Honda, was previously engaged entirely in the manufacture of weaving machines, looms, etc., and went into the motorcycle business after the war with great profit. The principals had visited Triumph in this country which put me on rather a better basis for discussion. They were courteous and willing to discuss any aspect of their business with me. Their factory was even more mechanised than that of Yamaha and very self-contained, making its own castings, forgings, presswork, etc.

Honda: The last factory I visited was Honda. This particular factory was only three years old, up to the minute, being windowless, air-conditioned and designed specifically for the purpose of efficient motorcycle production. The Hamamatsu factory is one of two, the other being outside Tokyo, with a third in the process of being built and equipped at a cost of £6,000,000. The chief of operations was Mr (Benjiro) Honda, the younger brother of the President, who was very pleasant, frank and courteous. Mr Honda expressed great respect and admiration for the British Motor Cycle Industry and said that, though some of our products were old fashioned, he was not deceived by this as he thought the "C" range of Triumph (350cc/500cc) was equally up-to-date in comparison with anything being made in Japan. This is our latest range, introduced three years ago.

The Honda factory was everything that one could desire as an up-to-date manufacturing conception for motorcycles, and although nothing I saw was beyond our conception and ability to bring about in our own factories, it should be borne in mind that we have not now, nor ever have had, the quantities of any one product that would justify these highly desirable methods being used. They had a large number of single-purpose, specially designed machine tools which reduce labour for any large component, such as a crankcase, to an absolute minimum. All components, except the very small ones such as gear shafts and gears more conveniently transported in trays, were moving on conveyors throughout the factory. Every section for the small, medium and large motorcycles being made was geared to a time cycle, all assembly being on moving bands. Paint and chrome were of high quality from automatic plants. The chrome, though not as good as we produce in our own industry, was apparently entirely without polishing, being coppered nickel and bright chrome on all large components, with quite tolerable finish. The surface finishes of machined parts and standards of accuracy were, I should think, better than our best work and most complex and elaborate equipment was used throughout on gauging, all developed in Japan.

Although wages are, roughly speaking, a quarter of ours, they were nevertheless extremely economical in the use of manpower. Apart from assembly, I saw very little handwork except for the odd frazing of castings to ensure they fitted spotting fixtures without trouble.

Engine and machine assembly was moving and all the components seemed to go together consistently and without difficulty, as indeed they had to in order to maintain the timed stations.

Testing in all factories was done on rollers geared to brakes which gave horsepower readings while the machine was stationary. A final run round the test track within the factory seemed to suffice to ensure roadworthy standards.

Packing of various kinds was very slick, with numerous tracks coming and going to take away the merchandise.

The whole was a dynamic experience and a somewhat frightening spectacle.

The capital investment in these factories is, of course, enormous and they are all self-contained, making their own iron and aluminium castings, forgings and, particularly, pressings. Their toolroom was very large, well manned and extremely busy, with elaborate and brand new press equipment.

There was no colour variation as far as I could see other than chrome and black, but one or two specials were being made for racing purposes in batches of 20.

They told me that they could see a reduction in the rate of acceleration of output for the home market and that they were, therefore, concentrating more on world markets.

When I returned to Tokyo finally, a meeting was arranged by Messrs Mikuni Shoko, my hosts, as it were, for the trade, press and one or two university professors to meet me, and I was asked if I would submit myself to questioning after giving a short address on the purpose of my visit. I naturally agreed to this and a highly placed official of practically every principal company attended, together with the national and technical press and one or two scientists, including the President of Tokyo University. They paid me, as a representative of the British Motor Cycle Industry, considerable respect and were kind enough to say that they acknowledged the great work that the UK had done during the last 50 years in the motorcycle Industry. They felt, however, that Japan afforded a unique opportunity for the motorcycle industry by virtue of the substantial prosperity now being enjoyed and the greater interest of young Japan in mechanical transportation.

It should be borne in mind that the motor car industry in Japan also is enjoying a great boom and, to give some idea of their approach, an Austin car is being made under licence in one factory and selling only 500 a month, but they have duplicated the complete automation of Longbridge even for these quantities, and I am bound to say the product is even better finished than that of this country. It should be clearly remembered that Japan is no longer copying Western products, apart from odd examples such as this. They are designing from first principles on the most scientific, logical and commercial basis and the whole gamut of so-called Western manufactured products in the automotive, electronic and domestic appliance fields is being pursued on an entirely new basis, for which Germany has long been famous, is far surpassed in both quality and price by Japan, and in radio it is well known that they lead the world for price and quality in the transistor field, tape recorders, etc.

It may appear in this report that I am inclined to emphasise and exaggerate but I am purposely avoiding any form of exaggeration. It is essential that our industry in general and the BSA Group in particular should know the facts and what we are up against in the retention of our export markets. Even our home market for motorcycles will be assailed and although personally I do not think the Japanese motorcycle Industry will eclipse the traditional style of machine that the British motorcyclist wants and buys, they are bound to make some impact on our home market by virtue of high quality and low prices.

Having familiarised myself with the situation as it exists, I have been giving considerable thought to what we might do, and a course to combat this situation, and I must confess that these answers are going to be hard to find. In the first place it should be borne in mind that the motorcycle industry has been big business in Britain. Its safety has to some extent been that it has never attracted big capital and big enterprise. We have never made to date, even in these relatively boom times, 1000 units of any one product in a week consistently, whereas many factories in Japan are currently doing this in a day. It is true that many of the large quantities in Japan are small motorcycles, but even the larger ones (250cc/300cc) are being turned out in quantities in excess of any equivalent model in this country and, therefore, it has never been feasible - and certainly not economically sound - to lay down manufacturing lines fully mechanised with complete single-purpose machine tool equipment of special design at every stage of manufacture.

Experience has shown that the British Motor Cycle Industry and our many export markets abroad want a range of motorcycles from each manufacturer. It may well be that we haven't had the courage to reduce our variety of manufacture so as to produce large requirements for any given model, but previous attempts in this direction have always led to a reduction in overall turnover. Therefore, with Japan, they have the manifold advantages of a large requirement for a single, developed article, and they have had the great courage to invest enormous sums of money with full confidence that their propducts will be purchased in sufficient quantities at home and abroad, and currently they are in full flight and are receiving snowball advantages from their enterprise.

I pointed out to the meeting that as Britain has opened up its doors to Japanese motorcycles, it is only fair that Japanese trade should should agree to similar measures for British machines, and in any case, as far as I could see, they had nothing to lose. Although this remark registered and there is some talk of liberalising British imports of motorcycles next spring, it is not thought by our importers that this will happen and, even if it did, in my judgment it would not result in the British Motor Cycle Industry participating significantly in the large Japanese home market owing to the very large price disparity. My thoughts are entirely directed towards the preservation of our existing export markets on which our companies depend to the tune of 30% to 40% of our output (Triumph 49%, BSA 35%, Ariel insignificant abroad as yet).

One of the most practical thoughts in this present situation would be to visualise opening up our own motorcycle operations in Japan, thereby obtaining the full advantages of their plentiful and cheap labour and having available a window for observation on the Japanese industry. We might even, should we consider this, obtain technical help which is not to be despised, particularly in regard to our future tooling and development.

By and large, the menace of Japanese motorcycles to our own export markets is that they are producing extremely refined and well finished motorcycles up to 300cc at prices which reach the public at something like 20% less. The machines themselves are more comprehensive than our own with regard to equipment, such as electric starting, traffic indicators, etc., are probably better made but will not appeal to the sporting rider to anything like the same extent as our own. However, they will make very big inroads into the requirement for motorcycles for transportation.

Our scooters, due to the poor roads in Japan, which follow a pattern of being a relatively good surface for reasonable distances, terminated by a series of very bad pot holes, the smaller wheeled scooter is not gaining favour. There are, however, a number of quite good scooters made but I do not regard this aspect as being too serious at this stage.

This report, reproduced exactly in Edward's own words, was accompanied originally by the two appendices mentioned earlier. Unfortunately, they are no longer available to be reproduced in a similar manner.

Met at the airport on his return by his chauffeur, Frank Griffiths, Edward was politely asked how he had got on: he summed up his impressions very succinctly. The visit had left no doubt in his mind that, unless the British motorcycle industry abandoned its head-in-the-sand attitude, there would be no-one making motorcycles in Britain in twenty five years' time.

Edward's relationship with Frank Griffiths was strangely ambivalent, perhaps because it extended way back to the time of his first marriage to Marion. During the desolate years after her untimely death, Frank often went far beyond his role of chauffeur, acting as Edward's cook and valet, or waiting at table and serving drinks when Edward had dinner or cocktail parties. In the summer months, Edward would take Frank to his yacht moored in Hampshire, and in the winter months Frank would accompany him to shooting parties, where he acted as his gun loader. When they had time to spare in London they would often visit a cinema together to see a Western, one of Edward's indulgences, and stop for fish and chips on their way home in the evening.

Edward preferred to sit beside his chauffeur whenever possible, rather than in the rear seat, as he liked to have "a clear view of the road ahead". Every journey was regarded as a challenge and began with him asking Frank if he could improve on their previous best recorded time. This amounted to an invitation to take risks whilst

Edward had a somewhat ambivalent relationship with his chauffeur, Frank Griffiths. Edward would sack him frequently, or Frank would hand in his notice, yet they had some kind of understanding that endured. They were travelling on the S.S. United States, on an early visit to America, when Edward took this photograph of Frank.

The Charane, *built in Munden, in the Netherlands, was owned by Edward from 1962-1971 when he was living at Abbotsvale. It was on the* Charane *that Edward entertained members of The Motor Cycle Industry's Executive Club on their ninth run on 14th/16th April 1967, when they stayed overnight at the New Forest Hotel, Ower, Southampton.*

overtaking in traffic against the flow in the opposite direction. When this 'back seat driving' began to irritate Frank he used to say "Would you like to take over Sir?" which usually resulted in a long silence. Needless to say, when Edward had a Daimler SP 250, travelling times reduced dramatically. His best personal driving speed was 131mph and it irritated him that Frank subsequently bettered it by 2mph!

Edward never lost his love of the sea and, for many years, had owned The Nomad II, which had provided him with a much needed means of relaxation. In 1960, he had commissioned from a boat builder in Holland a ketch built to his specification. 45 feet long, it had two sleeping cabins and a saloon and was built in the old-fashioned way with teak beams, a teak deck and brass fixtures. It replaced The Nomad II and was named Charane, a combination of the Christian names of his two daughters. Moored at Beaulieu for a while (but never at Cowes as others have suggested), it was used for several cruises around the Mediterranean, which meant sailing through the night. Edward considered himself a very experienced navigator, a fact confirmed by his chauffeur, Frank Griffiths, although there was a very embarrassing incident when the ketch ran aground in front of his own yacht club, the Royal Motor Yacht Club at Poole, the ultimate humiliation! Edward's family usually accompanied him, the womenfolk being mainly interested in visiting various ports along the way. He was never very happy about this as he was always impatient and anxious to be on the sea, heading for their ultimate destination.

Frank Griffiths, who sometimes fulfilled the dual roles of chief engineer and cook on board, was present when members of Triumph's senior management were invited aboard for what amounted to a 'work's outing'. There was also an occasion during April 1967, after Edward's official retirement, when he took members of the Motor Cycle Industries Executive Club to sea during their weekend at the New Forest Hotel in Ower, Southampton. Edward and Jack Wickes were founder members of the Club; at the time of writing, John Nelson is its President.

Inevitably, there were many clashes of temperament between Edward and his chauffeur which would end by either Edward sacking Frank or Frank handing in his notice! Neither took the other seriously, though, and their relationship continued unchanged until the early sixties.

When Edward returned to Coventry after his visit to Japan, he gave Bernal Osborne of *Motor Cycling* an exclusive interview, which was summarised in the 6th October issue. He also made a broadcast about his visit for BBC Radio Birmingham.

It was, of course, correct that at this time Honda was concentrating on small capacity models, and had already had a major impact on the commuter market with a well co-ordinated advertising campaign in the UK. By booking space in publications other than motorcycle

The Nomad II, *built in Cowes during 1926, was owned by Edward from 1950-1952 whilst he lived at Gibbet Hill Road. It was moored at Hamble, on the Solent.*

magazines, such as *The Lady* and horse riding publications under the theme "You meet the nicest people on a Honda", Honda acquired a foothold in areas where a motorcycle as a means of transportation may not have been considered seriously before. Previous advertising campaigns by British motorcycle manufacturers appeared almost

Edward and Jack Wickes were both founder members of The Motor Cycle Industry's Executive Club, more usually known as "The Club". In 1971, their seventeeth run took them to the Antrobus Arms Hotel, Amesbury, for the weekend. In this line-up Jack Wickes is second from the left on a Triumph fitted with a fairing. Also to be seen in the photograph are Bob Manns, Bertie Goodman, Ted Wassell, Arthur Bourne, Ken Whistance, Doug Hele and Mike Riley. "The Club" is still very much alive and active today. (Vida Wickes)

exclusively in motorcycle magazines, and achieved little more than preaching to the converted.

Later, in 1965, Honda entered the over 250cc market with the introduction of the so-called 'black bomber', the CB450 445cc parallel twin with its unusual torsion bar valve springs. Although, ironically, it was one of Honda's least successful models in the USA, Honda had done exactly what the British motorcycle industry had feared most. Three years later, Honda literally floored British manufacturers when the 736cc CB750 sohc four cylinder model made its debut, based loosely on Mike Hailwood's 1967 road racer. Nothing like it had been seen before; previously the only in-line fours, with the engine mounted transversely in the frame, were the MV and Gilera racers seen on the race track. Rumour has it that when news of the impending launch of this model in Japan reached Meriden it was greeted by stunned disbelief!

The advantage of hindsight brings to light at least one important factor. When it was known how the lower end of the UK market was about to be swamped by Japanese lightweights, the British motorcycle industry firmly believed that it would still have the upper hand when it came to selling larger capacity and more traditional models. Even Edward tended a little toward this view in his report, because he believed the Japanese lightweight model would attract more newcomers to motorcycling. What had been overlooked was brand loyalty. If someone buys a small capacity model on which to learn, and its gives cheap, economical, trouble-free service, the tendency is to buy another machine from the same manufacturer when trading up. This proved to be a key factor in the case of younger people who had little or no experience with British-made models, which increased as time progressed.

Dealers who dealt exclusively in Japanese motorcycles also scored in having high-profile salerooms, light and airy, with carpet on the floor and salesmen keen to close a sale rather than sit sprawled in an office drinking tea and studying horse racing form. Far too many of their British counterparts operated from rundown premises badly in need of a coat of paint, and with a workshop that was squalid beyond belief, confirming the view that motorcycles were dirty, messy vehicles that required frequent attention to keep them going. A dealer's reputation alone was not good enough, especially to newcomers who knew little or nothing about motorcycles. Dirty fingernails and grimy hands were still the order of the day, and old-established dealers resented young men in smart suits telling them how to run their businesses which, in all probability, their fathers had originally established.

Triumph's 1961 model programme concentrated mostly on the Tiger Cub range, with the addition of a third model, the high-performance T20S/L, which produced 14.5bhp at 6500rpm and had been based on competition experience gained during the 1960 season. Its engine had a 9:1 compression ratio, sports cams and close ratio gears, which suggested possible use abroad as a scrambler, although it could be used on the road equally well.

Whilst the other two models had mostly detail modifications, the standard T20 model had already been given a deep skirted rear fairing finished in silver sheen, and an increase of 60% in oil pump capacity, its drive to the distributor being better lubricated. The T20 was finished in silver and black, the petrol tank having a black top panel extending to the centre weld which was masked by a chrome steel strip. All Tiger Cub models now had a folding kickstarter.

The T20T trials model was similar to the previous year's model except for the dipswitch, which had carry-over contacts to prevent the headlamp bulb blacking out during a change from dip to main beam, due to the direct lighting. A tapping from one of the generator coils raised the output to the tail-cum-stop lamp, needed when riding at low speeds.

The 350cc and 500cc "C" unit-construction models incorporated further frame modifications to improve steering geometry and road-holding, and 'floating' brake shoes to more effectively centralise them and improve braking performance. The models fitted with the energy transfer ignition and lighting system had modified coil, condenser and alternator parts to ensure ignition timing setting was no longer as critical. A drop in size of one tooth of the gearbox sprocket

To match the semi-enclosure of the unit-construction twins, the Tiger Cub by now had a deep skirted rear fairing through which the front of the oil tank projected, and a two-tone coloured petrol tank. This did not apply to the Sports Cub, though, which dispensed with the rear fairing and had a rubber gaitered front fork.

improved flexibility of Triumph's 500cc models without any loss in performance.

The Tiger 100A's latest finish was in two-tone black and silver, and the 5TA Speed Twin continued with its brighter red colour, introduced the previous year in place of the traditional amaranth red. For the high performance models, a new cylinder head had been introduced, taking advantage of the lessons learnt in endurance events. Stiffened to withstand increased heat and stress factors, it also incorporated sound-damping pillars. All the "B" range models had their gearbox layshafts carried in Torrington needle bearings at both ends, and the gearbox adjuster was strengthened to prevent 'creep' by having dual adjusters.

A major improvement to the 6T Thunderbird was a new alloy cylinder head, which increased the compression ratio to 7.5:1. This, in conjunction with a modified camshaft, gave the engine a useful boost. The adoption of an 8 inch diameter front brake preserved the safety factor. This model also featured a new black and silver finish.

The Tiger 110 also had the compression ratio increased from 8 to 8.5:1, and new camshafts. The engine sprocket had been reduced in size from 23t to 22t, without any loss in performance, to improve flexibility. The T110's colour was changed to kingfisher blue and silver.

A new cylinder head was fitted to the T120 Bonneville, now redesignated the T120R to distinguish it from the American scrambler versions. It was given twin Amal Monobloc carburetters to replace the single remote float chamber arrangement used previously. Whilst the separate magneto ignition and the Lucas RM15 alternator were retained, the ignition setting was no longer manually controlled, an automatic advance and retard unit employed instead. Petrol tank capacity was reduced from four to three gallons, and the colour scheme changed to sky blue and silver. All 1961 models were fitted with an easy roll-on centre stand.

Roy Peplow and his 199cc Tiger Cub hit form again during October, demonstrating that he was still very much in the picture. He won the John Douglas Trial with a loss of only six marks, over a course that was heavily waterlogged in parts, and covered 57.5 miles around Winford, in North Somerset. Even Sammy Miller was brought to a standstill in one section and Gordon Jackson relegated to a First Class Award.

The 1960 Motor Cycle Show held at Earls Court during mid-November commemorated the Golden Jubilee of the British Industries Association, which was founded in 1910. To make the most of the occasion, exhibits came from twelve countries, including Britain, resulting in a total of fifty three stands featuring either motorcycles or scooters. Amongst them was Honda, the first Japanese company to take display space at this prestigious show and underline the validity of Edward's warnings about the impending threat to the UK motorcycle market. Honda had four models on display: two 124cc twins, the Benley and the Benley Sports, and two 247cc twins, the Dream and the Dream Sports. It did not escape notice that the standard Dream model had an electric starter, which some British manufacturers suggested was 'unmanly', and built-in trafficators. Bearing in mind their specification, the machines were realistically priced. Honda was already making a significant impact in road racing, and it seemed its machines would undoubtedly appeal to the rider who required 'something different', allied with good performance.

Early December saw four new appointments within the Triumph factory at Meriden. J.D. Brock became Export Marketing Manager, W.L. Robertson took over the role of Export Department Manager, and Neale Shilton's job was further expanded so that he became General Sales Manager with the added responsibility of overseas sales. John Nelson, who had joined Triumph in 1950, was promoted to Service Manager. He had worked his way through the works and Design and Development Departments to take on responsibility for the Development Department from 1953 to 1957

H and L Motors of Cainscross, Stroud, well known as a Triumph agent in the west, organised a 24 hour test during a weekend in December. Three standard Triumph solos, a 498cc T110, a 6T 649cc Thunderbird and a 348cc 3TA, ridden by a team of nine riders, covered almost 3000 miles from noon on Saturday to noon the next day. It was a non-stop run, following a course between Stroud and Bristol. No incidents were reported and the only machine to need attention was the 3TA, which had to have its rear chain adjusted. The 3TA recorded the best fuel consumption figure, a very commendable 89mpg.

Just before Christmas, Alec St. John Masters, who had joined Triumph in 1937, retired as Service Manager, handing over to his newly-appointed replacement, John Nelson. A dinner was held in Alec's honour at which Edward presented him with a camera. He will be remembered for the three books he wrote for C. Arthur Pearson Limited, *Triumph*, one of a series in the Motor Cycle Maintenance and Repair range, *Motor Cycling Holidays Abroad* and *Motor Cycle Sport*. Sadly, his retirement was short-lived: within a couple of months his obituary appeared in the motorcycling press; he was 64 years old and had been in poor health.

Triumph began the New Year well when John Giles won the Three Musketeers Trial on his 199cc Tiger Cub, with a loss of 9 marks. He was also a member of the Sunbeam MCC team that won the Club Team Award, thanks to help from Gordon Jackson (350cc AJS) and Peter Stirland. (350cc Royal Enfield). S.J. Milton on a 202cc J.A.H. Triumph won the 250cc Class Award.

The other event that dominated the New Year period was the

The compactness of the Triumph unit-construction engine prompted the building of a number of hybrid machines like this Grumph, which used a Greeves frame and cycle parts. (Author photo)

MCC's annual Exeter Trial, this year the occasion of its Jubilee. *Motor Cycling's* staffman, John Griffiths, fancied taking part, having ridden previously in the 40th Anniversary Trial. He phoned Neale Shilton to see if he could beg the loan of a Triumph sidecar outfit, and asked if Neale would like to accompany him as passenger. A dyed-in-the-wool motorcyclist, Neale accepted with alacrity, and offered one of the latest T110 models hitched to a Wessex single seat sidecar and fitted with trials tyres and Trophy Twin gear ratios.

The pair set off from the Triumph factory at Meriden in darkness to make their way to Kenilworth, one of the three starting points. Edward and Shirley made a point of being there to send them on their way, Edward uttering the words "Look after Shilton and bring him back safely!" He had ridden in the Exeter Trial himself in the past and was aware of its severity at this time of the year.

It was not a happy journey, with icy roads encountered in the dark, offset to some extent by the third wheel. After Exeter they encountered fog, too, but there was worse to come. The test hills at Fingle Bridge, Simms and Stretes Hill defeated them, yet, despite great adversity that included shedding the final drive chain, Shilton and Griffiths continued to the finish at Weymouth, having covered 295 miles. All chances of an award had gone and, of all those that started, only 20 qualified for a First Class Award.

Before the end of January came the welcome news that the 649cc TR6 Trophy Twin was back in production again. It had been temporarily withdrawn from the Triumph catalogue as the entire production had been booked for export, but pressure had been brought to bear by dealers and customers at the 1960 Motor Cycle Show.

Introduction of Triumph's unit-construction models, such as the 3TA and the 5TA, led to the origination of yet another popular competition special. With a little bit of ingenuity, the engine unit could be shoehorned into a 246cc Greeves scrambler rolling chassis, to produce a 490cc twin that weighed about 280lbs and made a quite potent scrambler. Home produced, the so-called Tri-Greeves weighed only 50lbs or so more than the original Greeves.

Neale Shilton was in the news again during early February after attending a motorcycle show in New York as part of a sales drive. Whilst there, he was able to confirm that Johnson Motors, Triumph's West Coast distributor, intended to sponsor a further attempt to better the World Motorcycle Speed Record, with Johnny Allen using two different models enclosed within a shell. The machines were again being prepared by Stormy Mangham, with a target speed of 410mph!

A private owner, Norman Eyre, won the 1961 Victory Trial riding a 199cc Tiger Cub. More to the point, he even beat the all-conquering Sammy Miller (497cc Ariel) in the tie eliminator, losing only four marks. Both riders had beaten John Draper's performance the previous year and, strangely enough, there was also a dead heat in the sidecar class between Ken Kendall (497cc Ariel) and A.J. Wakefield (498cc Triumph), Wakefield emerging the runner-up and presented with the Cranford Bowl. Also very much in the picture was Roy Peplow, who took the 250cc Class Award with his 199cc Tiger Cub.

Ken Heanes again won the 100 Mile Long Distance Scramble after completing 66 energy-sapping laps at Pirbright during late April. He had to battle all the way against John Giles, riding a similar 498cc Triumph. John had led for three quarters of the race but, just when it began to look as though he had the race in the bag, his throttle stuck open. The time taken to free it let Ken Heanes through and there was no catching him after that. Both had been riding for over three and a half hours.

A road test of the new 199cc T20S/L Tiger Cub was published in *Motor Cycling's* 27th April issue, leaving no doubt about its just under 80mph maximum speed, 12mph more than that of the standard T20 model. Apart from a high lift camshaft and a 9:1 compression ratio, an Amal 376/222 carburetter had been fitted in place of the standard Zenith instrument, with a 140 main jet. As may have been expected, the exhaust note was somewhat strident when it was ridden hard, although the silencer did its best to muffle the noise. The headlamp shell and switchgear was similar to that used on the ISDT models, and the front fork a specially shortened version of that used on the unit-construction twins, with two-way damping. Handling was described as firm, but good. For £165.0s.11d. it seemed to offer very good value for money.

After three years as Managing Director of Norton Motors and its subsidiary companies, Bert Hopwood had finally succumbed to Edward's advances. The latter confirmed in a statement that Bert would be appointed a director and General Manager of Triumph Engineering with effect from 27th May. He had been associated with the British motorcycle industry for the past 30 years and returned to Triumph with a vast amount of expertise. Later, when he advertised for a Development Engineer during mid-1962, the vacancy was filled by Doug Hele, who left when Associated Motor Cycles closed down Norton's factory in Bracebridge Street, Birmingham. With the transfer of Norton's entire operation to premises in Plumstead, Doug was unwilling to relocate in London. His partnership with Bert had begun when Doug joined Norton from Douglas (Sales and Service) Limited. As Bert said later in his book *Whatever Happened to the British Motorcycle Industry?*, "I was to enjoy a unique friendship, unequalled in my business life".

As Doug's appointment included responsibility for Triumph's racing activities, Frank Baker, in charge of the Experimental Shop, announced his intention to resign. Too valuable a man to lose, he was persuaded to stay on and take charge of Production Development. This was the year when Triumph won, for the first time, the big race in the Daytona 200, a prestigious American success for which Triumph had striven for so long. The winner was Don Burnett, riding a T100/SR and sponsored by the Triumph Corporation of America.

Triumph's 199cc Tiger Cubs figured well in the results of the 1961 Scottish Six Days Trial when Roy Peplow won the 200cc Class Award with a loss of 17 marks. Finishing third best, he was awarded the Nelson Challenge Trophy. The Jimmy Beck Memorial Cup went to Ray Sayer on another 199cc Tiger Cub, the best non-Scottish rider not winning another award. He too had lost a total of 17 marks.

Charles Grandfield who, amongst much else, had carried out the extensive testing of the 3TA unit-construction model, was another Triumph employee to retire, in May. At his farewell party Edward presented him with a set of tankards.

Ken Heanes won the Welsh Three-Day Trial at the end of May, a tough, 624 mile, international-style event based on Llandrindod Wells. He snatched the Welsh Dragon Trophy from under the very nose of John Harris by the merest fraction of a point in the bonus special marks section. Ken's mount was a 649cc TR6 Trophy Twin and John's a 246cc BSA.

In the same issue of *Motor Cycling* that carried this report was a road test of the latest 649cc T120R Triumph Bonneville 120, prefaced by the heading "Outstanding acceleration and high speed - without temperament". The maximum speed recorded on the MIRA Test Ground at Nuneaton was 108.2mph, with the rider laying prone. The

engine was reputably safe up to 7500rpm and it was alleged that although vibration was noticeable at all times, it was never excessive. As may be expected, the exhaust note generated by the small bore exhaust pipes was quite noticeable when the engine was used to full potential. Starting was easy but, when it came to high speed handling, it was classified as 'interesting' by the tester (Bruce Main-Smith)! The lights were below par on the test machine and the horn almost inaudible to the rider, though, hopefully, not to pedestrians and other road users.

After five years in office as Chairman of the Birmingham Small Arms Co. Ltd., Jack Sangster resigned and handed the reins to Eric Turner, Chairman elect. Sangster relinquished this post at his own request but remained a director of the company. His departure as Chairman coincided with BSA's centenary and also with the retirement of Tom Davis, Ariel's popular Sales Director. Edward presented Tom with a magnificent sunburst clock to mark his departure after 56 years of loyal service with the company.

If anyone had the slightest doubt about the validity of Edward's

John Holder (seated) and Tony Godfrey won the Thruxton 500 Mile Race held on July 8th 1961, on a 649cc T120R Triumph Bonneville. With them are Alec Bennett (the winner of five TTs, who now ran a motorcycle business in Southampton) and Harry Louis, editor of Motor Cycle. *(B.R. Nicholls)*

comments about the tremendous advances in technology being made by the Japanese, the results of the 1961 TT speak for themselves. Honda swept the board in the 125cc Lightweight Race by taking the first five places and setting a record lap and race record. Admittedly, Honda had signed a number of top level riders of international status, headed by Mike Hailwood, but without the machinery to match the rider's skills, nothing as sensational as this could have been achieved. To prove it was no fluke result, Honda made a repeat performance in the 250cc Lightweight TT where its riders again filled the first five places and set another lap and race record. Interestingly, entries had now been made by two of Honda's competitors, Suzuki and Yamaha, who had some very fast two-strokes.

At the July 500 Mile Endurance Race held at Thruxton, Triumph again carried off the spoils of victory when Tony Godfrey and John Holder shared a 649cc T120R Bonneville to win the overall classification. Run over 220 laps of this racing circuit close to Andover, Hampshire, the two Triumph riders managed to hold off a strong challenge from a 497cc Norton Dominator 88SS. Ominously, the 250cc class was won by a Honda CB72 that had covered 209 laps.

Ray Sayer won the Allan Jefferies Trophy Trial during the same month, riding a 199cc Tiger Cub. In what was alleged to be the closest ever finish in this trial, only one mark separated the first three riders. Elsewhere, John Giles was putting up an equally good performance on his 498cc Trophy Twin to snatch the 500cc Southern Experts Grand National from Matchless-mounted Dave Curtis. He won the George Holdsworth Trophy.

The Turners usually spent their summer holidays abroad, but this year a change of plan saw them visiting Cornwall instead. Shirley was now expecting a third member of the family and, before the end of the year, a son was born; Edward Amstel William Turner. The Turners had a habit of deriving Christian names from something or someone with whom they had associations. Amstel came from the Amstel Hotel in Amsterdam, and William was the Christian name of Edward's father, his eldest brother, and also Shirley's brother! They also always looked for at least one non-British god-parent or, in this case, both: Gisella, a West German au pair who had seen Shirley through her pregnancy, and 'Buster' Reinhardt, the agent for Triumph motorcycles in Denmark.

A formal family photograph, taken during 1961, with Edward Junior, the latest addition to the family.

The honour of putting a race-kitted 649cc Triumph T120R Bonneville through its paces fell to Bruce Main-Smith, a member of *Motor Cycling*'s staff at that time. He showed it was the fastest production roadster by clocking a speed of 116.5mph through the electronically-timed speed trap at MIRA's test track, near Nuneaton. To use his own words, the machine was "absolutely tireless as lap after consecutive lap was put in. All were at full throttle except three, when the throttle had to be eased whilst passing other vehicles". Peak revs of 7500rpm were used, apparently without any distressing vibration. Alternative equipment was now available, such as rearset footrests etc., for those who wished to use them for high speed work.

The British motorcycle industry seemed determined still to have Britain represented in the International Six Days Trial, no doubt influenced by the performance in the Welsh Three Day Trial, and because the 1961 event was to be based on home territory in Llandrindod Wells. Although smaller capacity two-strokes were now being included in the teams, Eric Chilton was down to ride a 649cc Triumph twin and John Giles and Ken Heanes 498cc models. All three were included in the Trophy Team. In the Vase A Team Roy Peplow forsook his 199cc Tiger Cub to ride a 498cc twin. Meanwhile, he chalked up yet another victory on his Tiger Cub, to win the Mitchell Trial after forfeiting only one mark.

If hopes ran high for the British teams in the International Six Days Trial they were soon dashed as the results subsequently showed. John Giles put up an immaculate performance to win a Gold medal without any loss of marks and also collected maximum bonus points. Sadly, he had to ease off when his team-mates encountered problems which put the Trophy Team out of contention. Ken Heanes had done equally well during the first three days, until one of the constant mesh pinions in his gearbox shed a tooth during one of the special tests. Eric Chilton had suffered a somewhat similar gearbox problem on the first day when a third gear pinion seized on its shaft. Roy Peplow only just managed to avoid a collision with a car on the first day, although the resultant full-lock slide that followed broke a leg off his machine's centre stand. He collected maximum bonus points at the special test on the fifth day and won a Gold medal without loss of marks. Britain finished 8th and last in the International Trophy competition, and the Silver Vase 'B' Team third.

The Triumph model range for 1962 brought about some changes in model specifications and a new T100S/S 490cc unit-construction version of the Tiger 100. In effect, a 'sports' variant, it owed some allegiance to the competition models ridden by Gordon Blakeway, John Giles and Roy Peplow, distinguishing features being an abbreviated 'bikini' rear fairing and a separate detachable competition-type headlamp with plug-in electrical connections. With a compression ratio of 9:1, sports camshafts and a 1 inch bore carburetter, the T100S/S boasted a power output of 34bhp and was regarded as a companion model to the T120 Bonneville.

An amalgamation between the T110 and TR6 models had resulted in the TR6S/S, a designation coined and catalogued by the Sales and Publicity Departments which did not appear in either the engine or frame numbers. There were also TR6R and TR6C models, their model code relating to road and competition/off-road models respectively. It marked the beginning of Meriden's acknowledgement of the demands for alternative specifications for East and West Coast variations of the same models for the US market. In the Tiger Cub range, the recently introduced 199cc T20S/S model replaced the older T20SL and T20T Tiger Cub models, to leave the only other alternative, the standard T20 model. These changes reduced the range of models available for 1962 to a total of eight.

The 'slickshift' gearbox, which had failed to make much of an impression, was now discontinued and a quick release clutch cable anchorage was fitted to the 348cc and 490cc twins, thanks to lessons learnt during the International Six Days Trial. There were also many other detail modifications made throughout the entire range, most of only a small but beneficial nature. The 3TA, 5TA and TR6 Thunderbird models continued much as before, as did the two scooters (and their BSA counterparts). Optional extras were now available for the latter in the form of a spare wheel and a rear luggage carrier. Sales remained at a low level.

The 649cc T120 Bonneville, Triumph's flagship, remained the top of the range model and, as mentioned earlier, could now be obtained with optional high speed 'extras' if high speed motorcycling was to be the main objective. The passage of time would show that it was one of the more outstanding motorcycles of its era.

Gordon Blakeway adapted well to his 199cc Tiger Cub to win the Travers Trophy Trial in October with a loss of four marks. He was also a member of the team that won the Best One-Make Team Award, in company with Ray Sayer and R.A. Brown.

Motor Cycling's 'man in the Midlands', Bernal Osborne, was again quick off the mark to secure a road test on the new 490cc Triumph Tiger 100S/S, a unit-construction with fitted with a bikini-type rear fairing that gave little hint of its semi-sports performance. Problems with the ignition system had now been overcome successfully. The engine would start easily when the main ignition circuit was switched on, just as readily as it would when an emergency start was necessary. Performance-wise, a maximum speed of 95mph was recorded over a flying lap at the MIRA test track, with the rider lying prone. Fuel consumption averaged out at 82mpg during 500 miles of normal road usage. The new model's most distinctive feature was the absence of the familiar Triumph nacelle at the top of the front fork due to the use of a separate, detachable, competition-type headlamp. It also meant the speedometer had to be bolted to the top yoke of the fork assembly.

John Giles managed to put one over on Sammy Miller (497cc Ariel) in the West of England Trial held at the end of October. He lost 7 marks on his 199cc Tiger Cub, less than half those lost by Sammy, the previous year's winner. A week later, Roy Peplow, riding a similar Tiger Cub, denied Jeff Smith the chance of a hat trick in the Perce Simon Trophy Trial. He had the edge on Jeff's 343cc B40 BSA and won by a two mark margin.

Chapter 13: Heading for retirement

BSA's new unit-construction twins, the 499cc A50 and the 654cc A65, were announced at the beginning of 1962. They were to replace the existing A7 and A10 twins, and were listed initially as 'Star Twins' in accordance with the name already in fashion which related to the company's single cylinder models. Both had been completely redesigned, with development entrusted to Len Crisp who, after 26 years with BSA, reached retirement age at the end of 1961. He had been in charge of BSA's Experimental Department since 1935, and had been involved with most of the company's products during that time.

Edward had little direct involvement in the design of these models even though he was now in charge of BSA's Power Unit Divison. Rather than be accused of bias in favour of Triumph, he asked Don Brown, who was visiting Meriden from Johnson Motors, to appraise the project for him. Edward issued instructions for Don to be driven to Small Heath, where he was received in a chilly atmosphere. There he was shown an A65 and presented with the research and development drawings and the bill of materials. Previous experience as an apprentice tool and die maker, and as an aircraft engine mechanic, left him well qualified to comment as requested. Far from being impressed he had found BSA's latest twin unexciting from a styling point of view, being accustomed to the slim and attractive lines of the Triumph twins. When Edward joined him for dinner that evening, he summed up his impressions by saying that its bulbous appearance and fat crankcase made BSA's new twin look like a pregnant Bantam!

Roy Peplow won a tough Vic Brittain Trial on his 199cc Tiger Cub, beating the runner-up, Scott Ellis, on a similar mount by a margin of three marks. Held in the Clee Hill area of Shropshire, an abundance of water had been the biggest deterrent in some of the sections, especially the Crumpsbrook watercourse, where all but one of the sidecar entries failed. C.J. Davey, also riding a 199cc Tiger Cub, was awarded the Buckingham Cup for being the best Wolverhampton member over forty; he lost 127 marks which illustrates the severity of the course.

Ivor Davies, Triumph' former Publicity Manager, was further promoted during February when he was appointed Advertising Manager for the Motorcycle Division of BSA.

As mentioned earlier, he had joined Triumph on 1st January 1946 as Publicity Manager on his return from India and Burma, after wartime service with the Royal Corps of Signals.

Although the manufacture of the TS2 Tigress 249cc scooter was terminated during October 1963, there had been an attempt to utilise the engine unit in a attractive-looking, lightweight, three-wheel microcar styled by Jack Wickes. Two prototypes were made of the Ladybird; an 'open' version with handlebars by which to steer it, and a 'saloon' which had a roof but no sidescreens and a half steering wheel. The bodywork pressings for both had been made by Carbodies, a BSA subsidiary which made the bodywork for London taxis. It became another abandoned project, allegedly for a number of reasons varying from it being underpowered to indifferent handling at higher speeds.

Early in February 1962, Edward received the only accolade he would ever have from the industry to which he had devoted his entire working life when he was elected President of the British Cycle and Motor Cycle Manufacturers' and Traders' Union. He was invested with

Stirling Moss was a keen scooter enthusiast; he lived in the centre of London and found that a scooter offered an ideal means of getting around the traffic-laden streets. This specially posed Triumph publicity photograph shows him making friends with a mounted policeman's horse whilst crossing Trafalgar Square on his twin cylinder Tigress.

The Ladybird three-wheel car, fitted with a twin cylinder Tigress scooter engine. Initially a promising idea, it got no further than the prototype stage as its engine was noisy exhaust-wise and, more importantly, it proved unstable in the higher speed range.

the President's regalia by Henry Yates, the retiring President and Managing Director of Brooks, best known for its cycle and motorcycle saddles. In his address, Edward inferred that there was likely to be a shortage of motorcycles in the spring as the result of factory cut-backs over recent months. Total production of British motorcycles had fallen from 193,600 in 1960 to 144,200 in 1961, largely due to the increase in competition from overseas manufacturers. He also commented on the alarm being expressed about the mounting number of casualties resulting from accidents that involved motorcyclists. He highlighted recent developments that were helping to reverse this unsatisfactory situation, one of the most promising being the use of high hysteresis, or 'cling' rubber, in the manufacture of motorcycle and scooter tyres. It had helped greatly in improving adhesion on slippery road surfaces, especially in the wet.

Later in the month it was announced that Triumph would be making available a limited number of Tiger Cub competition models, replicas of those used so successfully by the works trials riders. Peter Fraser went to investiagte and meet up with Henry Vale and Roy Peplow. Given an opportunity to ride one of these new models, he found its overall weight had been pared down to 210lbs. Triumph was fortunate in having very dedicated enthusiasts who left no stone unturned in seeking perfection. Henry was in charge of the competition shop and was well known for his meticulous attention to detail. This also applied to his able assistant, Vic Fiddler, who accompanied Henry as his spanner man to competition events overseas as well as in the UK.

Until 1954 Henry had ridden, with reasonable success, as an amateur in trials and scrambles, on either a BSA or a Triumph, and benefited from this first-hand experience. It was he who was responsible for building the ISDT twins that had been so successful in the late forties and early fifties. All the time he worked at Meriden, Henry saw Edward on only three occasions, one of them when he

Scott Ellis, a promising newcomer who won the 1962 Victory Trial, put up the best performance by a rider under 21 years of age with his Tiger Cub. He had further successes in the Cotswold Cups, the Kickham (best solo), the Wye Valley, the Bemrose and the Scottish Six Days trial. His concentration in the 1962 Clayton Trial is clearly evident in this photograph. (B.R. Nicholls)

was running an engine on test late at night. Edward looked in to see what all the noise was about, but when Henry offered to explain he showed little interest! Henry remained in charge of the development shop until Edward retired, and stayed with Triumph until late 1975.

A newcomer to the Tiger Cub trials riders rose to prominence during the 1962 season: Scott Ellis put up the best performance by a rider under 21 years of age in the Victory Trial. He achieved further successes in the Cotswold Cups Trial, the Kickham Trial (best solo), the Wye Valley Trial, the Bemrose Trial and the Scottish Six Days Trial.

The reason behind Edward's patent application of 1959 for an automatic transmission system became apparent during March 1962. It formed the basis of another Triumph scooter, the Tina Automatic. Powered by a 99.75cc, two-stroke engine, it featured trailing link front suspension and pivoted fork rear suspension with a single spring unit. The major selling point was the novelty of its automatic transmission system, which had neither conventional clutch nor change-speed gearbox. Instead, it incorporated a centrifugal clutch which took up the drive as engine speed increased by opening the throttle and then relying on the opening and closing of two pulleys driven by a vee belt to govern the speed of the machine on the road. As the Tina catalogue put it so succinctly "no gears! no clutch! ... it couldn't be easier".

Edward's had decided to use the name 'Fairy' for the new scooter, so, whilst Don Brown was still with him, he took the opportunity to disclose the details. Don knew only too well that the word Fairy would have unfortunate connotations in America, where it was used to describe a homosexual. Acquainted with these facts, Edward

'it
almost
drives
itself !'

TRIUMPH
Tina
AUTOMATIC
MADE IN ENGLAND

As the Tina automatic catalogue clearly says: "It almost drives itself!'

reacted by smashing his fist on the desk; the literature relating to the scooter had already been printed! He called for Jack Wickes and gave him a severe berating for not having researched the proposed name sufficienty.

It begs the question of why Triumph should have decided to market another scooter at this time, bearing in mind that the two Triumph and BSA Sunbeam scooters mentioned earlier had not been successful, putting their continued production in doubt. Britain's scooter 'boom' was now in decline and Lambretta and Vespa retained the dominant positions they had held in this market ever since introduction. One can only assume that the intention was to capitalise

on the use of an automatic transmission system which made the scooters so easy to use. Virtually anyone could ride one after only a few minutes' tuition, without having to familiarise themselves with a clutch or the need to change gear. As early advertising slogans put it "No gears, no clutch, goes at a touch" and "It almost drives itself".

Edward was keen to hold the initial launch at Meriden, to which Triumph dealers would be invited, followed by a buffet luncheon. By the time arrangements had been finalised and a date agreed, he was due to make his annual visit to the USA, so he asked Bert Hopwood to deputise for him. Bert was decidedly unhappy with this prospect, as was Frank Baker, who had been involved with development work.

A nicely posed photograph showing a Tina automatic scooter outside the modern Coventry Cathedral. Part of the ruins of the original Cathedral, destroyed during the blitz of November 1940, can be seen on the left.

inflator, a licence holder, twin pannier bags and a legshield bag. Othe accessory manufacturers soon caught on and Avon was soon able to offer an alternative screen, and what it described as a 'stowaway', a kind of pannier.

An unorthodox feature of the scooter was a switch on the handlebars which had 'start' and 'drive' positions. It was necessary to know how to use the switch correctly as it had to be in the 'start position before the engine was started. It brought a governor into action to prevent engine speed from rising sufficiently to bring the centrifugal clutch into action and engage the drive. Once the rider was properly seated, the switch could be moved to the 'drive' position and the scooter driven away by using the throttle alone. A good idea in practice, but if the switch happened to be in the wrong position, as could so easily happen, the result could be very interesting!

Hughie Hancox recalls a particularly embarrassing occasion when Edward came unstuck in this way. He had decided he would ride the scooter himself after some press release photographs had been taken and, when he had finished posing with it, he prepared to start it. Someone drew his attention to the significance of the handlebar-mounted switch, only to be brushed aside with the words "Yes, I know all about that". Unfortunately, it would seem that the previous rider had left the switch in the 'drive' position and, after kickstarting the engine, Edward took a fistful of throttle! The Tina took off like a scalded cat and veered across the drive, hitting one of the high kerbstones that lined it. The deflection of the front wheel caused the scooter to fall on one side and deposit Edward on the grass in an undignified manner. His smartly tailored suit now bore evidence of his impromptu departure from the scooter seat, and he was in pain. He had broken his ankle and the factory nurse was called. There was a deathly hush amongst those present, which included a few from the works staff who had wandered outside to witness this spectacle for themelves.

After this incident, consideration was given to adding a pair of retractable small diameter wheels, which would be positioned close to the scooter's rear wheel, and similar to the stabilisers fitted to a child's bike. Easy to raise and lower, they were intended to form what was described as an 'easy park' device, but the idea had to be abandoned in view of the many problems inhibiting sales of the Tina. Another idea was a rear brake pedal that could be operated by either foot. Unfortunately, experience showed it tended to confuse a rider, who became unsure of which foot to use when an emergency braking situation arose. It was changed to a single foot pedal on the left.

Other faults with the Tina included a tendency for the drive belt to invert itself on its pulleys and lock the transmission solid when the scooter was ridden at speed. As the level of complaints - mostly from women - steadily rose, they were tactfully handled by Stan Truslove, who dealt with many lady riders. However, remedial action had to be taken and a revised version, the T10 Automatic, replaced the Tina a couple of years later.

Ironically, a problem with that all-important handlebar switch lingered on, becoming an embarrassment during the T10 launch. The switch was now re-located under the seat and pre-tensioned so that the weight of the rider, when seated, would depress it to select the 'drive' position automatically. A slim, attractive, young girl was used to demonstrate at the launch to show how easy it was to ride After she had started the T10, the commentator followed up with words to the effect that she would now drive off to the hairdresser by merely opening the twistgrip throttle. She twisted the throttle in vain as the scooter remained stationary, much to the embarrassment of the commentator. The underseat switch had been tensioned to change to the 'drive' position when depressed by a ten stone weight and she weighed only eight!

In their opinion, they felt it inadvisable to hold a launch at this time because the scooter was still virtually unproven, only a nominal mileage having been covered to date. Fortunately, of the three prototypes available, none as yet had shown any serious faults, so they were pressed into service for launch day. Only later was it found that when the transmission system failed and jammed solid, as it did all too often, the scooter had to be abandoned by the roadside because it had no neutral and could not be pushed. To be recovered it had to be lifted bodily off the road.

Priced at £93. 9s., the Tina was claimed to be capable of 40mph and had shown no vices on the road. It would shortly be available with a number of optional accessories, in the form of either a complete pack for £10. 10s. or for purchase individually. These accessories amounted to a handlebar fairing and mirror, a pannier carrier, a tyre

Under normal circumstances he believed the company's business could continue along present lines without his aid. However, he was also aware that present turnover could be increased by at least £20 million if the company was to take on entirely new business. A combination of the BSA Group's existing facilities and his own expertise had suggested a way in which this objective could be achieved. He had some sympathy for the Chairman's problems and this, coupled with his genuine desire to help BSA, had led to his proposition.

Worldwide - with the exception of Russia and Japan - motor cars were attracting a turnover of in excess of £10,000 million; in 1960, the British car industry's turnover was between £800 and £900 million. It was

Other prototype deratives of the Tina included a three-wheel version with a small luggage-carrying platform behind the rider, rather like a miniature pick-up truck. About a dozen were made and used around the Meriden factory, eventually to be sold off when the factory closed many years later. There was even a four-wheel version, created by joining two Tinas together with bridging metalwork. The right-hand handlebars were retained and linked to the left-hand steering head by a metal rod so that both front wheels would turn in unison. The two separate engine units were retained, also, and control co-ordinated by including a junction box in the throttle cable that operated both carburetters simultaneously. Only one of these was made and use restricted to the factory site for moving parts from one building to another. From all accounts anyone in the way had adequate warning of its impending approach as it sounded just like an angry wasp! In view of the problems experienced with the Tina, this version was known within the works as 'double trouble'.

It had been evident for some while that Edward was keen to break into the automobile industry. Although his appointment to the Daimler board had spanned a period of only four years, he had established his credentials and received acclaim for his design of the revolutionary, high performance SP250, and the 4.2 litre V-8 engine for a limousine. If anything, this increased his desire to continue in this kind of work and, during the first half of 1962, he drafted an outline plan to place before Jack Sangster with which to implement this. Before he did so he sought the advice of his solicitor, J. Whiting Smith of Wragge and Co., in a private and confidential letter dated 8th May 1962. His letter stressed his plan was intended for the private consideration of his Chairman and it was important that it was not seen by BSA's board or any other individual because it could easily be misinterpreted. Edward considered that BSA was not in very good shape at that time. He believed that, although the motorcycle business was incapable of significant growth, it would continue to show a reasonable return on capital for a few more years to come. What disturbed him was that its future no longer appeared to justify his undivided effort for the few active years that lay ahead of him.

Edward's belief that a car could be created without great capital expenditure by using BSA's existing facilities. Within four years it would give BSA a permanent place in the car industry and make a contribution similar to that of Daimler, with whom BSA had been associated until Jack Sangster sold the company to Jaguar in 1960. He envisaged a medium-size car capable of carrying five passengers, with an air-cooled engine, which would sell for £1000-plus. He believed he was probably the only person in the industry capable of designing it. In doing so he would work unaided until the design work had been completed, after which a number of design draughtsmen would be needed, and later, development engineers.

The plan would be implemented in two stages. The first would have as its objective the need to get the business on a profit-making basis, with capital requirements within the resources of the Group. After the prototype had been tried, proven and costed, and met all requirements, production would commence on an initial basis of 200 to 300 cars a week. This would be more or less accomplished with existing funds, employing personnel mostly from outside the Group so that the technical staff would not be weakened. Although the design and construction of the prototype would be Edward's first consideration, it was also his intention to create an entirely separate nucleus of an organisation that would not be dependent or rely on any of BSA's personnel at that time, with one or two exceptions. Stage one would involve his full-time participation for a two-year period, although he would be available during this period for consultation on motorcycle matters. He would not, however, expect to be involved in executive duties.

Stage two would require more financial and production conception [sic] than the product itself. As the car had been designed to have worldwide appeal, production would amount to ten times the initial figure of 200 to 300 a week. Implementation of this stage, Edward believed, would be well within the capabilities of the Chairman.

From a personal point of view, Edward's main concern was to ensure his family had a secure future, as far as 20 years ahead.

Another record-breaking attempt on the Bonneville salt flats took place during August 1962. Using a 649cc Triumph engine in a streamline shell, prepared by Joe Dudek, Bill Johnson achieved a mean speed of 224.57mph over two runs, which was later ratified by the FIM. Now Triumph officially held the World Motorcycle Land Speed Record. Bill Johnson was a truck driver and not related to Bill Johnson of Johnson Motors.
(John Nelson)

His present salary from BSA yielded about £1000 per annum, after paying surtax on the remainder of his estate, which did not provide much incentive to do a conscientious job other than that of Managing Director of BSA's Motorcycle Division on a part-time basis. To compensate for this he intended asking the Chairman to devise some means to reward him if he was directly responsible for producing upwards of an extra £2 million profit for the Group within four years, but not at the expense of anything produced at that time. Any risks taken by BSA would be negligible, most of the initial work being abstract and using a considerable amount of paper long before metal could be worked. He was quite willing to underwrite his efforts out of his own pocket, and only when BSA was called upon to back a virtual certainty would investment be needed.

Overall, it was Edward's intention to lay the foundation for an entirely new type of motor car, which would not only put his company in business but also establish a long line of cars which the public would buy every year for an indefinite period.

J. Whiting Smith's reply was pessimistic, suggesting it would be unwise for Edward to remain on BSA's main board if he went ahead with his plan. If he did not resign it could be inferred that he would be in a position to influence BSA's board in its dealings with him, and he could be open to criticism from shareholders and the press. There was no reason why he should not rejoin the board when development of his car had been completed and he had sold the company to BSA. If his project succeeded as envisaged, he could then rejoin BSA with increased status and responsibility. In the meanwhile, there was no reason why Edward should not continue to give advice as a consultant to the motorcycle companies within the Group, at an appropriate fee.

From this one may assume that Edward was discouraged, and Jack Sangster never acquainted with the proposition, which was subsequently abandoned.

The Welsh Three Day Trial was viewed as a prelude to that year's International Six Days Trial, and Triumph took it very seriously. In the 1962 event, Gordon Blakeway put up the best solo performance in the fast schedule category on a 349cc twin, without any loss of marks. Dick Clayton, riding a 490cc 'unit' twin, won the slow schedule, and did so without losing any marks, either. Ken Heanes, always a star performer, was another who lost no marks. Riding a 649cc twin, his was the best performance provided by an over 350cc machine.

When riders were selected for the 1962 ISDT, there were two Triumph riders in Britain's International Trophy Team; Ken Heanes (649cc) and John Giles (490cc). Roy Peplow (349cc) was a member of the Vase B team. In the event itself, Britain was runner-up in both the International Trophy and Vase B competitions. John Giles, Ken Heanes, Roy Peplow and Eric Chilton lost no marks, the first three gaining a Gold medal and Eric Chilton a Silver. Gordon Blakeway retired. In an analysis of the results, of the 50 Britons that had entered, 25 had retired. 15 had won Gold medals, 4 Silver, and 6 Bronze. John Giles had given the best performance by amassing 583.724 marks out of a possible 600.

The big news during August 1962 was another record-breaking attempt by Bill Johnson on the Bonneville Salt Flats, using a 649cc Triumph engine enclosed within a 17 foot long steamlined shell. Running on methanol at a compression ratio of 11:1, the machine had been prepared by Joe Dudek and, in a preliminary run, a speed of 230.07mph was recorded, however, as this was prior to the record-breaking attempt it would not have been recognised by the FIM. A

had the full 'bath tub' rear enclosure, with the exception of the 3TA and Speed Twin models. Also noticeable was the fitting of twin exhaust pipes and silencers to models that previously had a siamese system. The electrical system was improved by having separate ignition and lighting switches mounted in the headlamp nacelle.

The Bill Johnson/Joe Dudek record-breaking Triumph took pride of place on Triumph's stand at the Motor Cycle Show, with both Johnson and Dudek in attendance. At the show, Edward presented each of them with an engraved silver salver. Also on display was John Giles' ISDT Tiger 100 and a Tiger Cub of military specification, as a reminder that a considerable number were supplied for use by the French armed forces. Amongst those who made a special visit to the Triumph stand to see the record-breaker for themselves were Donald Campbell and Lord Brabazon.

Surprise last-minute entries on the eve of the show were two lightweight motorcycles, the 49.9cc Ariel Pixie and the 74.7cc BSA Beagle, both of them ohv four-strokes. Earlier in the year Honda had added seven new ultra-lightweights to its range of UK imports: the 49cc C100, C102, C110 and C114 models, the 87cc C200 and S90 sports models, and the so-called miniature 49cc 'monkey bike". All were powered by a push rod operated ohv engine, the C100 and C102 models a cross between a moped and a scooter which was initially classified as a 'scooterette'. They were soon referred to as step-thrus, a much more acceptable name that described them more accurately. The C100 and C102 were the first of the Super Cubs, the C102 having an electric starter. Both had three-speed transmission with an automatic clutch. Although it could not have been realised at the time, these were the forerunners of what are probably the most reliable motorcycles ever made, destined to sell worldwide in millions. To market them, European Honda Trading Limited had been set up, with premises in Kingston-upon-Thames. A road test on a C110 Super Cub Sports model published in *The Motor Cycle* towards the end of the year gave an indication of why they were proving so popular: the 49cc C110 weighed 146lbs, was capable of just under 50mph and retailed at £109. 19s.

To demonstrate their reliability, a Honda endurance test was set up at the Goodwood motor racing circuit near Chichester in West Sussex during November. With Geoff Monty in charge, three machines were ridden around the track non-stop for 24 hours a day, over a 7 day period, by 20 riders. Apart from the main objective of demonstrating reliability in a very positive manner, the test was also intended as a bid for the Maudes Trophy, a prestigious award held by BSA since 1952. It was awarded to the manufacturer whose machines had, in the opinion of the Auto Cycle Union, performed the most meritorious certified test in any one year. Conditions throughout Honda's test were most unpleasant; torrential rain, a bitingly cold wind and ice forming on the track at night. Yet everything went according to plan and Honda was awarded the Trophy.

few days later the record-breaking attempt was successful (subject to FIM ratification), with a mean speed of 224.57mph over two runs. It looked as though Triumph would at last hold the World Motorcycle Speed Record after being so blatantly cheated out of it in 1955.

Early in September it was disclosed that, henceforth, the automatic scooter would be referred to only as the Tina, and would be supplied by Triumph, BSA or Ariel. Although the scooters were being assembled at Meriden, the engine was built by BSA in the old Sunbeam works. Carbodies supplied the bodywork pressings, and Motoplas the plastic mouldings.

When Triumph's plans were unveiled in advance of the 1962 Motor Cycle Show, there were two significant changes to the model range. The T120 649cc Bonneville engine was converted to the unit-construction type, and the Tiger 90, a sports version of the 3TA twin, was introduced. The Bonneville was the last of the twins to have a unit-construction engine/gearbox and, unlike the 500cc twins, it retained its original bore and stroke dimensions of 71 x 82mm. The conversion also involved the use of a new design of frame with a lower tank rail, which was used for the other large capacity twins also. The new T120 Bonneville produced 46bhp at 6500-7000rpm, which meant a top speed in the region of 102-110mph.

With regard to the Tiger 90, it was needed to provide a higher performance version of the 3TA, carrying out much the same role that the ill-fated Tiger 85 would have done in relation to the 3T model, had it not been for World War 2. Otherwise, it was largely a question of detail modification to upgrade the other models still further, with the exception of the addition of a limited number of Tiger Cubs being made available as replicas of the 'works' trials models.

Most noticeable amongst the updating modifications was inclusion of twin contact breakers within the timing cover so that a distributor was no longer required. Distributors had been a constant source of trouble due either to variation of the points gap as a result of worn bushes in the distributor assembly, or oil finding its way on to the points because of damaged or worn seals. Also welcome was the use of knurled edge rocker inspection caps retained by springs. The older type had a tendency to work loose through high frequency vibration, with the need to re-tighten them after every long run to prevent them unscrewing completely. The 649cc twins now featured a cylinder head with more fins, and there were fins cast into the rocker boxes.

The lesson learnt from the USA resulted in what were known as 'bikini' rear fairings being fitted to the twins, that had previously

A copy of the original press release announcing Edward's retirement with effect from 1st January 1964. It was issued from the BSA Chairman's office.

The British motorcycle industry was well aware of the impact this test would have, but was still convinced that the impending flood of imports from Japan was of no real concern, as Britain still made the best large capacity models. If anything, the industry identified a need to make more small capacity models in view of the number of potential new riders being encouraged to take up motorcycling by the Japanese products.

This was a line Edward tended to take now that he was acting as the mouthpiece for the Industries Association as its President. Inwardly, though, he must have had quite different thoughts in view of his visit to Japan when he had seen for himself all that was going on. Even so, he still had no reason to suspect that Japanese manufacturers would soon break into the marketplace by introducing sophisticated models of more than 250cc capacity.

At the Motor Cycle Show dinner Edward introduced the new Ariel and BSA ultra-lightweight models by saying: "Our aim is to provide a pair of machines - exciting things to ride - which will appeal to those interested in motorcycling as such rather than as a mere means of transport. A two-stroke lightweight model would certainly be cheaper to make, but the four-stroke has much better fuel consumption and is an altogether more sporty proposition. We have incorporated a four-speed gearbox, the better to take advantage of the high rpm which the new unit has been designed to withstand ... Nylon bearings have been used to cut maintenance to a minimum".

The introduction of these two new models seemed to represent a setback in commonalising design features so that parts became more interchangeable. Although the engine units were little more than a miniaturised version of the Tiger Cub unit, which confirmed they were Edward's designs despite having differing capacities, there was a marked difference between Ariel and BSA cycle parts. When drawings reached the respective production departments, they were thought to be some kind of elaborate joke! The public at large did not think much of them, either, and sales were well below expectations. The situation was not helped by the fact that neither model was available until almost a year after launch. Sadly, the models compared unfavourably with their Honda counterparts, and production came to an abrupt halt during August 1965, along with that of BSA's Dandy scooter.

A full account of Bill Johnson's record-breaking attempt was published in the 29th November issue of *The Motor Cycle*, and made interesting reading. That the FIM subsequently ratified the attempt as the new World Motorcycle Speed Record must have pleased Edward immensely.

1963 started off well when John Giles took the best 200cc award in the St. Davids Trial. Unfortunately, the uncharacteristically bad weather and heavy falls of snow during the weeks that followed took its toll on trials events.

Soon after he had returned from his yearly visit to the USA in late January, Edward held a press conference at Small Heath on 1st February to give an update on the current export trading situation. It seemed things were going very well, and the BSA Group would achieve a turnover of almost $6 million by the end of the financial year. This represented a new record as turnover was little short of $1 million up on the normal level of business. Edward found the Americans good people with whom to do business and considered the future in the USA to be very bright. It was possibly the only country in the world to offer such prospects. He acknowledged the growing threat of Japanese influence on the marketplace, which would necessitate British manufacturers concentrating on small capacity machines to meet the challenge. Already the BSA Group had plans in that direction. Exports needed sound backing from the UK market as overseas sales still accounted for 32% of total UK production.

From 1963 the Industries Association had decided to revert to a yearly Motor Cycle Show by holding alternate events regionally in order to attract those unwilling to make the yearly pilgrimage to Earls Court. The show this year was held in the Olympic Hall at the Winter Gardens, Blackpool, in mid-May and, in his capacity of President of the Industries Association, Edward made the customary address at the showtime dinner. The pertinent part of his speech ran as follows: "Because Britain's roads and the distances between towns allow only somewhat restricted travel, there is now a need for smaller, lighter, more economic and cheaper motorcycles. The £300 machine is beginning to have a limited appeal and it is important that manufacturers concentrate on new designs, techniques and approaches so that motorcycles bear a closer relationship to any other commodity". The show was well attended but nothing like the number that usually visited the London events.

A road test carried out on Neale Shilton's personal 649cc Triumph Saint 177 EUE, the model used for law enforcement purposes on which Neale had once covered 400 miles in 7 hours, was published in the 29th August issue of *The Motor Cycle*. The test was conducted by Bob Currie, the magazine's Midland Editor. The bike's acceleration was impressive, as was its maximum speed of 102mph.

In the Scottish Six days Trial Ray Sayer was on form to win the award for the best 200cc with his Tiger Cub, whilst in the Allan Jefferies Trial, Scott Ellis gave an excellent performance to win the Best Solo award with a loss of only 10 marks.

The 1963 ISDT was little short of disastrous for the British teams, which finished 7th in the International Trophy competition and last in the Vase. Of the Triumph riders, John Giles (490cc), Ken Heanes (649cc) and Roy Peplow (349cc), all of whom were in Britain's Trophy Team, won Gold medals. Eric Chilton (649cc) was awarded a Silver medal but Dick Clayton (490cc) and Scott Ellis (349cc), the latter of which had been drafted into a Vase Team, retired.

As if to make amends in the later West of England Trial, back on his Tiger Cub Scott Ellis won The Motor Cycle Trophy with a loss of only two marks, one mark less than Ray Sayer on a similar model. Ray claimed the best 200 award. In the Cotswold Cups Trial that followed a fortnight later, it was Scott's turn for the best 200 award. Held on the same day, Gordon Farley, riding a Tiger Cub, emerged as the best 250.

Triumph's 1964 model range was announced at the end of October and, with no new models planned, it was largely a question of detail modification once again. These included introduction of 12 volt electrics on the 649cc Thunderbird models. Front fork design had been changed to provide better damping and, as the springs were now fitted externally, protected by flexible bellows-type gaiters. All the twins with rear enclosure now featured the abbreviated 'bikini' panels, and standardised throughout were twin contact breakers in the timing cover, rubber-mounted oil tanks (previously found only on the Tigers) and magnetic speedometers. Internal modifications to the crankcases resulted in improved oil scavenging, and a new design of push rod cover tubes and their sealing washers helped eradicate a past potential source of oil leakage. The twins also benefited from a new ball and thrust mechanism to lift the clutch, introduced previously on the 649cc twins only.

As the trials season came around again it was still Scott Ellis who made the news with a best 250cc performance in the Hoad Trophies Trial and the best 200 award in the Mitcham Vase Trial that followed a couple of weeks later. In mid-November it was confirmed that production of the 249cc Triumph and BSA scooters had ceased. The BSA B1 single cylinder, two-stroke scooter would now be the only one available, apart from the Tina, which was to continue in production until replaced by the updated and improved T10 version.

For publication on 17th December 1963, the Birmingham Small Arms Company Limited put out a simple press release. As from 1st January 1964, Edward would be relinquishing, at his own request, his executive appointment as Managing Director of the three motorcycle companies in the Group, BSA Motorcycles Limited, the Triumph Engineering Company Limited and Ariel Motors Limited. He would, however, remain on the boards of these companies so that his wide knowledge of the motorcycle industry would be available to them. He would also remain a director of the parent company and would be concerned with the design and development of new products. The announcement - reduced to only a few brief lines of text and easy to miss - appeared in the following week's issue of *The Motor Cycle*, now the only weekly motorcycling publication in magazine format.

With Edward's departure assured, Bert Hopwood had every expectation that he would assume the role of Triumph's Managing Director, as had been promised when he agreed to rejoin the company. Sadly, it did not happen. Eric Turner, Chairman of BSA Company Limited, had other ideas, and was convinced that this appointment

should not come from within. It was his opinion that if an existing member of staff was promoted to Chief Executive, the management team would be broken up because the others would take exception. He was strongly in favour of appointing a newcomer to the industry for this key position and, after getting the board to agree, Harry Sturgeon became Managing Director of BSA's Motorcycle Division. Previously, he had held an executive position in the aircraft industry and had the reputation of being an accomplished salesman. He took up his duties in May 1964.

Edward was remote from all of this as he had timed his departure for a three month visit to Australia to coincide with the issue of the press release about his resignation. Taking his family with him meant visiting the girl's school with Shirley to seek the approval of their headmistress for this extended leave of absence. It was granted on the understanding that they would be going on a trip around the world, which would be an education in itself. They were asked to send regular reports of their travels to their geography mistress, and it was agreed that Edward would teach them maths. They departed on the SS Oransay just before Christmas 1963, calling at Gibraltar, Port Said, Aden, Penang and Singapore on the way. When they reached Australia they called at Perth, Adelaide and Melbourne before finally docking in Sydney. They stayed there for two months, visiting relations, although Edward was seldom with them as he had business contacts to make.

From Sydney the Turners flew to Hawaii, where they were feted by the local Triumph dealer, then onward to California which included a visit to Disneyland at Anaheim to coincide with Charmian's birthday. Their next stop was Baltimore, where they were met by Mr and Mrs McCormack of TriCor and taken to their home in Maryland. The trip ended with a few days' stay at the Plaza Hotel in New York.

There was a sequel to this trip. Edward was aware that his Secretary, Nan Plant, and Brit Eriksen, their Norwegian au pair, had spent the winter months during their absence with a dismal family in an unheated house in Cornwall. He made amends by asking them to join the family for a few days in Paris durng April, which they gratefully accepted.

Christmas 1964 was spent on a cruise to the Cape Verde Islands, via Madeira. It marked the beginning of the inevitable breakdown of Edward's second marriage and, in all probability, avoided the painful

Brit Eriksen agreed to look after the children for a three year period after Edward and Shirley's divorce, when he was given custody. Brit returned to Norway at the beginning of 1968.

nostalgia of a last old-style Christmas in the family home. The 30 year age gap between the couple had by now become even more noticeable, with Edward very set in his ways and Shirley aware it was now or never if she was to get out of the marriage before it was too late. The occasional trips abroad afforded little compensation for the fact that she had become trapped in the wrong life.

The main concern was who would look after the children, which ultimately went in Edward's favour, even though it left him with the responsibility of their welfare. His thoughts turned to Brit Eriksen who, by now, had returned to her native Norway to start her first year at university. He wrote to her, using all his persuasive powers, and implored her to come back. Fortunately, she agreed as her first year at university had not been to her liking and life in Coventry seemed to offer a much better proposition. She agreed to do so for a three year period, to satisfy the Home Office requirement for a work permit, and arrived during January 1965. Edward and Shirley's separation had been agreed some while before, but she had agreed to stay on so that she could supervise the transfer of responsibilities herself.

Brit returned to Norway at the beginning of 1968, as expected. Having resigned from the parent board of BSA during January 1967, Edward was no longer committed to living in the Midlands and thought it would be a good idea to move closer to Poole where his boat Charane was moored. The drive to and from Coventry was proving both long and boring. He found a house at Charlton Marshall in Dorset, relatively close to Blandford and Wimborne. It had been built on the site of an old Celtic barrow and occupied a commanding position on a hill at the northern edge of the village, with countryside views for miles around, Dating from the early Victorian period, it had two really spacious downstairs rooms and a small conservatory attached to the dining room. More isolated than Abbotsvale, its grounds took the form of rough parkland, studded with trees down the hill, which presented a somewhat bleak and windswept outlook in the rain. The only public transport link with Blandford was a rather infrequent bus service.

By far Edward's greatest accomplishment at this time was the design of a 350cc, double overhead camshaft, twin cylinder motorcycle for the BSA Group, intended to offer a head-on challenge to its Japanese competitors. It seems probable that work on this project commenced early in 1968, or possibly late 1967, with production scheduled to start in 1971. This is confirmed in Bert Hopwood's autobiography as he refers to his correspondence about the project with Lionel Jofeh in October 1968, the BSA Group's Managing Director at that time. Understandably, Bert was annoyed that his former boss had been invited to design this machine with the promise of the loan of some of his own design team, and that he was to organise the work. With some justification, he recommended that, in future, Edward should be dependent on his own resources to carry out design work as he was no longer part of the Group and was negotiating royalty payments for the project. It was the beginning of an ever deepening rift between the two designers who, in their Ariel days, had enjoyed a convivial working relationship.

Edward's prototype, which was to be marketed by Triumph as the Bandit, and by BSA as the Fury, was available for test during late 1968. On almost every count it met with Bert's disapproval, which was particularly unfortunate as Edward had already told his American contacts of its existence, which created a demand that could not be fulfilled for at least a couple of years. Although Bert agreed it was a good-looker, he regarded it as "extremely badly engineered and very unreliable", to use his own words. Percy Tait, however, who carried our most of the road testing, found it reached 112mph at the MIRA test track and rated it highly. The outcome was that Bert Hopwood

Having made so many presentations himself, Edward is now on the receiving end, and looks well pleased with his gift.

and Doug Hele undertook its complete redesign, which included a conversion to a 180 degree crank throw so that the pistons no longer rose and fell in unison within the cylinder bores. Eventually, the bore and stroke dimensions of 63 x 56mm were the only original design parameters that remained unchanged. Not that it mattered very much. Although 12 prototypes had been made at Small Heath for the launch in November 1970, which had been organised on a lavish scale, the BSA Group now found itself faced with considerable financial problems, which led to the Group's collapse; neither the Fury or the Bandit went into production.

Had they have done so they would have been an attractive proposition, with a specification that included a five-speed gearbox, chain-driven overhead camshafts, a forged crankshaft with an integral flywheel, and twin carburetters. Power output was claimed to be 34bhp at 9000rpm and dry weight was 345lbs. They were to have retailed at £380, inclusive of Purchase Tax, with an additional £21 for an optional electric starter. Two street scrambler versions had also been projected but they suffered the same fate.

Returning to Edward's domestic situation, without Brit's help, two separate housekeepers were taken on, both of whom proved unsatisfactory. Edward's retirement was not working out as he had hoped, especially as neither of his daughters had any real enthusiasm for his boat. To make matters worse, he was now going through the unpleasant task of preparing for a divorce, and having his private affairs aired in public from the witness box. Even his financial status was threatened when Harold Wilson's Labour Government instituted

David Green (second left), Edward and Jack Wickes (far right), with some of the members of the Umberslade Hall design team and the prototype 350cc Triumph Bandit twin, in the early 70s.

realise that Charlton Marshall was not an ideal location in which to bring up a couple of teenagers, and that the novelty of living in a small village in Dorset was beginning to wear off for them; he was now finding it pretty boring himself, particularly during the winter months.

In his search for somewhere to live abroad his obvious leaning would have been towards California, where he had many friends and enjoyed the lifestyle. Unfortunately, it had its disadvantages, too because he had three children to educate and, from a financial viewpoint, he would have to face up to the 'dollar premium'. After much consideration the Bahamas seemed to offer the best compromise as the currency was sterling and there were no financial constraints.

He found the ideal location during February, but before he could make any definite arrangements, he had to be available for his divorce petition which was scheduled for the following month. His lawyer asked Brit if she would be prepared to testify in his favour, to which she agreed. Fortunately, no-one was subjected to cross-examination in the witness box as on the morning of the hearing a settlement was agreed out of court. Edward mentioned his Bahamas plan to Brit, asking if she would would be prepared to come with them; he was pleased when she accepted

a special 'one-off' tax levy over and above the normal income tax return, aimed at those whom they considered could afford it. Although of less significance, the final blow came just before Christmas when he was caught speeding once too often and had his driving licence taken away for a short period. It triggered serious thoughts about the practicality of living abroad.

The problems continued to mount to the extent that Edward once said they would tax a man half his age. He was beginning to

The left-hand side of the Bandit prototype showing the twin Amal Concentric carburetters and the 'cocktail shaker' silencers, reminiscent of those fitted to the 1938 Tiger 100. Later substantially redesigned, neither the Bandit nor its BSA Fury equivalent went into production due to the collapse of the BSA Group.

his invitation. To her it sounded a lot of fun. In April 1969 they left England to set off and start what seemed to be a new life.

They settled in an American-style, split level house on Tarrytown Drive, near Freeport, on Grand Bahama Island, where they would remain for the next couple of years. Edward began to enjoy the social life, especially as there were plenty of open-air parties where all age groups were invited and intermingled freely. The American-style, easy-going atmosphere was more conducive to family life, in complete contrast to the final uphappy years of Edward's marriage where he had got used to seeing most of his friends away from home. He also found he could live more modestly on his retirement income, yet continue to give everyone a good quality of life. Because they were in a safe environment, young Edward, now just under ten years old, was the one who benefited most from this freedom.

It was here that Edward regained his interest in music, for it will be recalled that, in his younger days, he had a fine baritone voice. It was much to his regret that he had never learnt to play the piano like his sisters Maud and Winnifred. He loved opera and had revelled in listening to Caruso in his youth. Often he would play records by Wagner or some other opera at high volume in the early hours of the morning, which disturbed the rest of the family when they were still feeling a bit fragile from a previous party.

He also set himself up as a radio ham, harking back to his days during the 1914-18 war when he served as a Telegraphy Officer in the Merchant Navy. Now the equipment he used was more sophisticated so that he could communicate verbally without having to resort to Morse code. He made many new friends as a result, which helped lessen his sense of isolation. Living on a small island with huge roads meant there was nowhere much to go. Although at one time he started to write his memoirs, he didn't get very far with them, whch was a great pity as there are so many parts of his life about which there are only faint recollections. He did, however, in 1973, record on tape for Jim Lee, who had worked as a tester for both Ariel and Triumph, an brief account of the early part of his career. A brief interview with Val Page was included on the same tape.

Just when everything seemed to be falling into place, his health started to deteriorate. His diabetes got worse and his vision was impaired for something like six months before remedial medication began to be effective. He had been his own worst enemy in this respect as he was not very good at keeping to a recommended diet. American-style food was too much of a temptation and he somehow held the belief that ice cream did not have any sugar in it!

When his diabetes problem was at its worst he was unable to move about as much as he wanted, nor enjoy whatever was available to him. This warning depressed him as he realised that if his health should break down further he would be better off where medical facilities were better. Even life on a 'desert island' was beginning to wear a little thin, especially when the climate was very hot and humid at certain times of the year. When young Edward started preparatory school he knew he needed to be on hand so that he could take him out and spend as much time with him as possible. As his two daughters were already poised to start their own social lives in England, he knew it was time for them all to pack their bags and return home.

Exactly why Edward should have chosen the village of Ockley, in Surrey, is not known, but that is where the family settled during 1971 at Newlands, in Weare Street. He had no connections there, but, presumably, it provided the opportunity of living in a country environment whilst being close to the London he had loved whilst a boy. He also kept a flat in London, which he finally relinquished at the beginning of 1973. Unfortunately, very little evidence exists about his involvement with the motorcycle scene at this time, or, for that matter, much about any of the freelance work he undertook. It is known that at some time during this period he roughed out a design for a motorcycle with an in-line, four cylinder engine. Known as the Turnerdyne, a coloured picture of it hangs on one of the walls in his youngest daughter Charmian's house in London.

Edward also wrote a couple of articles for *Books and Bookmen* one of them about the Wankel rotary engine that was attracting a great deal of attention at that time. BSA had taken out a licence to make it from Fichtel and Sachs, a German company that held the patent rights. BSA experimented with it for many years and although a machine with an engine of this type was marketed under the Norton name, it never met up to its inventor's expectations. The design of the combustion chamber was not ideal because its shape was restricted by virtue of the design parameters. In consequence it tended to be a pollutant and also suffered from a high rate of fuel consumption, two major environmental disadvantages. It is known that he designed a collapsible boat, a fully-automated car parking system, and even invented a device for saving soap so that the last remaining sliver was not wasted!

On the morning of 15th August 1973, at home in Ockley, Edward seemed to be more energetic than usual and was moving furniture around. After lunch he took his customary afternoon nap on the sofa in his sitting room, but when Brit came to bring him his afternoon tea there was no response. He had died peacefully in his sleep from a coronary thrombosis. Perhaps it is as well he did not live long enough to see the final demise of the Triumph Engineering Company. He had seen it coming and had been very upset by the way in which the industrial climate had deteriorated through labour disputes and the so-called 'winter of discontent'. He had always viewed his own contribution to industry as part of the larger picture, not relating directly to his own immediate area of concern.

The funeral was organised by Nan Plant, Edward's former secretary. It was expected that he would be buried alongside his first wife, Marion, but, on making enquiries, Nan found this was not possible because the graveyard had been hit by bombs during the air raids on Coventry. Finding an alternative site, such as a country churchyard, presented a problem as Edward did not belong to any congregation and attended church only for weddings and funerals. Consequently, he was cremated at Randalls Park Crematorium, Leatherhead, on 22nd August, the crematorium that served the area in which he had lived. His ashes were interred in the Garden of Remembrance beneath a stone that bore his name and dates of his birth and death. In the Book of Remembrance at Randalls Park the simple entry 'mechanical engineer' was appended against his name, an understatement if ever there was one. His former wife Shirley, and staff from what remained of the Triumph Engineering Company, were there on this very sad occasion.

Even though the Triumph Engineering Company is no longer in existence Edward left behind a massive legacy in the form of so many motorcycles that bore his trademark. There are more Triumphs and BSAs in existence today than any other classic design, and the Triumph Owners Motor Cycle Club has a very large, worldwide membership.

Fortunately, the name and assets of the old company were acquired by John Bloor before they faded into oblivion. At the time of writing Bloor's company, Triumph Motorcycles Limited, is now the leading British motorcycle manufacturer, with state-of-the-art, multi-cylinder designs that offer a serious challenge to their Japanese counterparts. Now that Edward would have found most gratifying.

Chapter 14: The American market

The American market made such a massive contribution to the overall success of the Triumph Engineering Company during the post-war years that it merits a chapter of its own - and not just as an afterthought. It was a difficult market to break into, because the requirements of American motorcyclists differed in many respects from those of their British counterparts. For example, competition success was all-important in bringing the Triumph name to the fore, as was the provision of machines with a macho appearance that underlined their sporting pretentions. These requirements conflicted with Edward's policies relating to direct factory participation in competition events, and his move toward semi-enclosure; areas in which he was forced to compromise if headway was to be maintained. As recounted in the text that follows this prologue, a win at Daytona in 1962, coupled with ratification of Triumph's World Motorcycle Speed Record that same year, also helped underwrite Triumph's enviable record of success in the American market.

With typical shrewdness, Edward had foreseen the potential that lay ahead when he encouraged Bill Johnson to forsake his career as an attorney and form Johnson Motors Inc. to act as Triumph's West Coast distributor. The number of motorcycles manufactured in Britain had reached a total of 147,000 in 1928, over 59% of them destined for overseas markets, a figure which would not be bettered for a good many years. Yet, of this number of exports, very few went to North America, mainly because of widely differing market requirements. In America, the large capacity vee-twin reigned supreme because motorcyclists had been accustomed to this type of motorcycle almost since the US industry began. Big, ruggedly-built machines with large capacity engines were popular in view of their ability to run for long periods with only minimal attention. Furthermore, because America is such a large country, a wide variety of climatic conditions was likely, and had been taken into account by those who designed these machines.

In less affluent times a large proportion of the British working population was dependent on a motorcycle as a cheap and convenient means of commuting. In consequence, most people tended to favour a small capacity two-stroke which, despite relatively poor performance, had few working parts and was cheap, reliable and easy to maintain. Those who also wished to make the most of their leisure time at weekends were usually more in favour of a larger capacity four-stroke, often one with sporting aspirations. The most popular capacity was 350cc which, compared with a 500, had a lower insurance rating, lower road tax, better fuel economy and the ability to carry two comfortably with little noticeable loss in performance.

Perhaps the most important difference was that the distance between large towns and cities in America - usually with good interconnecting highways - could be covered by a vee-twin at a higher sustained cruising speed. In Britain these distances were much smaller and the roads more torturous, with higher traffic density. Large capacity models were at a disadvantage, not only because they were heavier and more thirsty, but also because the opportunity to use them to maximum performance occurred less frequently. Until the vertical twin made its appearance during 1937, a single cylinder model was by far the more popular choice in Britain.

Before World War 2 the average American rider regarded the British motorcycle as a frail and somewhat unreliable machine that would have to be purchased by special order and take some eight weeks or so to arrive. Spare parts would be available from the manufacturer's agent only, who would also have to provide supporting servicing and/or major overhaul facilities. The average American dealer was unlikely to be familiar with anything other than a domestically produced product, and might well adopt a hostile attitude because he had not supplied the machine in the first instance. British motorcycles held most appeal for those who wanted something 'different' and were prepared to put up with the inconveniences. But, when the early Triumph Speed Twin production models started to appear in 1938, the situation began to change.

Of the small number of British motorcycles sold in America, the best known importer was Reggie Pink. He had founded his business in 1926 and had his showroom in the Bronx district of New York. Although he did not deal exclusively in British machines, he had represented Ariel since the late twenties. When Jack Sangster formed the Triumph Engineering Company in mid-January 1936, Triumph was added to his list of agencies. Although never a factory-approved distributor, Reggie operated a franchise arrangement with other dealers when Triumph's new range of Tiger singles began to arrive. He stocked only a small number of machines for prospective purchasers, and ran his business largely on mail order lines, but as he was located on the east coast, those who lived in the west found themselves at a disadvantage.

In 1936, whilst working as an attorney, Bill Johnson bought a Salsbury motor scooter. It aroused his interest in two-wheel transport to the extent that he began to buy British motorcycling magazines. A year later he came across an Ariel Square Four and was so intrigued by its engine that he acquired a 600cc model from British and American Motors. This brought him into contact with Edward Turner, with whom he corresponded about its technicalities. A friendship grew through this regular exchange of correspondence and Edward was perceptive enough to sense that a hitherto largely unexplored but promising export market existed for both Ariel and Triumph in California. When Bill Johnson decided his vocation was in the motorcycle business, importing British designs which would appeal to American motorcyclists, he joined forces with an accountant friend,

Wilbur Ceder, to raise the necessary finance. They bought British and American Motors which had a modest showroom in Avocado Street, Pasadena, and was up for sale. The two partners became joint directors; Johnson fulfilling the role of President and Ceder that of Secretary-cum-Treasurer.

They retained the original company name initially and, in the spring of 1937, Johnson signed an agreement to begin importing Ariel and Triumph motorcycles into Southern California. Getting started was not as easy as the two partners had anticipated, especially when their plans to take advertising space in the motorcycling press caused something of a hiatus. When their advertising agency submitted full-page layout copy to *The Motorcyclist*, the magazine's editor had misgivings about giving such extensive coverage to a newcomer who intended to compete with America's home-based motorcycle manufacturers. In the knowledge that exposure of this nature might offend his regular advertisers and result in loss of advertising revenue, he sought advice from the American Motorcycle Association, with whom the magazine had an 'understanding'. The AMA's response was that steps should be taken to dramatically reduce the size of the advertisement. When Johnson got to hear of this he claimed it would violate his constitutional rights. After seeking legal advice, the magazine's publisher found it would be difficult to justify the proposed action, (especially when dealing with a former attorney!), so the advertisement was printed in full, as originally intended. If anything it helped increase advertising revenue for the magazine as other specialist importers of British motorcycles took note and had their own advertisements soon afterwards!

British and American Motors' advertising campaign was backed up by a three-day 'open house' at the Avocado Street showroom, where members of the general public could see the latest British models on display. The usual harbingers of doom, who had predicted Johnson's and Ceder's imminent financial ruin, were now even more convinced of this when it was disclosed that the pair had sent invitations to their competitors! Space had been offered for them to display the latest American models alongside their British counterparts. That the astuteness of Johnson and his partner had been underestimated soon became apparent when something like 15,000 visitors attended during the display's three day duration. Hap Alzina, California's Indian distributor, was one who had taken advantage of the display offer, and had shown a number of Indian models. Impressed by the level of response, he broke the ice and offered British and American Motors an Indian franchise for central Los Angeles.

It was during the summer of 1939 that Edward visited America for the first time, to at last make personal contact with Bill Johnson. Jack Sangster had suggested the visit to give him the break he sorely needed to help recover from the tragic death of his wife, Marion. Already Sangster had agreed to Edward's own request to relieve him from having to run both Ariel and Triumph, as he was finding this dual role too much of a burden. It allowed him to concentrate more fully on the development of Triumph's business, especially as a foothold had now been gained in the America market after he had encouraged Bill Johnson to acquire British and American Motors and represent both Triumph and Ariel.

Unfortunately, it had not been possible to ship one of the new Speed Twins to Pasendena in time for Johnson's 'open house' days, although this had little affect on the way in which the business was building up. It soon became necessary to take on employees and, by the time Edward set foot in Pasadena, the first two Triumph twins had arrived. He was there when the company sponsored a Tiger 100 in a track racing event. Right from the beginning, the two partners had shown a keen interest in all aspects of off-road motorcycle sport, and Ceder, in particular, was an ardent follower of speedway racing. Triumph motorcycles began to benefit from increased public exposure, the more so after Bruce Pearson was sponsored by British and American Motors during the 1940 season. Riding a tuned Tiger 100 he won 32 out of the 36 events he entered.

In 1940 Johnson took up Hap Alzina's offer of an Indian franchise. The outbreak of World War 2 on 3rd September 1939 meant British manufacturers would soon be fully engaged in making motorcycles solely for use by the armed forces, with little or no prospect of any being exported for civilian use. Even obtaining spare parts for those already in service would present an ever-increasing problem. The acceptance of the Indian franchise encouraged Johnson and Ceder to move their embryo business to new and better sited premises at 1240 West Pico Boulevard, Los Angeles. At the same time they changed the company name to the more appropriate Johnson Motors Inc, which was soon shortened to 'JoMo'. An unexpected bonus from selling British-made motorcycles was that Johnson Motors also acquired the exclusive rights for distribution of the original equipment accessories, such as Amal carburetters, BTH magnetos, Dunlop tyres, Lucas electrical components, Renold chains, and Smiths speedometers.

An advertisement published in *The Motorcyclist* during 1940 told American motorcyclists all about Triumph's intentions in America. It expressed the hope that export of the twin cylinder models and spare parts would be permitted to continue, despite the outbreak of World War 2, and carried a photograph of a somewhat grim-looking Edward with the caption 'Edward Turner, The Triumph Chief'. A photograph taken of JoMo's new showroom at about the same time depicted a Tiger 100, a Speed Twin, and an Ariel Square Four, with a row of Indian twins behind them. A second Tiger 100 took pride of place in the showroom window.

Although British manufacturers had published details of their 1940 model ranges in Britain's two weekly motorcycle magazines, the chances of any of them actually being made were very slim. Petrol rationing began soon after the outbreak of war, and it was obvious it would be only a matter of time before manufacture of motorcycles for civilian use in Britain would cease 'for the duration', to use an oft-quoted phrase. Already government controllers were permitting the release of raw materials to the motorcycle industry only on the understanding that at least 75% of the output would be allocated for export.

As related earlier, Triumph had intended to market a nine model range in 1940, one of which would have been the new 349cc 3T twin. Its launch had originally been timed to coincide with the 1939 show, but, due to the war, it had to be cancelled. Without the show, the 3T would have no launch platform. If it had been advertised in America it was unlikely to have created much of a demand at that time: a 21 cubic inch engine with a 19bhp power output would not appeal very much to the average American motorcyclist. This was subsequently confirmed when it made a (delayed) appearance in 1946.

There was no mention of 1941 models by British manufacturers as those who had contracts for the supply of motorcycles to the armed forces were working flat out to produce the numbers required. The others diversified into other work of national importance, making a wide variety of components to help the war effort, which ranged from munitions to parts for aircraft and electrical equipment such as generators. It was no longer possible to supply machines for the export market either, or, for that matter, to maintain a spare parts service to keep existing models on the road. A similar situation would soon face American motorcyclists when their country was dragged into the global conflict. Johnson Motors Inc. had to concentrate on repair work to keep going, although this too was affected by wartime conditions with fewer motorcycles on the road and spare parts becoming increasingly difficult to obtain. Eventually, JoMo also became involved in work to further the war effort.

As the war in Europe began to wind down, it inspired three American businessmen to investigate how the US motorcycle industry might forge stronger links for the importation of British motorcycles after the ceasefire. All three men considered that a wider variety of choice was long overdue. One of them was Alfred Rich Child, a much respected salesman and entrepreneur who, as an expatriate, had joined Harley Davidson as a salesman in 1920. In 1924 he had started an import operation in Japan which blossomed into a manufacturing operation when he made, under license, the Rikuo, a Japanese version of the Harley-Davidson. In a bid to acquire the sole importation rights in North America for BSA, Child risked life and limb to make three separate and extremely hazardous sea crossings of the Atlantic, one of them on the day before the Allied invasion of France. His meetings with BSA's Chief Executive, James Leek, at which Jack Sangster and Edward were present, ultimately paid off. Impressed by their visitor's business acumen, an agreement was reached during 1945 which gave him the sole distribution rights for BSA and Sunbeam. Ariel and Triumph, the latter still a privately-owned company, had their own representation through Johnson Motors Inc. of California, who Edward wished to continue out of loyalty to Bill Johnson.

A full account of Edward's three month visit was published in the 18th October 1945 issue of *Motor Cycling*, contrasting the difference of departing from the grim austerity of post-war Britain to the welcoming bright lights and warm hospitality that awaited his arrival in America. He made a relatively fast Atlantic crossing to New York in eight days by obtaining a berth on a diesel-engined freighter. From there he managed to book a seat on a night flight to Chicago, where he spent two and a half days before flying onward to Los Angeles. There, he was met by Bill Johnson who took him to stay at his home. During his visit he was able to look in on several embryonic motorcycle and scooter manufacturers, and take a ride on some of their prototype designs. Later, when he accompanied Johnson on a visit to San Francisco, the pair called on Dudley Perkins, the main distributor in California of Harley-Davidsons, and Vern Gardner, who ran the Square Four Motor Service across the bay, in Oakland. Both Perkins and Gardner were also keen to see British motorcycles being imported in even greater numbers, because they believed it would help fill the gap created by the lack of variety amongst their own country's products - even if they were likely to be more costly.

When the time came to return to Britain, Edward needed no convincing that America seemed to offer the best prospects for a considerably extended post-war export market. Already he had in his sights a projected sales target of 1000 Triumphs a year, which, at that time, would represent something like 60% of current output. Even so, he had inner concerns about how American manufacturers would react to this intrusion, and what action they might be forced to take to limit the damage to their own business expansion plans.

Now that war had ended, Edward negotiated a change in his contract which amounted to half-time employment. It enabled him to make six-monthly visits to North America on an annual basis to explore business opportunities, which included taking in American trade shows and exhibitions held during the winter months, and race meetings such as Daytona and the Big Bear Run. With regard to Daytona, it was here at this prestigious race meeting that British manufacturers were keen to achieve an impressive win, and Norton and BSA seemed as though they might well be able to do just that.

In a letter to Jack Sangster dated 19th May 1948, Edward broached the question of starting up a dollar-earning company in America. As the result of many conversations with American motorcyclists, it had become obvious that a machine built more on British lines would be most acceptable to them, with the proviso that it would need to have an engine capacity greater than 500cc, yet be neither larger in size nor heavier than a 500. Of the two major American manufacturers, he believed that Indian did not have a good understanding of the motorcycle business, whereas Harley-Davidson understood it well but was firmly of the opinion that a big twin was what the American public required. In Edward's opinion, it would be possible to design a machine around American manufacturing facilities to be made in the States at a price very much lower than the cost of shipping a similar model from Meriden. An added advantage was that it would have a much greater appeal as it would be aimed specifically at the American market.

The intention would be to build up a business of around 5000 machines a year, so that a profit-making company would quickly be established to form the nucleus for further development and expansion. It would be staffed entirely by American nationals, inclusive of management, and enable Edward to spend his yearly six months away from Britain promoting the American company. Jack Sangster would then have a half-interest in Edward's spare time away from Meriden.

With regard to the possible affect on existing Triumph business in America, Edward was of the opinion that this could be advantageous. Distribution at the time of writing was still sketchy as it was not yet possible to ship enough machines effectively to cover the whole territory. If the objective was to have a Triumph dealer in every important town, a dealer who dealt exclusively in Triumphs would need to receive adequate supplies to safeguard his livelihood. Both Indian and Harley-Davidson always insisted on exclusivity of their product, as was the customary practice in America for most products. An American company producing something new would be well received, and a dealer could be required to sell Triumph motorcycles alongside American machines to make enough profit to remain in business and provide the necessary back-up sales and service facilities.

When such a business had been established it would give Edward the opportunity to pursue an aspiration he had long held; to break into the automobile field. In his travels he had seen an opening for a small, high performance car. Built with a relatively small capital outlay, it would not compete with the cars from Detroit, but, in his opinion, an enormous turnover could be built up in something like five years, terminating with an equity of great value created from virtually nothing. Any such proposition would, of course, have to come later, preferably after any loans and share capital held by American interests had been redeemed. It would leave Jack Sangster and Edward as sole owners of the business.

Edward ended his letter to Sangster by requesting a quick response as he needed to consider other options to replace income he had lost from Triumph due to his half-time employment arrangement. There was a noticeable coldness in the correspondence that passed between them, as all of Edward's letters started "Dear Mr Sangster", whilst Sangster's replies were always addressed "Dear Turner".

Jack Sangster's response, in a letter dated 1st June, was somewhat curt and began by expressing his disappointment that the dollar-earning projects Edward had in mind two years ago had failed to materialise. The unusual half-time arrangement Edward had with the Triumph Engineering Company had been in operation for 18 months, and it now seemed that the setting up of a development company, or its equivalent, in America as originally envisaged no longer seemed a profitable operation.

He believed the only proposition which would be practical (and the only one in which he would be prepared to take an interest) would be one in which the control of the American company would be vested in the Triumph Engineering Company to the extent of 56%. Assuming a capitalisation of £250,000 in the form of £125,000 Ordinary Shares and £125,000 Preference Shares, he would be willing to invest £70,000 in Ordinary Shares and believed a good case could be made to persuade the Treasury to grant the necessary permits. The outstanding balance he believed could be obtained from American sources.

As an official of the US company who devoted the other half of his time to its interests, Edward could be remunerated on a scale which would more than compensate for the reduction in his salary at Meriden. Furthermore, it would still be possible for him to accumulate capital out of income over there with certain safeguards. An agreement between the UK company and the new American company would provide for the former to supply the technical know-how for the latter over a three-year period for a reasonable fee. This would be subject to prior appointent of a satisfactory all-year-round manager at Meriden.

It would seem there had been some earlier discussion about setting up a development company at Meriden, to which Sangster next referred. He considered it a far cry from the dollar-earning activities of which Edward had once had high expectations, and had led to him to agree to his request for half-time leave of absence. The taxable profits that might accrue would not be very attractive to either of them, and he viewed with considerable misgiving the possibility that any independent business activities carried out at Meriden would inevitably lead to friction and dissatisfaction within the company.

As usual, Sangster's letter ended with a sting in the tail. He drew attention to Edward's expense account for his visit to America during the autumn of 1947, which he had requested should be re-adjusted. He also referred to what he described as 'the Indian matter' and asked for an overdue report about how the situation had been left or how it was to be cleared. Presumably, this was a reference to Edward having been shown the drawings of Indian's prototype vertical twin, the model 249 known initially as the Scout, on which he had been asked to comment. He made the observation that he considered its main bearings to be inadequate, a criticism that went unheeded yet subsequently proved correct. (This so-called 'little operation' undertaken for Indian had, in fact, received Jack Sangster's approval, as confirmed in an air mail letter he sent to Edward c/o the Plaza Hotel, New York, on 4th October 1947. It may, however, have been given retrospectively.)

An intriguing and highly confidential transcript of a meeting between Edward, Jack Sangster and a third party referred to only by the initial 'M', dated 12th November 1948, gives a fascinating insight into an attempt to resolve the Indian 'problem'. Although the purpose of the meeting was "To discuss the percentage offer on the American proposition", it was used by Jack Sangster as an opportunity to tell 'M' what he thought of Edward, which was little more than a character assassination!

Sangster began by saying that Edward was an extremely awkward man, to which 'M' replied that he was probably a difficult man himself. In fact, he believed everyone was difficult in business if they had any ability. Surprisingly, Sangster said that in spite of the prosperity and success he had enjoyed since his association with Edward, the unpleasantness he also had to endure had taken the gilt off it. He went on to say that Edward did not have a regard for contracts, citing as an example that when he made contact with

Edward once mentioned that he had ridden a motorcycle at 110mph. That occasion is captured here as he gets ready to ride Rod Coates' Grand Prix model, complete with open megaphones.

Ralph Rogers of Indian, and suggested Edward might meet him, Edward went over there and did a design job for Rogers without consulting him. Edward repudiated this immediately as no design work had been carried out. He also said that he would not have his integrity attacked or reflection made on his honesty, to which 'M' demurred saying he did not think Sangster meant to question his honesty. Significantly, Sangster said nothing. 'M' then stated that he never had the slightest doubts about Edward's honesty.

With regard to the percentage, it is notable that the paper presented to Edward outlining the terms stated 30%, whereas when Sangster spoke to 'M' he mentioned 33 % without comment. 'M' already had the paper in front of him.

Edward then brought the interview to a close by saying that although they were slanging each other without heat in a gentlemanly way, the echoes of such interviews are felt long afterwards, and as far as he could see they served no useful purpose: nothing had been decided.

Sangster's parting comment was that when Edward joined the company 20 years ago, he had been paid £450 a year, but now had assets of £100,000.

During early February 1949, New York held its first car and motorcycle show at the 69th Regiment's Armoury, at which six countries displayed their motorcycles. Although British machines were much in evidence, their manufacturers did not support the show directly and were represented by US distributors. A small show by British standards, BSA and Sunbeam were represented by the Rich

Child Cycle Company, and Triumph and Ariel by Johnson Motors Inc. Harley-Davidson and Indian occupied the most prominent positions in the display; the latter rumoured to have new 'British style' single and twin cylinder models at the prototype stage. Both Edward and Jack Sangster attended the show, at which Lew Roberts, Triumph's New York agent, was also present. On display were Triumph's latest twins, featuring the stylish headlamp nacelle that contained the instrumentation previously accommodated in a panel set into the top of the petrol tank. There was also a cutaway of a Mark 1 spring wheel. A new Triumph Grand Prix racer drew the most attention. It had been shipped over for Rod Coates to ride in the forthcoming Daytona races. Rod was an employee of a New Jersey dealer selling Ariel, Triumph and Vincent motorcycles.

Also in America at the same time as Edward and Jack Sangster was Graham Walker, editor of *Motor Cycling*, making his first visit. His main objective was to find out why only one person out of 600 in America rode a motorcycle, whereas the corresponding ratio in the British Isles was one in 100.

Walker had to contend with an ambitious but tiring 10,000 mile road and rail itinerary to be completed in 38 days, starting off with a 900 mile journey by road to Daytona. There, he witnessed Floyd Emde win the 200 Mile Race on a 45 cu. in. side valve Indian, and 19 year old Don Evans the 100 Mile race on a Norton. Unfortunately, Rod Coates' debut in the 100 Mile Amateur Race on his Grand Prix Triumph came to a premature end when he was sidelined by unspecified mechanical problems. At that time, the race was held on Daytona beach and Graham was unimpressed by the very lax crowd control that allowed spectators to venture much too close to the speeding riders.

After Daytona he made his way to Pasadena by a circuitous road journey, calling on Johnson Motors to see for himself its set-up, with which he was much impressed. Whilst he was in the Los Angeles area he attended the Trail Blazers Annual Dinner at the Santa Ana Hotel, as Guest of Honour, and gave a film show of British events with his own added commentary. There followed a round of other local dealerships, including those who handled Indians and Harley-Davidsons, before setting off by train to visit Harley-Davidson's factory in Milwaukee. He did so with some initial trepidation as he was aware that the company was supposed to have an influential interest in motorcycle sport through the American Motorcycle Association, the equivalent of Britain's ACU. Furthermore, he also knew its views about competition from overseas manufacturers and the nationalistic approach to it. However, any such qualms were quickly dispelled when he received

an open arms welcome and was escorted around the factory by Bill Davidson.

All too soon, Walker was back on the train again for a night-time, 400 mile journey to Toronto where he gave another talk and film show to 1000 motorcycle clubmen gathered in the Goodyear tyre plant. A subsequent visit to local dealerships brought to light the surprising fact that, although no motorcycles were manufactured in Canada, a tax was levied on all British imports!

Montreal was the next stop on his itinerary, again to visit local motorcycle dealers, before he caught yet another night train to Springfield, Massachusetts. Here he was "royally entertained", to use his own words, by Ralph Rogers, President of the Indian Motocycle Company. His visit to the factory included a close look at the latest two prototypes, the twin cylinder Scout and the single cylinder Arrow models, which were still on the 'secret' list. They were the machines mentioned earlier that had been designed along British lines, in an attempt to break away from the stereotyped vee-twins with which the company had for so long been associated.

His conclusions at the end of his visit were that the lack of variety amongst American motorcycle manufacturers tended to discourage prospective purchasers, and that whilst a closed shop distribution system seemed to work well in theory, it did not do so in practice. He also believed that isolation of the American Motorcycle Association from the international sporting scene delayed progress; the AMA's refusal to give its individual members voting powers allowing policy to be dictated by the more influential manufacturers. As for the motorcycling press, neither of the two monthly magazines enjoyed a large circulation, which meant American motorcyclists were 'starved of news' about their hobby. He was of the opinion that whilst there was ample evidence of unlimited expansion in motorcycle sales, this would only happen if it was given a push in the right direction. This seemed unlikely to happen whilst the AMA and the American motorcycle industry continued to sit tight and not abandon their introspective attitudes.

In mid-1949, Johnson Motors Inc. took advantage of a golden opportunity to relocate to Pasadena when it purchased an impressive building originally built for a car dealer. The two-storey building at 267 West Colorado Street (later renamed West Colorado Boulevard) had large floor-to-ceiling display windows and second floor office accommodation. The Parts Department lay to the rear of the showroom area, and there was a separate entrance to the well-equipped Service Department at the rear. A considerable amount of money was spent on refurbishment, claimed as not far short of $100,000. Support for off-road sporting events was later stepped-up when these new premises became the starting point for the annual 500 mile Greenhorn Enduro Run.

After the move had been completed, Johnson relinquished the Indian agency he had acquired from Hap Alzina. At that time, the Indian Motocycle Company was beset with problems that threatened its future. When the war in Europe was showing signs of coming to an end, contracts for the

The premises of Johnson Motors Inc. at 267, West Colorado Boulevard, Pasadena, were originally built for an automobile dealership. The whole of Triumph's and Ariel's west coast operation was run from here.

Bill Johnson's impressive sign had a dark sage green background. This photograph was taken during Edward's visit to California in 1947, where he is seen with Bill.

by a small capacity, Evinrude, two-stroke engine and featured an unusual torque converter drive. It was one of these scooters that first caught Johnson's eye when he was in Honolulu, arousing his interest in the potential of powered two-wheelers.

Johnson and Ceder were determined to make their new premises a showpiece, and banish once and for all the perceived image of drab, unattractive, dirty premises staffed by men in oil-stained overalls. They were, in fact, anticipating what the Japanese motorcycle manufacturers would be doing several decades later - giving the motorcycle an entirely new image to attract completely new customers.

The business continued to expand and, before the end of 1949, Johnson Motors had in excess of 100 dealers retailing Triumphs and Ariels, thanks to the pioneering efforts of Andy Anderson and Pete Colman, who had criss-crossed the country to set them up. It became increasingly obvious that Harley Davidson was enforcing a solus agreement in its own dealer network to preclude any attempt to take on an additional Triumph franchise. When the news leaked out about a threat to stop the supply of new motorcycles and spare parts if any Harley-Davidson dealers reneged on this agreement, it incurred the wrath of the Federal Trade Commission, which lost no time in advising Harley-Davidson of the dire consequences that would result if the Commission found evidence of any such illegal contracts.

Arrival of the 650cc Thunderbird in America provided the incentive for increased sales, even if the early models were painted in an unattractive colour, and were underpowered, having been fitted with an undersize carburetter. A large number of machines were already being purchased for off-road sporting use and, with so many American-made parts available for customising and/or enhancing performance, it was easy to improve on the performance of the 500cc, over-the-counter models. A 650cc twin was exactly what American motorcycle enthusiasts had been requesting and sales began to increase dramatically, irrespective of the fact that export models had been built to UK specification.

Rod Coates' win of the 100 Mile Amateur race at Daytona in 1950 couldn't have been better timed, because it coincided with the Norton team finishing 1st, 2nd and 4th in the 200 Mile Experts race. A British machine finished third, too; a BSA ridden by Tommy McDermott. Rod was again riding a Grand Prix Triumph and had finished ahead of an ohc Norton. Interestingly, Ed Kretz, an extremely successful rider who had ridden for Indian until its demise, had changed allegiance to Triumph. He stood an excellent chance of winning and had led the Experts race for a considerable distance until a slipping clutch put him out of the running.

The 1950 New York Show of British cars, motorcycles, and bicycles was held later this year on 16th April, having been transferred to the Grand Central Palace. It was again attended by Jack Sangster and Edward, in company with other executive members of the British motorcycle industry, including James Leek of BSA Cycles Ltd., and Major H.R. Watling, Director of the British Cycle and Motor Cycle Manufacturers and Traders Union. The motorcycles were to be found on the first floor, Bill Johnson having ensured four Thunderbirds were prominently displayed, along with Rod Coates' Daytona Amateur 100 Mile race-winning Grand Prix model. Other Triumph exhibits included a Trophy Twin, a black 3T twin and a Speed Twin fitted with two-way radio equipment for use by the police. Numbering ten in total, most of the Triumphs were fitted with the new dualseat.

Jack Sangster and Edward had another important duty to perform whilst there: finalising arrangements for the establishment of an eastern distributorship for Triumph motorcycles. For some time

manufacture of motorcycles for the armed forces were unexpectedly terminated by the US War Department. Indian suffered particularly badly from this as no allowance had been made for machines already completed, or for the spare parts needed to keep them running. Indian held a particularly large stockpile of machines which had been completed under the original contract, along with a hefty inventory of component parts. When a flood of ex-military machines was released for sale to civilians at cut-rate prices, a dramatic fall in the level of new models sold followed, giving rise to financial problems that all but annihilated the money provisionally allocated for post-war development projects. Control of the company slipped out of the hands of the DuPont family, and passed to Ralph B. Rogers, a young industrialist who held a majority shareholding. With doubts being expressed about the future of this once-big company, Johnson decided now would be an opportune time to drop his Indian franchise.

As an aside, in addition to the Triumph and Ariel enterprise, Johnson Motors also sold the Mustang, a somewhat unorthodox, step-thru type of machine with small diameter wheels. Powered by a rather feeble 314cc single cylinder side valve engine, it was made in nearby Glendale and sold alongside the Motor Glide scooter, a somewhat similar machine which the company had been retailing for some while. It, too, had small diameter wheels, and was made in Inglewood by the Salsbury Corporation. The Motor Glide was powered

The interior of the Johnson Motors showroom, with the adjoining spare parts department. Two Tiger 100s can be seen and two Ariel twins, which suggests this photograph was taken circa 1948/9.

Edward had not been happy with the existing set-up in which Johnson Motors Inc., a private company, held the sole US importation rights for the machines made at Meriden. Johnson Motors had worked hard to establish nationwide dealerships, but, in such a large country, Triumph representation was seriously over-stretched and only patchy at best. To compound the problem, Ralph Rogers of the ailing Indian company had already reached a US distributorship arrangement with a number of other British manufacturers, after forming the Indian Sales Corporation with capital from Brockhouse Engineering, of Stockport. This meant British machines could be re-badged as Indians for sale in America. Only the Brockhouse-made, 250cc, side valve Scout would leave the Stockport factory with an Indian transfer already on its tank. Intended for the American market, it was arguably one of the worst and most inappropriate motorcycles ever made for sale in the US.

Edward had seen how Alfred Rich Child and Hap Alzina had made significant progress in the American market by having separate BSA distributorships in the east and west, and realised that Triumph should be operating along similar lines. Unable to find a private company in the east that would be the equivalent of Johnson Motors, the decision was made to create an entirely factory-owned outlet with direct responsibility to Meriden. This action was taken on the advice of the Market Research Association of America, which also suggested Baltimore, in the state of Maryland, as an appropriate location. The setting up process

had to be a covert operation, working from rented accommodation, so that Harley-Davidson was kept unaware of the existence of the embryonic Triumph Corportion of America for as long as possible. Harley-Davidson would hardly welcome this extension of Triumph's business!

Finding the right person to head-up the new company was not too difficult. Denis McCormack was Vice-President of the Market Research Association and, by birth, a Coventrarian, although he had become a naturalized American citizen. Having the necessary

How the Johnson Motors sales representative delivered new motorcycles during the early post-war years.

Motorcycle manufacturers were always keen to get their machines associated with movie stars for publicity purposes. Bill Johnson must have had good connections with the studios to be able to get Rita Hayworth to pose on a screen set with Edward and Bill Johnson on this early post-war Speed Twin.

background and experience, he filled the post of President admirably and had similar views to Bill Johnson when it came to running an ultra-smart and highly efficient business.

Later in the year a lease was obtained on a building in Joppa Road, Towson, a suburb of Baltimore. On 1st October 1950, McCormack, his secretary, Phylis Fansler, and Earl Miller, an accountant, moved into their new premises to commence operations, supported by an advertising campaign in the motorcycling press. As the advertisements proclaimed, Triumph now had two separate operations, one in the east and one in the west, and, in theory at least, nationwide representation. The new distributorship took over something like 60% of Johnson Motors' territory and in an area that comprised 70% of the total population. Johnson was, if anything, relieved about this and, in compensation, was made a Vice-President of the Triumph Corporation

and given a token share in the equity. It was largely an honorary position as he had no personal involvement in the day-to-day running of what was soon referred to colloquially as 'TriCor'.

One of McCormack's early TriCor appointments was Jack Mercer. An anglophile, Mercer was well-known in Britain for his freelance contributions about the American motorcycling scene in *Motor Cycling*. He also sold British motorcycle books and magazine subscriptions. A very likeable man, full of bonhomie, he was the ideal person to take on TriCor's eastern territory as its sales representative. A month after starting he was joined by Rod Coates, who was appointed TriCor's Service Manager. Rod brought with him a wealth of first-hand practical experience as both a development engineer and an experienced competitor. Because of his engine tuning abilities he was also put in charge of TriCor's racing department.

There was also a need for someone who had been factory-trained at Meriden to be available at Baltimore, to ensure that factory procedure was observed when it came to servicing and repair work. Edward seconded David Jones from Triumph's Experimental Department, who welcomed the opportunity despite being committed to a minimum stay of twelve months. Now the basis could be laid for regular service schools, where dealers and their mechanics could become acquainted with the correct factory service procedures. It was well-known that new recruits at Meriden were told there were three ways of doing things: the right way, the wrong way and the Meriden way. Presumably, doing it the Meriden way meant doing it correctly, but taking short cuts whenever they could be taken with safety!

At the 1951 Daytona race meeting, the first Triumph home in the 100 Mile Amateur race was ridden into second place by Peter Freytag, and in the 200 Mile Experts race that followed Triumphs finished 3rd, 4th and 6th. These results were particularly encouraging as Triumph had a better presence there this year. TriCor had now been officially launched and a banquet for Triumph personnel was held at Daytona Beach's Bath & Tennis Club. Attended by more than 200 Triumph dealers from across America, it presented an excellent opportunity for those from the west coast to intermingle with their colleagues from the east. Edward, Bill Johnson and Denis McCormack were all there, the last mentioned now able to disclose his identity. At the banquet, these three congratulated Bobby Turner who, at an AMA records meeting held on Daytona Beach, had achieved a two-way aggregate speed of 129.24mph through a one mile speed trap, riding a specially-prepared 649cc Thunderbird.

After the banquet Edward took the opportunity to tell those present about Triumph's plans. He was also able to allay fears expressed by some dealers that the current boom in Triumph sales would later lead to machine shortages. He confirmed there would not be a shortage of machines during the current year, or, for that matter, in 1952: he had taken the necessary steps to ensure this in recognition of the efforts they had made to achieve record sales.

Because of all the exposure that Triumph was getting, and the detrimental affect it was having on sales, Harley-Davidson decided it was time to act. The company petitioned the United States Tariff Commission on 21st May 1951 for higher duties on the imports of foreign motorcycles, on the grounds that British manufacturers were guilty of 'dumping'. Harley-Davidson claimed that since the British government's devaluation of the pound during September 1949, machines imported from Britain were selling for something like 25-30% less than its own equivalent models. However, the case was somewhat flawed because, in reality, Harley-Davidson did not have any models that were comparable with British imports! Be that as it may, Harley-Davidson claimed it had suffered serious loss of business as a result, and had been forced to lower its prices.

The Commission sat on 9th June and, when his turn came to testify, Denis McCormack put up a spirited defence. He believed that the 40% surcharge Harley-Davidson had recommended, and its proposal that the number of British machines imported be limited to that of pre-war levels, would put importers out of business. Something like 2000 dealers involved in the import business would find themselves having to face up to severe financial problems, and it should not be overlooked that the dollars earned by Britain through these imports were used to purchase American manufactured products such as foodstuffs.

McCormack was ably supported by Alfred Rich Child, who was well aware of the marketing ploys adopted by the American motorcycle industry and their restrictive practices from his days with

Sales and service schools played a very important role in keeping the American dealerships completely up-to-date with current developments and the techniques employed at Meriden. If Edward himself could not be there, he ensured that one of his senior staff was present. These regular schools were run by both Johnson Motors Inc and the Triumph Corporation of America. The continuation of this arrangement was reaffirmed when Edward made his first post-war visit to California in July 1945.

Harley-Davidson, which involved, amongst other things, price fixing. Neither Indian nor Harley-Davidson, the two major manufacturers, had made any attempt to develop lightweight models to compete with the imported machines, although they had a virtual monopoly in big capacity heavyweight vee-twins which meant the buyer's choice of machine was limited.

The lengthy hearings continued for almost three weeks and resulted in Harley-Davidson's petition being rejected on the grounds that it was unsustainable. The company had no similar models with which to meet the challenge offered by the imports, and had not attempted to make them. British manufacturers heaved a huge sigh of relief: had the petition been successful, the proposed surcharge - and the strictly controlled import quota - would literally have put them out of business as far as exports to America were concerned. Dollar earnings were vital in helping to pay off Britain's wartime borrowings and safeguard the post-war recovery programme.

Towards the end of June, Jack Mercer submitted a report to *Motor Cycling* about the Laconia road race meeting held in New Hampshire. Although the 100 Mile Championship race had been won by a Norton, this annual meeting held at Bellnap Country Park was soon to become a happy hunting ground for Triumph riders in their never-ending battle with Harley Davidsons. On this occasion, the first Triumph home was placed fifth, although it was not until 1953 that the first victory was scored when the Championship was won by Ed Fisher. Davey Jones won the 25 Mile Novice race at record speed and Sherman Cooper the 50 Mile Amateur race, to make it a 'hat trick' for Triumph. Attended by an estimated 20,000 spectators, this was another prestigious event that provided good publicity for Triumph.

By the end of the year British motorcycle exports had reached a peak of 91,700, and the number of Triumphs dispatched to America had more than doubled, heading toward the 3000 mark. Apart from

At the service schools, demonstrations were given on how to strip and rebuild an engine and other component parts 'the Triumph way', as in the case of this Tiger Cub engine.

the Thunderbird, the 1951, all-alloy engined Tiger 100, with its diecast close pitch fin cylinder head and barrel, and the Trophy Twin fitted with a similar engine, had each made a significant contribution.

No-one could deny that the Trophy Twin was one of the prettiest twins ever made. Weighing only 295lbs, it was an instant success with the off-road fraternity; not even its spring wheel was considered a disadvantage in desert races. Only long distance races gave pivoted fork rear suspension the decisive edge.

There could be no denying that American interest in road racing and off-road events had played a major role in promoting the sale of Triumphs in the USA. From earlier chapters it will have been apparent that Edward was very much set against factory involvement in road racing and similar events, although he was prepared to sanction works-sponsored riders in motocross and trials. The earlier arrival of the Grand Prix model had created quite a stir and, although only a fifth of total production had been exported to America, the machine became something of a legend. Indeed, it is probably fair to say the Grand Prix model received more acclaim in America than it did in Britain, despite its shortcomings.

The problem was, of course, that it conflicted with the 'no racing' policy Edward had so clearly laid down, even though he had given a hint that Triumph might find factory support for production racing more acceptable. Now he had grudgingly to accept the fact that American competition successes were largely responsible for the sale of Triumphs in such considerable numbers! It left him with little option other than to turn a blind eye to it, comforted by the fact that the support was coming from either JoMo or TriCor, with no direct factory involvement. Even so, he must have had some initial misgivings in consenting to produce a complete tuning kit for converting an alloy-engined Tiger 100 to production racing specification. Yet it was a

logical move following the demise of the Grand Prix model, allegedly due to pressure applied to Meriden by Pete Colman of JoMo.

Sunday 6th May 1951 marked the occasion of the first Catalina Grand National. There was a tendency to compare this event with the Isle of Man TT, since both involved the ascent of a mountain and each was held on an island that lay off the west coast of the mainland. There the similarity ended, however. A lap of the Catalina course was only 10.3 miles in length compared with the 37.75 miles of the Isle of Man, much of the former consisting of unmade roads of a torturous nature and including fire breaks through forests with innumerable tight turns and hazardous drops should a rider overshoot. It was, in effect, more akin to motocross than a road race. The main 100 mile race was won by Walt Fulton, a former very competent Harley-Davidson rider who had switched allegiance to Triumph. He rode what was virtually a standard 6T Thunderbird with a specially tuned engine. British-made machines took the first five places, and also won the 250cc and 125cc races run the previous day.

When the 1952 model range was announced, production of the 349cc 3T twin had ceased, not that many in America were concerned as it had been a slow seller. Various excuses were made for its demise but, in all probability, production was discontinued because it had always been the odd man out, differing in several ways to its 498cc counterparts. Those at Meriden were working flat out to produce all the 500cc and 650cc twins they could and the 3T could conveniently give way.

The New Year heralded the first of TriCor's yearly service schools, held on 22nd January. Ninety dealers made their way to Baltimore, those who wished to do so staying on for an extra day for advice about engine tuning and machine preparation given by Rod Coates and Davey Jones. These three to five day schools were well attended and went a long way toward ensuring that dealers and their mechanics were kept up-to-date with technical developments. They also promoted adoption of factory service procedures so that they would be carried out 'the Triumph way'. Edward was very much in favour of them and made sure that if he could not be there himself, some senior person from Meriden deputised, such as Jack Wickes or Triumph's Service Manager, John Nelson. Direct representation from Meriden was regarded as essential.

JoMo followed suit shortly afterwards, with Pete Colman in charge of the schools and direct representation provided by a senior person from the Meriden factory.

Competition success continued and, after a near-miss in the 100 Mile Championship at Laconia, when Ed Fisher finished second, reward for the Triumph riders came at the AMA 100 Mile Dirt Track Championship at Langhorne, during September. Triumphs took the first four places, with Rick Fisher winning at a race speed of 88.81mph. Triumph also had a runner-up in the Michigan 500 Mile Jack Pine National Enduro Championship, riding a Trophy Twin. It must have been a tough event as out of the 339 starters only 46 completed the course!

The 1953 model range brought in the Tiger 100C. The race kit parts mentioned previously had been discontinued and, instead, a production racing version of the over-the-counter Tiger 100 could be purchased with all these parts ready fitted. The other new model to appear on the American market was the T15 149cc Terrier. It may seem strange that such a small capacity, single cylinder model would have any attraction for American enthusiasts, especially in view of the low level of sales of the now discontinued 349cc 3T twin. However, the fact that it had the appearance of a miniaturised single cylinder Speed Twin in almost every respect meant it appealed to some. Product loyalty (sadly, a vital factor that was overlooked in later years) could not be ignored, and if a youngster or a lady rider bought a Terrier, it often meant a later upgrading to one of the larger capacity twins. The T15 was also purchased by competition riders, although it was not designed for this use. It made an ideal off-road competition lightweight after a few modifications had been carried out.

1954 was of greater significance as it marked the introduction of the new 649cc T110 model, the first Triumph twin to feature a cradle frame with pivoted fork rear suspension. The high performance engine benefited from a heavier crankshaft assembly that ran in larger diameter main bearings, enlarged inlet valves and ports, and a larger choke size carburetter. The engine produced 42bhp with air cleaner and silencers fitted, and, as denoted by the model designation, the T110 was capable of 110mph in standard road trim. A indication of its capabilities in this direction was the use of an 8 inch diameter front brake fitted with an air scoop. Adding to the list of attractions was the new shell blue sheen finish, which was also applied to the other models in the range with the exceptions of the Speed Twin and the Terrier. In short, the T110 represented everything the American enthusiast had been seeking for so long.

Edward finally capitulated and sactioned the production of a specially built production racing machine for sale in America. The 498cc TR5/R was similar in most respects to the already very successful T100/R model, differing in having the pivoted fork rear suspension frame and a selectively assembled engine that had been bench tested prior to installation. In order to satisfy AMA Class C regulations, the TR5/R was supplied with a quickly detachable lighting set, similar to that already in use on the standard production TR5 Trophy Twin.

Also new for 1954 was the T20 199cc Tiger Cub; in effect, a Terrier fitted with the new 63 x 64mm all-alloy, close pitch, fin engine. It retained the plunger-type rear suspension of the Terrier (the only two Triumph models ever to feature this type of rear suspension). If the Terrier had an unexpected impact on off-road riders, the Tiger Cub was destined to make an even bigger impression. It, too, was finished in the new shell blue sheen colour and, with its upswept exhaust pipe, looked a very purposeful mount.

The frame, with pivoted fork rear suspension, was fitted to the entire model range for the 1955 season, with the exception of the two lightweight singles. It would be only a matter of time before the Tiger Cub had a similar form of rear suspension due to a new design of frame, whilst the T15 Terrier was discontinued. For those models fitted with magneto ignition it was now necessary to fit one of Lucas manufacture, because BTH had ceased production of this vital component that had given such good service.

The change of frame was just one of several modifications to the Trophy Twin which, from the American viewpoint, were considered overdue. In Britain, the charm of this model had been its low overall weight (295lbs), and 'soft' low compression engine that made it eminently suitable for use in trials. In America there was very little interest in trials, a slow-moving sport that attracted few spectators. The 1955 Trophy Twin came with a much improved engine, performance-wise, having a compression ratio of 8:1, and the internals, such as camshafts, were similar to those used in the T110 engine. The power output had, in consequence, been boosted to 33bhp at 6500rpm, at the expense of increased weight of the new frame, which had gone up by no less than 65lbs. This would not have been well received by trials riders in Britain, but in America the reaction was the exact opposite. The Trophy Twin had, at last, become really competitive in desert races, especially those of long distance which previously had been dominated by Matchless and AJS singles.

In October, JoMo decided it was time to call a halt to retail sales and act solely as a wholesaler, to enable it to concentrate more on supplying the dealer network in the west, and ensure adequate servicing facilities were available to them. TriCor had already re-located at the beginning of the year when the lease for its premises in Towson expired. Rather than extend the lease, TriCor moved to purpose-built premises in Joppa Road, Timonium, another suburb of the city. The move had been underwritten by a company formed by Jack Sangster for just this purpose, Sangster Holding Inc., to keep it under the control of the parent company. The new building had been completed and was ready for occupation in January 1956. The inventory and accounts system had already been computerised under Earl Miller's guidance and the company had taken on representation for Steib sidecars.

The controversial issue of 1955 was Triumph's bid for the World Motorcycle Speed Record, when Johnny Allen achieved a two-way average speed of 193.72mph at Bonneville within a streamlined shell powered by an unsupercharged 649cc Thunderbird engine. (The full account of this long, drawn-out saga is given in Chapter Ten.) Had it not been for the petulant attitude of Piet Nortier and FIM President, Augustin Perouse, both of whom resented the AMA not having sought membership of the FIM, there can be little doubt about its authenticity as a World Record. Fortunately, because the record had been achieved on American soil and had been supervised by AMA officials, it could not be disputed as an American record. Triumph was still able to benefit from where the spin-off mattered most.

Another break-through occurred in 1956 when the first Triumph model designed specifically for the American market was launched. It was the TR6 Trophy, virtually the latest TR5 Trophy Twin fitted with

Early in 1954 the Triumph Corporation of America moved into its own purpose-built building in Joppa Road, Timonium, a suburb of Baltimore. It had been financed by Sangster Holdings Inc. to keep it under the control of the parent company.

a 649cc engine. Two versions were available: a competition version aimed at the desert racers in the west, and for those in the east, a road legal version with smaller diameter wheels and an 8 inch front brake. The latter model was the so-called 'street scrambler' soon to be widely known as the 'Trophy-bird'. The new TR6 model made an impressive debut in the 1956 Big Bear Run when Arvin Cox, Bud Ekins and Bill Postel took the first three places after dominating the race and constantly challenging each other for the lead.

The TR6 highlighted the need for models made for the two different markets in America, equipped in a style that differed from that of the standard British specification models. Hitherto, they had been shipped from Meriden only in small numbers, to special order. There was, however, a side issue now that necessitated a special US model coding to differentiate between what were basically near identical models. As a result, a road-going machine with a standard exhaust system layout was given the suffix /A, and one with an upswept system /B. An economy version (which usually meant the tachometer was omitted) carried the suffix /C. The coding was used for the 498cc and 649cc twins.

Other model changes for 1956 included a competition version of the Tiger Cub, the T20C, and the decision to discontinue production of the T15 Terrier. There had been signs that the Terrier had come to the end of the line when models began to appear with an all-black finish. Otherwise, the programme followed what previously had been announced in the 1956 model preview, with colour scheme changes that related specifically to the American market.

Some changes within the JoMo organisation occurred around this time. Following the establishment of TriCor in the east, the dealer network was still somewhat sparse, amounting to some 90 or so retail outlets in the 19 western states. Don Brown, a former broadcaster, journalist, and competition rider, was appointed Marketing Executive. His initial task was to manage the field sales force after researching the potential for sales in the 19 western states. His area of responsibility included the acquisition of new dealers, implementation of dealer policy, and sales promotion. At that time, Wilbur Ceder acted as Administration Manager, handling all the detail that Bill Johnson did not wish to become involved with. This included responsibility for ordering and co-ordinating the supply of machines with the Meriden factory. Pete Colman, through Wilbur, was responsible for the co-ordination of service and technical matters.

Don's market research showed that considerable potential still existed for expansion, as Triumph machines were outsold by Harley-Davidson and BSA products in rural areas. To rectify this situation, Don set up Service Depots, a scheme that was quite novel in the west. These Service Depots would put up a Triumph sign and purchase from JoMo on a cash basis new Triumph motorcycles at the normal

dealer discount, and spare parts at 25% below the suggested retail price. In this way a competitive situation that conflicted with already established dealers was not created. The whole scheme took two years to implement fully, but within the first year over 100 Service Depots had been established, effectively doubling JoMo's dealer network.

The next step was to convert these Service Depots into regular Triumph dealerships, providing the opportunity to drop those existing dealerships which had not come up to scratch. Wilbur had been determined the Service Depots should be capable of providing a first class service in accord with JoMo standards which, in view of their rural location, had made their selection all the more difficult. Over a period of three to four years, this programme contributed substantially to the expansion of the Triumph dealer network, and was directly responsible for a hefty increase in sales in the western area of America.

1957 proved to be a year of setbacks, beginning with a longshoremans' strike on the east coast during February. The strike lasted long enough to delay delivery of three shipments of new motorcycles from the Meriden factory.

Whilst Don Brown had been fully occupied with expansion of JoMo's dealer network, Rod Coates of TriCor had been developing an extensive range of after-market accessories and performance enhancing parts, some of which were manufactured by outside suppliers to comply with TriCor's exacting standards. They were listed in the company's 28-page Accessories and Equipment Catalogue, which was destined to become the 'bible' of Triumph enthusiasts.

Announcement of Triumph's 1957 programme was not as well received as it might have been because the range included a new 348cc twin, the Triumph Twenty-one. It marked the introduction of a new unit-construction engine and gearbox, and also the 21st Anniversary of Edward's first twin cylinder model, the legendary Speed Twin that had caused such a sensation at the time of its launch. It happened to be coincidental that 21 was also the capacity of the engine measured in cubic inches, the customary way of denoting car and motorcycle engine capacity in America.

A 21 cubic inch engine was unlikely to attract a great deal of attention in the American market as already had been evident with regard to the earlier 3T twin, but to compound the situation, the new model had an even greater disadvantage; pressed steel enclosures. These gave the Twenty-one the appearance of a cross between a motorcycle and a scooter. A deep section front mudguard made it look more like a heavyweight; this feature was accentuated by the bodywork that enclosed the rear end of the machine, covering the oil tank and upper half of the rear wheel, serving also as the rear mudguard. In Britain, the rear enclosure ensured that, in no time at

146

all, the Twenty-one was dubbed the 'bath tub' model. When the first of these models arrived in America during the second half of 1957, it received a similar reaction.

It was immediately obvious that styling of this nature would not meet with the approval that had been anticipated. Many prospective purchasers regarded it as effeminate and, although a similar reaction had already made itself less strongly felt in Britain, there was a greater sense of disappointment in America. It was one of very few occasions when Edward had attempted to project a new style, intended, in this instance, to provide rider and pillion passenger with better weather protection, which had failed to meet its objective. Those in the western states, where better weather and participation in off-road motorcycle sport was more evident, were the most resistant. To help maintain sales, dealers were forced to remove the enclosures so that the new machine could be given that macho look beloved of American riders. It was by no means uncommon to find a stack of unused enclosures at the rear of a dealer's premises, as Jack Wickes discovered when he called on Bud Ekins in Los Angeles.

From Edward's point of view the enclosures represented a genuine attempt to attract newcomers to motorcycling; those who previously had regarded motorcycles as dirty, oily machines in need of constant maintenance to keep them on the road. He had mentioned this intention when he gave an earlier lecture to the Institution of Mechanical Engineers, and was by no means the first to have produced a machine intended to create a new image. The industry had, unsuccessfully, spent millions of pounds trying to perfect a machine with this objective. Ironically, it was the scooter that came closest to achieving this goal during its unprecented popularity in the 1950s.

Included in the 1957 model range was the TR5AD, an optional twin carburetter version of the TR5A, a US distributor-inspired model that was not of Meriden origin. The cylinder head, with its widely splayed ports, was known at Meriden as the Delta head. It had larger diameter inlet valves and formed part of a 'package' that included 9:1 compression ratio pistons, racing camshafts and associated cam followers, interference fit racing valve springs, and bronze valve guides. When asked whether Triumph could supply a similar cylinder head for the 649cc twins, Edward had always been very wary, suggesting on many occasions that to do so would be the quickest way to end up in the bankruptcy court. Exactly what he meant by this is not clear: it has been suggested he may have fought shy of using a twin carburetter set-up on anything other than a 498cc twin because he was of the opinion it would be at the expense of a rougher running engine, the risk of overheating, and loss of low speed tractability.

Four different versions of the T20 Tiger Cub were now available in America, and it was on one of the competition variants that Ralph Adams won the 200cc class in the 1957 Catalina Grand Prix. A further six of these models finished in the top ten, and Johnny Smith won the 165cc class on a Terrier. In recent years, the Tiger Cub had become a popular model and helped swell the ranks of those who did well on a Triumph in this event.

Toward the end of the year yet another problem had begun to manifest itself; an ever-growing stockpile of unsold machines taking up valuable warehouse space. JoMo was the worst affected as its inventory of unsold models included a large number of Ariel Red Hunter singles, and some of the Triumph stock was two years old! If more machines than the market would bear continued to be ordered, the point would eventually be reached when, in about two years' time, no more new machines would have to be ordered from Meriden for at least a year or maybe longer, until the backlog of unsold machines had been cleared.

It was a national problem because JoMo's territory abutted that of TriCor. When it came to the end of the year and holdover machines were heavily discounted to get rid of them, some of the eastern dealers got wise to this and would make arrangements with those in the west to buy some of them. Denis McCormack viewed this practice with disapproval and wrote to Wilbur Ceder about it. The arrival of his letter more or less coincided with Don's report on the situation, which suggested that all marketing should be put in charge of a central office. Bill Johnson was sympathetic, although realised there would have to be a substantial cutback in orders for next year's models if such a plan was to be implemented. Without knowing how Edward would react, he suggested Don should take his programme to Meriden and discuss it with him. If Edward agreed and something could be worked out between them, he would then give it his blessing. With the help of Bill Robertson, Don worked out a programme whereby a substantial one-off cutback for one year only would be made in JoMo's orders to clear the backlog, followed by more formal and methodical co-ordination of ordering and distribution thereafter.

By the beginning of 1959, JoMo was organised in such a way that all matters, including factory technical specification changes relating to improving the model range, were all co-ordinated through Don's office. Production scheduling was carefully monitored and, within a year of the new programme being implemented, nearly $100,000 had been saved on warehousing charges alone. It was now possible to pre-sell by accepting advance orders from dealers and monitoring them so that machines would be dispatched direct from the factory and go in and out of the warehouse quickly, without running up several months of warehouse charges. Denis McCormack was impressed by this rearrangement and asked Don to call on him on his return from Meriden. Don stayed at TriCor for a couple of days and such a good understanding existed between the two men that a lasting friendship developed.

Another Triumph innovation that failed to generate much enthusiasm made its debut in 1958. This was the infamous 'Slickshift' gearbox which permitted gearchanges to be made without using the clutch, if desired. However, motorcyclists had become accustomed to having a clutch lever on the handlebars and using it to change gear, and preferred to continue changing gear in the conventional manner. When new models started to arrive with a Slickshift gearbox, feeling was strong enough for some buyers to request a conventional gearbox instead. Yet, if the clutch lever had been removed from the handlebars and an automatic gearbox fitted (should such a thing have existed at that time), it is doubtful there would have been many takers for that either. When the Japanese offered big capacity models with a centrifugal clutch and automatic transmission in later years, they, too, failed to make a impact. Another of Triumph's attempts to attract newcomers to motorcycling (it had been expected to appeal to learners in particular) had failed, even though it eliminated the need to co-ordinate clutch and gearlever to achieve a 'clean' gearchange.

A new T20/J Tiger Cub, a model never seen in Britain, had been included in the 1958 model programme. It was the Tiger Cub Junior, with a power-restricted engine. As an 'entry level' model it was aimed at attracting youngsters, particularly students. In Britain, the minimum age to apply for a licence was sixteen at this time, whereas in America the age limit was fourteen. US legislation at that time restricted to 5bhp the power output of a machine that fourteen to sixteen year olds were eligible to ride. Despite its 199cc capacity, the Junior Tiger Cub met this requirement by the simple expedient of fitting a smaller bore carburetter with a restricting washer in its inlet to the engine. These modifications gave the engine a certified rating of 4.9bhp at 5700rpm. The advantage of this approach to power limitation was that when the rider reached his seventeenth birthday, removal of the restricting inlet washer and fitting of a larger bore carburetter would restore the engine to full performance capability. Needless to say, as the restoration of full power was so easy to achieve, many did this prematurely and quite illegally!

Don Brown saw promotion of the Tiger Cub Junior and the Twenty-one models as a way to encourage newcomers to motorcycling. Through JoMo's dealer network, he set up a motorcycle instruction programme for learner riders, who were taught the basic rules of the road and how to ride safely. Not only did this help reduce the road accident casualty rate, but the increase in motorcycle sales encouraged TriCor to set up a similar scheme.

The Big Bear Run, like those that preceded it, was a long distance desert racing event in which riders covered 155 miles from start to finish. The 1958 event attracted an amazing 834 entries, the majority of whom rode British motorcycles. This year's winner was Roger White, riding a Triumph TR6; it is worth recording that Bud Ekins repeated his 1957 win the following year on a similar mount.

What went on behind the closed doors of the Experimental Department has, of necessity, to remain a well-kept secret. When the availability of a twin carburetter splayed port cylinder formed the subject of a Triumph Technical Information Bulletin in 1958, it came as no real surprise. Both JoMo and TriCor had been pleading for this for some considerable time, as it was high on the 'shopping list' of American enthusiasts who were always seeking the ultimate in performance. Many had resorted to modifying the twin carburetter head already available for the 498cc twins so that it could be used on a 649cc engine, but to do this required experience and certain equipment.

A twin carburetter 649cc model was indeed at the experimental stage at this point in time, in the capable hands of Frank Baker. A prototype engine was already showing promise, sufficient to underline the need for a one-piece crankshaft to successfully withstand the increased power output. When a complete machine was available, tests were carried out at the Motor Industry Research Association's proving ground. Even Percy Tait, one of the works testers who could always get the best out of any Triumph, was surprised to learn he had been electronically timed at 128mph! Costings for the new model were favourable, and after JoMo and TriCor had been advised and signified their whole-hearted approval, the green light was given to go ahead. Some frantic rescheduling of the production programme at Meriden followed, so that the new model could be included in the 1959 programme.

Although the new twin had been designated the T120, it still had no name, and it was not until almost the last minute that it was agreed. In recognition of Johnny Allen's record-breaking venture at Bonneville in September 1955, Bonneville it had to be, especially in view of high sales prospects anticipated in America. By the time Triumph's annual review of the following year's models had been published during late October, motorcyclists had been made aware of Triumph's new flagship model, which headed a nine model range. What was destined to become a legend in company history was about to arrive, bearing the World Motorcycle Speed Record Holder transfer.

The problems which had initially blighted sales of the Thunderbird in America, and the reaction to the Twenty-one model and the Slickshift gearbox, have already been described. Because of these it might have been expected that, by now, Edward would have a better understanding of what that country's motorcyclists desired most, but if so it was not very apparent when the first Bonneville models arrived. Despite the high performance capabilities of this new model,

only the British specification model was available to be shipped. The headlamp nacelle, the large capacity petrol tank, deep section mudguards, and a wide, two-level dualseat all detracted from the image it should have had. This was all the more perplexing because the Bonneville had been produced with American requirements in mind! The 649cc Trophy was, in the opinion of many, Triumph's most popular model at that time, and a twin carburetter version of the locally modified US market TR6A would have been appreciated more than the latest high performance model, which somehow just did not look right.

It was a problem that dealers had to recognise and overcome by ordering a Bonneville cylinder head and an extra Amal Monobloc carburetter, to effect the satisfactory conversion of the much leaner looking, locally modified US market TR6A. TriCor issued a dealer bulletin outlining what was needed to do this, and suggested it should be done only as a last resort if the sale of a Bonneville was likely to be lost. TriCor also recommended the dealer should make a charge of $100 to cover the cost of the conversion.

Fortunately, it did not take long for Meriden to realise the error of its ways: the 1960 Bonnevilles exported to America arrived without the nacelle and with a rubber-gaitered front fork, a chromium-plated headlamp taking the nacelle's place. Other modifications included slimmer front and rear sporting mudguards, high-rise handlebars and a different, slimmer dualseat. It was the beginning of the realisation that models shipped to America would have to be built to meet American customer requirements if projected sales targets were to be met.

Another surprise was that the 1959 Speed Twin had a unit-construction engine and all the enclosures already featured on the Twenty-one. The good news was that the new 490cc engine was a short stroke, with bore and stroke dimensions of 69 x 65.5mm compared to the old 498cc engine's measurements of 63 x 80mm. Those who prepared engines for competition work saw great possibilities in it, and such was the level of interest that both JoMo and TriCor provided instructions on how to convert the unit-construction engines to meet AMA regulations. Later, both suplied ready-converted engine units.

The 498cc TR5 Trophy Twin had now been dropped from production and another import from Meriden came to America: the twin cylinder 249cc Tigress scooter. Now that Triumph had been acquired by the BSA Group, the identical B2 BSA Sunbeam scooter also came in as a parallel import, available only through the BSA dealer network. Amalgamation of the two separate dealership networks was still some way off, and would not take place whilst Edward remained in charge of Triumph's affairs. The scooter was another model regarded with indifference in America, so there was not much potential for scooter sales. Its inclusion meant that the Triumph range in America comprised sixteen different models, more in number than those available in Britain. However, this apparent discrepancy was accounted for by American dealers stocking several different versions of the same model, denoted by the amended model code as outlined earlier. Sales of the twins continued to increase unabated, but the scooter was considered by most dealers to be little more than an expensive inconvenience.

A new threat now appeared on the horizon when American Honda occupied premises on West Pico Boulevard in Los Angeles. The first Triumph dealer to break rank and join the 'opposition' was Ed Kretz, who took on Honda representation without first notifying either Don Brown or Wilbur Ceder of JoMo. Already American Honda had attracted a number of ex-Triumph personnel to join its staff, including Walt Fulton, of TriCor. Kretz's defection came as a rude shock and sent a ripple through the trade. Triumph policy at that time forbade any major metropolitan dealer from taking on any other line that would be directly competitive with its own without first discussing such a proposition with JoMo. In view of his national reputation as a highly successful competition rider, Kretz's move was seen as likely to influence other dealers to follow suit and defect.

A meeting with a group of local Los Angeles dealers was convened at Johnson Motors' premises to provide an opportunity to discuss JoMo's fears that its dealers believed that taking on Honda representation would not affect Triumph at all, and that JoMo should not be hostile about it. As it turned out, the dealers were right, but, as JoMo did not have the luxury of hindsight, it did something that was rather arbitrary and upset dealers in the short term, but which probably proved the best move it had made in a long time. JoMo cancelled all dealer contracts that gave exclusive territorial rights and replaced them with new agreements that were non-exclusive with regard to these rights. In effect, JoMo said that if a dealer took on other machines, JoMo reserved the right to take on other Triumph dealers, wherever considered appropriate. This move was not well received initially and, for a while, relationships with dealers were uneasy.

As the situation developed, Bill Johnson asked Don to set up a meeting with one of American Honda's senior Japanese executives, and this was duly arranged through Jack McCormack, a former JoMo employee now working for Honda. American Honda was curious about Johnson Motors which, at that time, had a very good reputation as a promotional-minded company, and was keen to learn something about JoMo's operation. Held in Bill Johnson's office, those present at the meeting comprised Bill Johnson, Wilbur Ceder, Don Brown, Pete Colman, Jack McCormack and Hirobumi Nakamura, American Honda's Sales Manager.

During the course of conversation, Bill Johnson asked Honda's Japanese executive how many machines he thought he could sell, and, after thinking for a minute, Nakamura said 5000 units. Bill Johnson replied that this could probably be achieved if he worked very hard, as the machines were cheap. He didn't know how much Honda had spent on promotion, but supposed that this level of machine sales could be realised by the end of the year. Honda's man remained silent for a further minute then held up his hand: he meant 5000 units a month. Bill Johnson almost fell off his chair and said "There is no way anyone can sell that number of machines in a month"!

After the meeting Bill Johnson asked Don to carry out some research on the situation, as he had received a letter from Edward who wanted to know about American Honda and what the future held. A week later Don's report to Bill was complete, and was forwarded to Edward. Bill had been sceptical about the report because Honda intended to develop a range of models specifically for the American market. Although Honda's current model range was ugly, a tremendous promotional campaign had attracted a new class of rider which included, for the first time, those new to motorcycling. It began to look as though JoMo had possibly underestimated the extent of the Honda threat, not that the situation had been monitored in isolation. Denis McCormack had also been seeking information about American Honda's activities from both and through the Meriden factory. TriCor was more remote from the centre of American Honda's operation as Honda had begun operations on the west coast, virtually on JoMo's doorstep.

When he received Don Brown's report, Edward made immediate plans to visit America and asked Bill Johnson to collect together a representative selection of Japanese motorcycles so that he could evaluate them himself. He rode every single machine, including the Meguro twin that was a virtual copy of the BSA A7. His verdict at the conclusion of his extended test session was "too good to be true". It was this that inspired him to visit Japan to see the situation himself. His initial belief was that the Japanese were trading on cheap labour but did not stand much chance of competing directly, nor intended to do so. If they did, he believed they would run into unexpected increases in cost. Without any doubt, Edward had a better understanding of the Japanese situation than anyone in Britain - or, for that matter - in America, and was the first motorcycle manufacturer to take the iniative and find out for himself exactly what was going on in Japan.

Edward's observations prompted Don Brown to change his marketing strategy. He sent out a letter to all dealers stating that JoMo no longer believed Japanese motorcycles offered a competitive threat. Furthermore, due to multi-dollar advertising campaigns, and because Honda machines had a reasonable re-sale value, Honda had attracted a new class of customer, so dealers could take on representation if they wished. Don's letter greatly relieved the tension that existed between JoMo and its dealers, and proved such a success that a copy of it ended up in American Honda's office!

Honda had attracted a new class of dealer, one which had a large amount of money at its disposal. It greatly increased the desire amongst dealerships to become a Triumph representative also, which, in turn, meant dealers could be located more strategically. Additionally, the trade-up feature caused sales volumes to escalate: it was on these very points that JoMo was able to capitalise.

The preview of the 1960 programme revealed that Triumph had twelve models available for the American market. The range would now include a third unit-construction twin, the T100/A, as the Tiger 100 had been the next in line to have a 490cc short stroke unit-construction engine and 'bath tub' bodywork. It would appear that Edward was still determined to press ahead with his predilection for semi-enclosure, irrespective of customer reaction. Although this type of styling had given rise to less controversy on the home market than it had in America, the hierarchy of JoMo and TriCor brought pressure to bear on Edward through Triumph's Export Manager, A.J. Mathieu, to supply model variations which would more closely meet customer requirements.

It is easy to understand why dealers were no longer prepared to accept models which would have to be modified if sales targets were to be met. Already, more than half of Triumph's production potential was being exported, a significant proportion of which was scheduled for shipment to America. The arrival of the first 1960 Bonnevilles is another good example of what may well have triggered off this plea. Described in the sales cataolgue as the T120 Bonneville Super Sports model, it was still identical to those that had arrived earlier. Not having the new duplex tube frame mentioned in the 1960 model preview that was intended for the T110 and T120, the Bonnevilles were obviously holdovers from the 1959 season. It has even been suggested that had this, and the previously strong representation, not been made by the American distributors, the Bonneville would have had bodywork similar to that of the other unit-construction models, when it was redesigned with a unit-construction engine for the 1963 programme!

American needs had, however, been met by two Bonneville variants, the TR7A And TR7B, which were based on the TR6 Trophy and concocted by the two US distributors. The TR7A was a Road Sports model and the TR7B was listed as a Bonneville scrambler. These and similar machines with US model codings were not factory produced models. They were often based on standard models that had been held in stock for too long, the conversion being carried out by the distributor's staff whilst the machines were still in their crates. They did not stamp the revised model coding on the crankcase as a prefix to the engine number.

When the new season's 649cc models began to arrive with the new duplex tube frame, warranty problems started to arise. Edward had omitted the lower tank rail and the top tube, and the steering head had to bear additional stresses. The new frame transmitted more vibration which caused the tubes to crack or even fracture completely in the vicinity of the steering head. Warranty claims began to flood in, and, as mentioned earlier, there was a fatality in the Big Bear Run when a competitor's frame broke unexpectedly. To Edward's credit, remedial action was swiftly taken and a lower tank rail added to the frame's structure to stiffen it.

Unfortunately, it was a case of curing one problem and creating another. The modified frame now transmitted even more vibration, so that petrol tanks began splitting, giving rise to even more warranty claims! It was not until another, different frame appeared in 1962 that these problems were finally overcome.

At this time trouble was also being experienced with the Lucas electrics, supplied as original equipment, being unreliable. This had been particularly evident on the unit-construction models which relied on AC generator output for both the ignition and lighting, matters coming to a head when the Lucas Energy Transfer System was adopted. It would function efficiently only if the ignition timing was spot on; any small variation and the engine would not run properly or, worse still, fail to start. This problem led to lengthy, high level discussions with senior Lucas personnel which initially did not achieve very much. Eventually, the problem was resolved, but not before Lucas's reputation had been harmed.

This problem was exacerbated by the motorcycle manufacturers to whom the equipment was supplied. Cost was all-important and even fractions of a penny mattered. Corners often had to be cut if the supplier did not wish to lose a valuable contact. This also applied to other original equipment accessory manufacturers. Ideally, Meriden should have had someone in overall charge of quality control, but Edward remained adamant that this was unnecessary.

There were many who regretted the passing of the 498cc TR5A Trophy Twin, and it was not until the unit-construction Speed Twin and T100A models appeared that potential for an updated version was seen in their short stroke engines. For the 1961 season, Triumph offered two reincarnations of the 498cc T100, based on this engine, which comprised a road-going model, the TR5A/R, and a competition model, the TR5A/C. These were genuine factory made models in the form of variants for the east and west coasts. Otherwise, the 1961 model

Johnson Motors, Inc.
DISTRIBUTORS OF BRITAIN'S FINEST MOTORCYCLES

ARIEL   **TRIUMPH**

CABLE ADDRESS "JOMO"   •   267 WEST COLORADO BLVD.   •   PASADENA, CALIFORNIA

As you may know, I have come to California to pay my last respects to Bill Johnson who was one of my closest friends and I think we all feel a deep sense of loss at his passing. The purpose of this letter, however, is to make clear to all Triumph dealers my company's continued support for Johnson Motors, Inc. Fortunately, Mr. Johnson had for many years set up a smooth running and efficient organization, the management and principals of which are personally known to you.

As Managing Director of Triumph Engineering Company Limited of Coventry, U.K., I am entirely satisfied that Johnson Motors can and will continue to give you every support and help in the future as they have done in the past. We cannot say that we shall not miss Bill Johnson's wise and kindly influence on the business, but Mr. Fleming, Mr. Ceder and myself will give all future operations our close attention and Mr. Don Brown, in common with the other executives of Johnson Motors, Inc., will continue to vigorously pursue the business in our mutual interest.

Wishing you continued success, and I am sure you will join with me in offering Mrs. Johnson and all personnel of Johnson Motors, Inc. our great sympathy for the loss of their founder and great friend of all of us.

Yours sincerely,

Edward Turner
Managing Director
Triumph Engineering Co., Ltd.
Coventry, U.K.

ET:us

The news of Bill Johnson's death, on 4th March 1962, came as a terrible blow, especially to Edward. This is the announcement about the future of Johnson Motors Inc., put out under Edward's signature, which had those graceful, flowing curves so representative of the models he designed.

range was basically that of 1960, with detail modifications. Those affecting the Bonneville included fully-floating front brake shoes, anti-vibration mountings and a froth tower for the oil tank, and a new, all-welded steel petrol tank with improved rubber mountings, retained by a central strap.

Unknown at the time, work was proceeding on the redesign of the Bonneville around a unit-construction engine. This had been prompted by the knowledge that BSA, now one of Triumph's main competitors in America, would be launching its new A50 and A65 unit-construction twins at the end of the year.

It was also planned to discontinue manufacture of the 649cc T110, which had enjoyed a long innings and, like the Bonneville, still had a separate engine and gearbox. It would, however, be overshadowed by the new unit-construction Bonneville, scheduled to became available in 1963: there was little point in updating it, too.

Bill Johnson died on 4th March 1962 at the age of 57, after what, at first, seemed to be a mild stroke that left him paralysed down one side. As Edward said when he returned home from Bill's funeral in California "He just turned his head to the wall and died". Edward had lost his best friend. As a memento of their friendship, Edward bought Bill's white Cadillac from his estate and had it shipped home (accompanied by a consignment of carrots!). He had travelled in that car with Bill on many occasions, which had an interesting history, having, at one time, been used by Vice-President Nixon. It must have caused quite a sensation when it was driven along Warwickshire's country lanes, with its left-hand drive, soft suspension and electrically-operated windows.

Apart from being very upset about Bill's death, it must have been a poignant reminder to Edward that his own business life was soon to draw to a close. Wilbur Ceder had taken over as head of Johnson Motors but, sadly, only for a short period. He died during May 1966. It was a case of 'all change' as far as Triumph's American representation was concerned as Denis McCormack retired during 1964, leaving Earl Miller to take over control of TriCor.

At last, Triumph got its long-awaited win in the prestigious Daytona 200, when Don Burnett, riding a 498cc T100/SR, held off Dick Mann's G50 Matchless by a matter of feet throughout the race. He had been runner-up the year before and, on this occasion, had lapped the entire field. The news came too late for Bill Johnson of JoMo as he had died only a matter of hours earlier. Dick Mann got his own back at Laconia a few months later when he took the winner's rostrum and it was Don who found himself runner-up.

As mentioned elsewhere, Joe Dudek built a record-breaking streamliner, using an aerodynamic shell based on the X-15 rocket-propelled aeroplane which, at that time, held the World's Fastest Aircraft Record. It was powered by an over-bored (667cc) Triumph Bonneville engine prepared by Pete Colman. Ridden by Bill Johnson (who was not in any way related to the late Bill Johnson of Johnson Motors), Dudek took the streamliner to the Bonneville salt flats for the annual record attempt session. Running on a nitromethane mixture, the Triumph averaged a two-way speed of 224.57mph over the flying kilometre to set a new World Motorcycle Speed Record. It could not be disputed by the FIM as it had been observed by the head of the FIM Technical Committee. The measured mile had also been timed at 230.269mph but, for technical reasons, this higher speed could be recognised only in America by the AMA.

The US market TR5A/R and TR5A/C models were discontinued after only a year, and replaced by other T100 variants, the T100S/R variant of the unit-construction T100 attracting no small amount of attention. As was so often the case with the 500cc models, the engine vibration factor was much less noticeable than on the 650cc twins. Model designations were now becoming difficult to memorise, unlike the model names to which purchasers had been accustomed in the past. This was compounded by distributors using their own designations for conversions they had carried out themselves on machines they had in stock. As a flood of different Japanese models began to hit the market, they, too, tended to use a similar system of numerical identification.

The new unit-construction T120 Bonneville models made their American debut during 1963 in the form of the T120R road-going model and the T120C Competition Sports version. Both featured the new frame that replaced the one that had given cause for complaint. By reverting to a single front down tube and a single top tube, less engine vibration was transferred to the rider and the frame itself, aided by the fact that the engine ran more smoothly. Unfortunately, high speed handling was somewhat doubtful and it was several more years before this new problem was eliminated completely.

None of the Triumph models had magneto ignition now, a matter which the older generation regarded with suspicion. Although the alternator-based AC systems had become more reliable, those who earlier had suffered the Energy Transfer system had good reason to be sceptical. Of the three 1963 490cc models, only the Tiger 100S/C competition model still adhered to this system, as did the T20S/R and T20S/C Tiger Cubs. Only the 5TA Speed Twin retained its distributor at the rear of the cylinder block. Wear in the bushes in which the distributor shaft ran caused variations in the points gap, and affected ignition timing. Sooner or later this resulted in a noticeable fall-off in performance and irregular running. The use of a distributor continued for only one more year.

Also new for 1962 was the 99.75cc Tina scooter. It was of little interest to America, which is, perhaps, just as well. Its automatic transmission was anything but trouble-free and, had it sold in significant numbers, it would only have brought discredit to the Triumph name and reputation.

There were still problems to be resolved relating to machines needed by the American market, as Meriden would have much preferred to have fewer model variations, and manufacture, instead, a simplified range of models that would meet customer requirements both sides of the Atlantic. Those in America seemed to think that Meriden never fully appreciated that both markets had good reasons for going their separate ways, a situation unlikely to change in the foreseeable future. It was all a question of profitability in the long run, as Edward knew only too well what was likely to happen once the Japanese manufacturers got into full stride. He had the shareholders to think of, too.

At the end of the year this problem was no longer Edward's concern as he handed over the reins to others and retired. He had a keen interest in Triumph affairs to the end and was pleased to have been retained on a consultancy basis. From this point on the wind of change began to affect Triumph's future and the downhill run began. It is perhaps fortunate that Edward did not live long enough to see the Triumph Engineering Company's final demise and all the misery and upheaval that preceded it. Combining the marketing and sales activities of Triumph and BSA was the final coup de grace.

Appendix 1: A tribute to Nan Plant

This book would not be complete without a tribute to Nan Plant, Edward's secretary and personal assistant for more than thirty years. Until now, her contribution to the Triumph story has been overlooked as she had always had a background role. A secretary of the old school, she performed a myriad of duties in a very efficient and quietly confident manner.

There were many within the company who, when called to the 'inner sanctum', or warned that Edward was about to appear on the shop floor, benefited from her helpful advice. When Edward was away for long periods on overseas visits, Nan could be relied upon to provide him with the latest production figures, and details of any other matters that required his personal attention. She was the one who answered telephone calls to his office, diverting the caller to someone else if there was no need to involve him personally. She was always addressed as Miss Plant, even by Edward. She would never have wished it any other way and, in any case, it is doubtful if anyone would have had the temerity to do otherwise!

Nellie Beatrice Plant, or Nellie B. Plant, as she always signed herself in her very neat handwriting, had been Edward's secretary since his first marriage to Marion. She had been educated at a technical school where the emphasis had been on office skills, such as shorthand and typing. During the period that followed the 1914-18 war, business opportunities for women were very limited.

Her father had returned from the war shell-shocked and in generally poor condition. He left his wife to live with another woman, forcing his daughter to care for, and largely support her mother alone. The relationship between mother and daughter was strained, but Nan's sense of duty - and the climate of the time - meant she was tied to her mother and could not desert her. She resented the situation bitterly initially, but eventually rose above it when she was in her early twenties. By sheer will-power she forced herself to adapt to the circumstances as they were.

One of the problems facing women of her age was that almost a million men died during the war, and many who might otherwise have had a happy marriage could not find a husband. In any case, Nellie had not seen the best side of the opposite sex: her father failed her, and the few bosses for whom she worked had been either difficult or unpleasant. When once she was asked by Edward's two daughters why she had never married, her answer was because she liked her bed, her body and her bath to herself!

She had worked in London before she came to Coventry and was a keen concert and cinema-goer. She also loved travel and had opportunities to do this through Edward, such as her visit to Paris as mentioned earlier.

Nan Plant, Edward's secretary, who was also a friend of the family.

Nan Plant's retirement party was obviously a very jolly affair. Her retirement present was a very handsome Murphy stereogram.

In her retirement she kept in touch with Phylis Fansler, her opposite number who worked for Denis McCormack of TriCor, and used to visit her in Baltimore. She also visited the Bahamas on one or two occasions whilst the Turner family was living there after Edward's retirement. His two daughters got to know her much better whilst he resided there because she used to supervise them at the beginning and end of each holiday. Later, she went to Maderia with a companion for a visit that had been organised by Edward's eldest daughter, Jane, during a a period of remission after her last illness. It was then that she disclosed what a great relief it was to have someone else organise all the arrangements after so many years of having to do it herself for others.

Although she was often on the receiving end of Edward's wrath when things were not going well, she was well able to stand up for herself. She was also skilled at knowing how to manipulate situations to her advantage when they seemed likely to provoke controversy. To quote an example; she knew that if she provided itemised accounts, Edward was likely to wave them through, whereas if they were presented separately they might cause a rumpus.

Typically, in her retirement she took it upon herself to look after and visit old people, some of whom were younger than her, but less fit. When she was almost eighty she also nursed a young woman who lived in the flat below her who was continually discharged from hospital and was slowly dying, until she was taken into a hospice. It was to the detriment of her own health and, it is believed, led to her own final illness.

Always loyal, when asked whether she thought Edward was a difficult man to work for, she invariably said that although he could be difficult, she found he was largely fair, interesting and worth working for. In short, she thought he was the best boss she had ever had.

It will never be fully known just how much Nellie contributed to the smooth running of the Triumph Engineering Company, or how many things she did to help others throughout her business career.

Author's note

This brief biography is based on notes kindly provided by Jane Meadows who, with her sister Charmian, held a great respect for Nan and considered her to be an essential part of the Triumph story.

Appendix 2: Sources of reference

Memories of ET, Jane Meadows (private document)
A Million Miles Ago Neale Shilton, GT Foulis, 1982
Whatever Happened to the British Motorcycle Industry?, Bert Hopwood. GT Foulis, 1981
British Motor Cycles Volume 5. Triumph Part One: The Company, Steve Wilson. Patrick Stephens Ltd, 1991
The Giants of Small Heath, Barry Ryerson. GT Foulis, 1980
The Story of Triumph Motor Cycles, Bob Currie and Harry Louis. Patrick Stephens Ltd, 1975
The Ariel Story, Peter Hartley. Argus Books Limited, 1980
Tales of Triumph Motorcycles & The Meriden Factory, Hughie Hancox. Veloce Publishing Ltd, 1996/1999
Triumph Tiger Cub Bible, Mike Estall. Veloce Publishing Ltd, 2000
It's a Triumph, Ivor Davies. GT Foulis, 1980
Triumph Thunderbird Superprofile, Ivor Davies. GT Foulis, 1984*
It's Easy on a Triumph, Ivor Davies. GT Foulis, 1990
Triumph: The Complete Story, Ivor Davies. The Crowood Press Ltd, 1991
Triumph Twins and Triples, Roy Bacon. Osprey Publishing Ltd, 1981*
Triumph Singles, Roy Bacon. Osprey Publishing Ltd, 1984*
Military Motorcycles of World War 2, Roy Bacon. Osprey Publishing Ltd, 1985
Triumph in America, Lindsay Brooke and David Gaylin. Motorbooks International, 1993*
Triumph Racing Motorcycles in America, Lindsay Brooke. Motorbooks International, 1996
Inside American Motorcycling, Harry V Sucher. Infosport Publications, 1995
Triumph Speed Twin: The development history of the pre-unit and unit construction 500cc twins, H Woolridge. GT Foulis, 1989*
Tiger 100/Daytona: The development history of the pre-unit and unit construction 500cc twins, JR Nelson. GT Foulis, 1988*
Bonnie: The development history of the Triumph Bonneville, JR Nelson. GT Foulis, 1979*
Triumph Bonneville Superprofile, John Nelson. GT Foulis, 1985*
Classic British Trials Bikes, Don Morley. Osprey Publishing Ltd, 1984
Glass's Guide Motor Cycle Check Book 1954-1962, William Glass Ltd
Daimler V8 SP250, Brian Long. Veloce Publishing Ltd, 1994
The Motor Cycle (various issues)
Motor Cycling (various issues)
Old Bike Mart (various issues)
The Classic Motor Cycle (various issues)
Classic Bike (various issues)
Motor Cycle News (various issues)
Classic Gas, the Newsletter of the Westland Classic Motorcycle Club, November 1997 issue
Interview and tape about his days with Triumph, Jack Wickes
Tape about Johnson Motors' Inc early days, Don Brown (USA)
The British Motorcycle Industry: interview with Edward Turner by Jim Lee, Ken Mellor 1973

Author's Note
Many of the above books and magazines are now out of print, a few of the books will have been replaced by a later edition or republished by a different publisher. Those marked with an asterisk (*) contain very comprehensive information about model specifications, often on a year-by-year basis. If in doubt about the availability of any title, please check with the publisher.

VELOCE PUBLISHING
THE PUBLISHER OF FINE AUTOMOTIVE BOOKS

Racing Line
by Bob Guntrip

RACING LINE

British motorcycle racing in the golden age of the big single

Bob Guntrip

Racing Line is the story of big-bike racing in Britain during the 1960s – when the British racing single reached its peak; when exciting racing unfolded at circuits across the land every summer; and when Britain took its last great generation of riding talent and engineering skill to the world.

V4793 • ISBN: 978-1-845847-93-7 • UPC: 6-36847-04793-1
Hardback • 22.5x15.2cm • 232 pages • 76 colour and b&w pictures

For more info on Veloce titles, visit our website at **www.veloce.co.uk**
• email: info@veloce.co.uk • Tel: +44(0)1305 260068

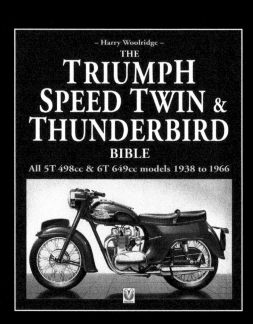
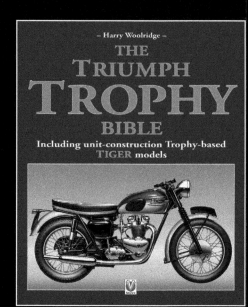

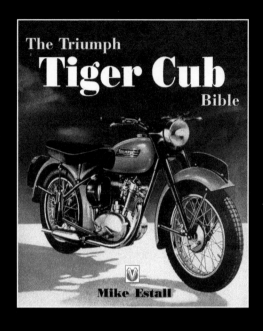
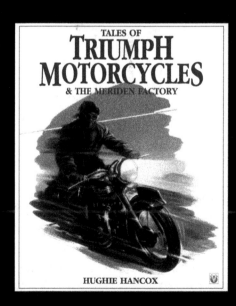

Velocette Motorcycles – MSS to Thruxton (Updated & Revised Edition)
by Rod Burris

The definitive development history of the most famous Velocette motorcycles, based on the author's earlier work, out of print for many years and much sought-after today. Includes the most comprehensive appendices ever published on this historic marque.

Hardback • 160 pages • 308 colour & b&w photos

ISBN 1-904788-28-9

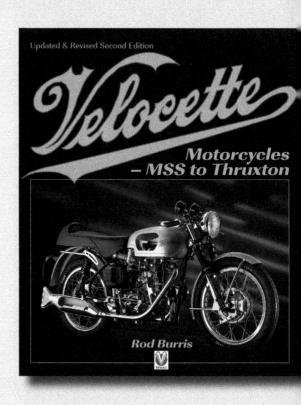

The Ducati 750 Bible
by Ian Falloon

When the great Ducati engineer Fabio Taglioni designed the 750 Ducati in 1970 there was no way he could comprehend how important this model would be. The 750, the Formula 750 racer and the Super Sport became legend: this book celebrates those machines.

Hardback • 160 pages • 163 pictures

ISBN 1-84584-012-7

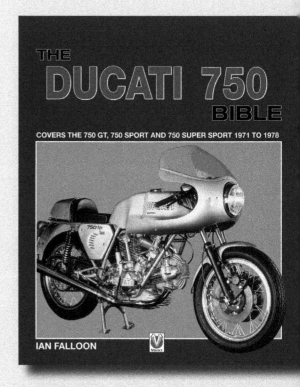

Index